ENVIRONMENTAL CONSERVATION AND BIOTECHNOLOGY

ENVIRONMENTAL CONSERVATION AND BIOTECHNOLOGY

Edited by

Dr. Avnish Chauhan
Department of Applied Science
Phonics Group of Institutions
Roorkee, Haridwar (Uttarakhand), (India)
avnishchauhan_in@yahoo.co.in

&

Dr. Pawan Kumar 'Bharti'
Centre for Agro-Rural Technologies (CART-India)
20, Jamaalpur Man, Raja Ka Tajpur
Bijnore (UP) - 246 735, (India)
E-mail: gurupawanbharti@rediffmail.com

DISCOVERY PUBLISHING HOUSE PVT. LTD.
NEW DELHI-110 002

Published by:
Tilak Wasan
DISCOVERY PUBLISHING HOUSE PVT. LTD.
4383/4B, Ansari Road, Darya Ganj
New Delhi-110 002 (India)
Phone : +91-11-23279245, 43596064-65
Fax : +91-11-23253475
E-mail : discoverypublishinghouse@gmail.com
sales@discoverypublishinggroup.com
parul.wasan@gmail.com
web : www.discoverypublishinggroup.com

First Edition: **2014**

ISBN: 978-93-5056-512-4

Environmental Conservation and Biotechnology

Printed at:
Aditi Fine Art Press
Delhi

Preface

Ancient people learnt to live with five elements of nature, the "earth", "water", "air", "light" and "cosmos" and actually worshipped them in reality and symbolically. We get lots of information about the relationships between man and nature and the human behaviours and indebtedness towards nature. Perhaps they were more aware and ecofriendly as compared to us. It is believed that even the cutting of branches could make his son invalid. Hindu homes worship peepal tree off widowhood; they worship of god Coconut tree is believed to be a symbol of fecundity and so Hindu women who nurse the desire to get a son worship coconut trees and eat coconut fruits as a "divine gift". Same respect with other plants like mango, banana, banyan, bailpatra tree etc.

But now man becomes selfish and exploited his natural resources in a manner that in a few next years it will become disappear from the earth as a result number of problems such as uncontrolled population, global warming or green house effects, El-Nino, deforestation, climate change, acid rain, water pollution, air pollution, soil pollution, thermal pollution, radiation pollution, ozone layer depletion etc. have been recognise. It must be remembered that if you disturb nature in one or another way definitely it will response you later or sooner.

Present day we are facing excessive pollution caused by industrialized agriculture where variety of chemical fertilizers and pesticides belongs to diverse chemical class are being used. Hence, these chemical fertilizers and pesticides have emerged as indispensible tool in modern agriculture. Their residue is contaminating the environment, hampers the balance of the eco-system and pesticides also destroy predator and parasites of the target organisms, leading to the reduction of beneficial species. They contaminate the ground water by leaching. Pesticides enter the food chain and lead to bio-magnification as their residues are found on fruits and vegetables.

This book provides comprehensive coverage of the fundamental principles and current practices and trends in the field of environmental pollution, conservation, agriculture, ecology and environmental biotechnology. This book updates the subject matter, illustrations and problems to incorporate new concepts and issues related to environmental conservation, pollution, agriculture, ecology, environment and biotechnology.

Particularly thanks are due to all contributors from South Africa, India; and publisher also for their contribution and assistance. I hope this book will be of benefit to both present and future colleagues, who teach, study and working in the field of environment, ecology, environmental pollution, agriculture and biotechnology.

–Editors

Contents

Environmental Conservation
A Challenge and Need of the Era

Avnish Chauhan*

* Department of Applied Science, Phonics Group of Institution, Roorkee, Haridwar, Uttarakhand, (India)

The word 'environment' may be defined as the 'physical, chemical and biological conditions surrounding an organism. First two conditions are abiotic and last one is biotic in nature.

1. **Physical Conditions** includes sunlight, temperature, pressure, soil etc.
2. **Chemical Conditions** includes water, oxygen, nitrogen, sulphur, phosphorus, carbon dioxide, pH, minerals etc.
3. **Biological or biotic conditions** includes:
   (a) Neutralisms
   (b) Negative Interaction
   (c) Positive Interaction
   (d) Both Positive and Negative Interaction

Our ancient people learnt to live with five elements of nature, the "earth", "water", "air", "light" and "cosmos" and actually worshipped them in reality and symbolically. We get lots of information about the relationships between man and nature and the human behaviours and indebtedness towards nature. Perhaps they were more aware and ecofriendly as compared to us. It is believed that even the cutting of branches could make his son invalid. Hindu homes worship peepal tree (*Ficus religious*) off widowhood; they worship of god Coconut tree (*Cocus nucifera*) is believed to be a symbol of fecundity and so Hindu women who nurse the desire to get a son worship coconut trees and eat coconut fruits as a "divine gift". Same respect with other plants like mango, banana, banyan, bailpatra tree etc.

But now man becomes selfish and exploited his natural resources in a manner that in a few next years it will become disappear from the earth as a result number of problems such as uncontrolled population, global warming or green house effects, El-Nino, deforestation, climate change, acid rain, water pollution, air pollution, soil pollution, thermal pollution, radiation pollution, ozone layer depletion etc. have been recognise. It must be remembered that if you disturb nature in one or another way definitely it will response you later or sooner. Our earth or blue planet is the only planet of the solar system which has the life supporting environment in this universe.

Environmental issues in India become more serious every day. The major issue is population growth and pollution in India. For the cause of population growth and industrial development there are much pollution in the world. The number of population growth and industrial development determines the total impact on the environment. Thus it can be said that environmental damage emerges from population, multiplied by the consumption unit per capita and environmental damages originating from per unit of consumption. (Sarkar, 2012)

Population

It is most important and most challenging task of the current world. Every year World Population Day is celebrated on July 11 every year to raise awareness of global population issues among common peoples. The event was established by the Governing Council of the UNDP (United Nations Development Programme) in 1989. The world population on July 9, 2012, was estimated to have been 7,025,071,966. Current projections show a continued increase in population (but a steady decline in the population growth rate), with the global population expected to reach between 7.5 and 10.5 billion by 2050. There are three Asian countries where 20% of the absolutely poor people are living in and in case of India this condition is worst as almost half of the total population in our country lives below the poverty line. One fifth of India's population lives in the rural areas, and the migration into cities and towns is at the rate of 2.2% every year (Goel, 1997). This migration has led to urbanization and 40% of the migrant population lives in slums (Goodland, 2000). Dharavi, the largest slum settlement in Asia, is in our country. 40% of India's urban population lives one-room houses, which contains an average of 4-6 persons. Our food production is enough to feed this 40% of India's urban population. In India 80% of the migrant population in the urban areas is not getting safe drinking water. They face the problems like urban slums, garbage and sanitation, which are associated with urbanization. Thus the "quality of life" becomes a critical question in India.

Table 1.1: Showing the Population of Different Nations

Country Population (Millions)	Country Population (Millions)
Year 2011	Year 2025
China 1,346	India 1,692
India 1,241	China 1,313
United States 312	Nigeria 433
Indonesia 238	United States 423
Brazil 197	Pakistan 314
Pakistan 177	Indonesia 309
Nigeria 162	Bangladesh 226
Bangladesh 151	Brazil 223
Russia 143	Ethiopia 174
Japan 128	Philippines 150

India has the second largest population in the world, with 1.24 billion people comprising 623.7 million males and 586.5 million females, according to the provisional 2011 Census report. In the last ten years, 181 million people were added and, since 1947, the population of India has more than tripled. Interestingly, the addition of 181 million people to the population during 2001-11 is slightly lower than the total population of Brazil, the fifth most populous country in the world. Significantly, the growth is slower compared to the previous decade. India accounts for 17.5 per cent of the world population. It is clear by the year of 2025 we will become world leader. In spite of this we don't have any rule and regulation to control ever increasing population.

Table 1.2: Comparison of Indian State Population with Other Countries

Population of Indian States Compared to a Few Countries in the World (in millions)			
Indian State	Population	Country	Population
Uttar Pradesh	200	Brazil	194
Maharashtra	112	Japan	128
Bihar	104	Mexico	107
West Bengal	91	Philippines	92
Andhra Pradesh	85	Germany	82
Madhya Pradesh	73	Turkey	75
Tamil Nadu	72	Iran	73
Rajasthan	69	Thailand	68
Karnataka	61	United Kingdom	62
Gujarat	60	Italy	60

Source: Census, Government of India/World Bank.

During 2001-11, as many as 25 States/UTs of with a share of about 85 per cent of the country's population registered an annual growth rate of less than 2 per cent, while 15 States/UTs have grown by less than 1.5 per cent per annum. The number of such States/UTs was only 4 during the previous decade, the report said. India has more than 50 per cent of its population below the age of 25 and more than 65 per cent below the age of 35. More population means more pressure on our existing natural resources and already these are under tremendous pressure and any further increase in population definitely there will be disastrous effects on earth.

Former Egyptian Foreign Minister and former Secretary-General of the United Nations Boutrous Ghali, who forecast, "The next war in the Middle East will be fought over water, not politics"; his successor at the UN, Kofi Annan, who in 2001 said, "Fierce competition for fresh water may well become a source of conflict and wars in the future," and the former Vice President of the World Bank, Ismail Serageldin, who said the wars of the next century will be over water unless significant changes in governance occurred. Daily water use per person is about 600 liters in residential areas of North America and 250-350 liters in Europe whereas per capita water use per day in sub Sahara region is a mere in 10 liters. In India it is about 50 liters per day. One flush of a western toilet uses as much water as the average person in the developing world uses for a whole days washing, drinking, cleaning and cooking. According to one estimates that woman in Africa and Asia walk an average distance of 6 km a day to collect water.

According to estimation of the *Central Ground Water Board of India* that the reservoir of underground water will dry up entirely by 2025 in many as fifteen states in India if the present level of exploitation and misuse of underground water continues. By 2050, when more than 50 per cent of the Indian population is expected to shift to the cities, fresh drinking water is expected to get very scare. Future wars between of within nations will be fight on the issue of water. *Centre for Science and Environment* (*CSE*) said that in parts of the capital city, the groundwater level is dropping by 10 meters (33 feet) each year. In 1995, World Bank vice president Ismail Serageldin predicted an acute water shortage for the new millennium: "If the wars of this century were fought over oil, the wars of the next century will be fought over water."

Water resources will come under increasing pressure in the Indian subcontinent due to the changing climate. Presently, more than 45 per cent of the average annual rainfall, including snowfall in the country, is wasted as natural run-off to the sea.

How much is where!

And you though, after the oceans. It's the rivers that contain the most water. Looks like you were wrong, as rivers contain only about 0.0001 per cent of overall water content in our earth, as this chart tell us.

Ocens-97.21 per cent

Icecaps, Glaciers-2.14 per cent

Ground water-0.61 per cent

Fresh water-0.61 per cent

Inland seas-0.008 per cent

Soil moisture-0.005 per cent

Atmosphere-0.001

Climate Change

Climate refers to characteristics weather conditions at a place or a region on earth. Weather is defined as the condition of the atmosphere at a particular place and time. It is characterized by parameters such as temperature, humidity, rain and wind. It should be member that the climate is vary place to place. Infact climate represents the state of atmosphere over a longer period (normally 35 years) of time. In simple terms shifting or altering in normal seasonal patterns (temperature, rainfall etc.) of the area is known as climate change. Climate change is a symptom of a sick earth. Our planet is suffering because of the way human activities are destroying and changing the surface of the Earth. One of the biggest reasons for climate change is global warming. Climate change is now widely recognized. According to one estimate the global mean warming of 0.45±0.15°C has been recorded over the last about years and for India the mean temperature has gone up by nearly 0.2 to 0.3°C during last 40 year.

Water Pollution

Water is the basic necessity for all life and the most serious environmental health problems are related to water. Perhaps the largest of the environmental issues in India facing the people of India is inadequate or lack of access to vital fresh water resources. As India's industries get bigger so will the amount of water they require and the amounts are already beginning to spiral. The rivers are on the front line of pollution in India. Millions of people depend on them for their livelihoods but they are slowly being polluted and destroyed by sewage, chemicals and other agricultural and industrial waste. Ganga is the most polluted river in India. Water used in India is such that 93% is used by the agricultural sector and 3.73% by the domestic sector. 80% of the fourteen perennial rivers in India are polluted with sewage. Industrial effluents, agricultural runoff, dumping of toxicants into the river and other large water bodies are the cause of water pollution. The Ganges River Pollution is now at such a high level that the amount of toxins, chemicals and other dangerous bacteria found in the river are now almost 3000 times over the limit suggested by the WHO as 'safe'.

Plastics and Other Waste

The American Chemistry Council. New York chemist Leo Baekeland invented the first true plastic material in 1907, Bakelite, which people still use today. The term "plastics" includes materials composed of various elements such as carbon, hydrogen, oxygen, nitrogen, chlorine, and sulphur. Plastics typically have high molecular weight, meaning each molecule can have thousands of atoms bound together. In other words plastics are macromolecules, formed by polymerization and having the ability to be shaped by the application of reasonable amount of heat and pressure or any other form of forces. This great human creation changed the world and brought comfort to our lifestyle(CPCB, 2009). Plastic bags have been introduced in 1970's (Williamson, 2003) and gained an increasing popularity amongst consumers and retailers. They are available in huge numbers and varieties across the world. It is estimated that around 500 billion plastic bags are used every year worldwide (Spokas, 2007; Geographical, 2005). Use of plastic is more dangerous for us. Plastic isn't in any urgency to degrade but the people of India don't seem to recognise this as they throw every unwanted item onto the floor wherever they are. Of course, the victims of this environmental issue in India are the future generations and the animals. The holy cows that are so integral to Indian life are slowly being killed from the huge amount of plastic bags they consume that eventually rap around their insides. Some areas are simply fed up with the lack of Government intervention and are using these initiatives. The average Indian consumption of virgin plastics per capita reached 3.2 kg in 2000/2001 (5 kg if recycled material is included) from a mere 0.8 kg in 1990/1991. However, this is only one-fourth of the consumption in China (12 kg/capita, 1998) and one sixth of the world average (18 kg/capita). This consumption led to more than 5400 tonnes of plastics waste being generated per day in 2000/2001 (totalling 2 million tonnes per annum)

It is to mention that no authentic estimation is available on total generation of plastic waste in the country however, considering 70% of total plastic consumption is discarded as waste, thus approximately 5.6 million tons per annum (TPA) of plastic waste is generated in country, which is about 15342 tons per day (TPD). CPCB, India. In India approximately 8 Million tonnes plastic products are consumed every year (2008) which is expected to raise 12 million tones by 2012. There are some interesting facts about the plastics and these are as follows:

- Annually approximately 500 billion plastic bags are used worldwide. More than one million bags are used every minute.
- A plastic bag has an average "working life" of 15 minutes.
- Over the last ten years we have produced more plastic than during the whole of the last century.
- Plastic accounts for around 10% of the total waste we generate

Hazardous Waste

The hazardous waste generated in the country is about 4.4 million tonnes, out of which 38.3 per cent is recyclable, 4.3 per cent is incinerable and the remaining 57.4 per cent is disposable in secured landfills. Twelve states of the country (including Maharashtra, Gujarat, Tamil Nadu, West Bengal, Andhra Pradesh and Rajasthan) account for 87 of total waste generation. The top five waste generating states are Maharashtra, Gujarat, Andhra Pradesh, Rajasthan and West Bengal.

Electronic Waste (e-waste)

The growth of e-waste has significant environmental, economic and social impact. The increase of electrical and electronic products, consumption rates and higher obsolescence rates lead to higher generation of e-waste. The increasing obsolescence rate of electronic products also adds to the huge import of used electronics products. The e-waste inventory based on the obsolescence rate in India for the year 2005 has been estimated to be 1,46,180 tonnes, and is expected to exceed 8,00,000 tonnes by 2012. There is no large scale organized e-waste recycling facility in India, whereas there are two small e-waste dismantling facilities functioning in Chennai and Bangalore, while most of the e-waste recycling units are operating in the un-organized sector.

Desertification

Globally, about 1,900 Mha. of land is affected by land degradation. Climate change, leading to warming and water stress could further exacerbate land degradation, leading to desertification. It is important to note that the climate sensitive sectors (forests, agriculture, coastal zones) and the natural resources (groundwater, soil, biodiversity, etc.) are already under major stress due to socio-economic pressures. Climate change is likely to exacerbate the degradation of resources and socioeconomic pressures. Thus India, with a large population dependent on climate sensitive sectors and low adaptive capacity will have to develop and implement adaptation strategies.

REFERENCES

http://cpcb.nic.in/upload/NewItems/NewItem_155_FINAL_RITE_REPORT.pdf

http://www.epa.gov/osw/conserve/materials/plastics.htm

http://en.wikipedia.org/wiki/Plastics_materials_in_India

Williamson LJ (2003) It's Not My Bag, Baby. *On* Earth: Environmental Politics People, 25(2): 32-34.

Geographical (2005). "Waste: An Overview." Geographical, 77(9): 34-35.

Spokas KA (2007). Plastics: still young, but having a mature impact. Waste Manage., 28(3): 473-474.

Sarkar, P.K. (2012). Environmental Ethics and Environmental Issues. *International Journal of Multidisciplinary Educational Research*, 1(2), 177-182.

Goel, P.K. *Water Pollution* New Age International Publication: New Delhi 1997.

Goodland, R. the Urgency of Environmental Sustainability; Where Next: *Reflection on the Human Future* edit. Poore, D. Paris UNESCO, 2000.

The Histopathological Effects of Detrergent 'Tide' on Some Tissues of the Fresh Water Snail, *Bellamya Bengalensis* Lamarck

P. Raghava Kumari*

* Lecturer in Zoology, S.K.R. College for Women, Rajahmundry, East Godavari Dist, A.P, (India) Pin - 533 103

ABSTRACT

In this study the fresh water snail (*Bellamyabengalensis*) one of the most abundant gastropods of river Godavari, is exposed to sub-lethal concentrations of detergent Tide for different periods of time for a histological study. The effects of sub-lethal concentrations of Tide on histology of foot, mantle, digestive gland and neurosecretory cells have been documented. Mortality was assessed and concentrations (LC_{50}) were calculated. LC_{50} increased with the decrease in mean exposure concentrations and times, respectively. The LC_{50} values obtained with the snails exposed to detergent (Tide) are 213.7 ppm for 24 hrs, 134.896 ppm for 48 hrs, 104.71 ppm for 72 hrs and 69.18 ppm for 96 hrs. The exposure of the snails to sub-lethal concentrations of the detergents resulted in prevalence of desquamation of the epithelial cells, changes in the number of mucocytes, disruption of glandular cells and atrophy of the columnar muscle fibres in the foot and mantle tissues of snails. The histopathological alterations examined in digestive gland are disintegration of basement membrane due to damaged epithelial cells, disruption of hepatic tubules, increase in internal luminar area at 104.71 ppm for 72 hrs, occurrence of cell debris in between the tissue at 69.18 ppm for 96 hrs.Cytological alterations observed in the neurosecretory cells are shrinkage and disruption of the cells, the enlargement of vacuoles in the cytoplasm, disorientation of nerve fibres or neuropile. The results are discussed, particularly in comparison to those of other aquatic organisms.

Key words: *Bellamyabengalensis,* TIDE detergent, Histopathological alterations, River Godavari

INTRODUCTION

Toxicology is the qualitative and quantitative study of adverse or toxic effects of chemicals. It is concerned primarily with the harmful effects of chemicals that are encountered by man either directly or indirectly. During the past six decades, rapid industrialization and agricultural development paralleled with increased health care have changed human life styles in various ways. This development is the chief cause of wide spread pollution ultimately with profound influence on our lives. The hazards of chemical pollution with unlimited, indiscriminate use of heavy metals, pesticides and detergents have enhanced toxic wastes into the environment. Toxicity is a relative property of a chemical which refers to its potential to have a harmful effect on a living organism causes injury or aberrations in tissues.

Detergents are common pollutants found in natural water ways. These are required in a wide range of our daily life for diverse purposes. Widespread use of synthetic detergents creates problems of water pollution. Such type of polluted water damages the life of aquatic organisms. In recent years, the use of detergents has increased by many folds all over the world. They may enter aquatic ecosystem along with domestic sewage or by direct washing effluents. The release of increasing quantities of detergents into aquatic environment and their accumulation in living and non-living systems endangers life, as they constitute an important group of environmental pollutants. The detergent may give rise to either local or systematic effects. Data concerning the toxic effect of detergent on vertebrates, invertebrates and especially fishes are available. After repeated exposures, detergents may accumulate and a sub-clinical or a clinical effect may appear. It would be appropriate to detect the histological changes before clinical symptoms start. Surfactants appear to be the primary toxic component in the formulations (Henderson *et al.*, 1959).Indiscriminate use of detergents may result in various biochemical, physiological and histological alterations in vital tissues of aquatic organisms. In some Spanish rivers concentration of anionic surfactants are higher than 5mg/L(Tarazonaet al., 1983). The histopathological studies are indicative of the pollution induced stress, it is gradually gaining popularity among toxicologists (Hinton et al. 1973). Those are morphological changes, inhibiting effects and behavioural changes. Besides the above, histomorphological change is considered to be an useful bio-assay tool in toxicity studies, as its application demands a high degree of competence and skill to make correct diagnosis (Warner, 1967).

Toxicity testing is an essential tool for assessing the effect and fate of toxicants in aquatic ecosystems. To evaluate the acute toxicity of a particular pollutant to a representative species in terms of mortality and time in a laboratory is necessary. The results of acute toxicity are generally expressed as a lethal concentration (LC) value. The LC_{50} effective dose is a concentration of which 50% mortality of exposed organisms occurs. The period of exposure for study of short term toxicity test is usually 24, 48, 72 and 96 hrs. This is a convenient way of expressing acute lethal toxicity of a given pollutant to the average individual. The exposure time plays an important role in LC_{50} values. The LC_{50} values derived from acute toxicity tests are best used to assess the margins of safety (Lloyd, 1977). The LC_{50} values decrease with an increase in exposure time (Gupta et al., 1981).

Studies on the acute toxicological effects of the various pollutants were undertaken in the nineteenth century. Carpenter (1924) published the first of her important papers reporting the lethal action of heavy metals on fish. The measurement of the toxicity of pollutants and bioassay method for acute toxicity was determined by Sprague (1969). Detergents are common pollutants found in natural water ways. According to Glaister (1986) structural changes caused by detergent may occur at any level of the biological organisations literally from molecule to mammals. The aquatic toxicology of surfactants on fishes has been studied for many years (Palanichamy&Murugan, 1991; Chellan et al, 2003). There is still scarce on the acute toxicity of detergent on histopathology of fresh water gastropods.

Exposure to moderate concentration of detergents can produce a variety of recognizable effects without actually killing an organism and these have been divided into morphological changes, inhibitory effects and behavioural changes (John, 1970). In a previous work we found that the *Lymnaeaperegra* is highly sensitive to the anionic surfactants, sodium lauryl sulfate (SLS) with a 96 hrs LC_{50} of 0.54mg/L (Jose and Oliva, 1987). No information exists in the literatures concerning the toxic effects of detergents for this snail. Therefore, the purpose of this study was to determine the acute toxicity of detergent to the freshwater mollusc*B. bengalensis* and to examine the histopathology of the detergent in the body after four days of exposure.

Due to the toxic effects of detergents, important organs like foot, mantle, digestive system, nervous system and other organs are damaged. The effect of the cationic surfactant lauryl trimethyl ammonium chloride (C_{12}-TMAC) was investigated on growth, reproduction, cellulolytic enzyme activity, and larval colonization of Asiatic clams, *Corbiculafluminea (Belanger et al., 1993).* The effects of heavy metals, insecticides and pesticides on the snails are extensive than detergents. Panwar et al. (1982) studied the toxicity of some chlorinated hydrocarbon and Pathological and biochemical disturbances of pesticide toxicity in *Vivipara bengalensis* is well documentedby Muley and Mane (1990). organophosphorous insecticide was investigated in *Viviparusbengalensis*. Viantet al. (2002) reported the copper toxicity on digestive gland of*Haliotisrufescens*. Boer et al. (1995) observed the ultrastructure of neuropathological effects of taxol on neurons of the fresh water snail *Lymnaeastagnalis*. Radwanet al. (1992) and Radwanet al. (2008)elucidated the affect of pesticides in the nervous system of *Thebapisana* and *Eobaniavermiculata*. The present study is devoted to evaluate the toxicological effects of detergents on *Bellamyabengalensis*.

MATERIALS AND METHODS

Acute Toxicity of Detergent

Snails *B. bengalensis* were collected from river Godavari in Rajahmundry, East Godavari District, Andhra Pradesh, India. Prior to toxicity testing, the snails were acclimatized for one week under laboratory conditions and aerated through an air stone. During acclimation the snails were fed on *Hydrilla* plants. The stock solutions were prepared with deionized water in 1 L volumetric flasks. Acute detergent toxicity experiments were performed for a four-day period using adult snails. Detergent solutions were prepared by dilution of a stock solution with dechlorinated tap water. A control with dechlorinated tap water only was also used. The tests were carried out under static conditions with renewal of the solution every day. Control and detergent treated groups each consisted of 10 groups of snails. No stress was observed for the snails in the control water until the end of the study. A total of 10 animals per concentration were used in the experiment. The experimental study was carried out in the laboratory at room temperature of 27.8°C. Each toxicity test ended 96 hours and mortality was recorded at 24, 48, 72, and 96 hours exposure intervals because acute toxicity tests were performed under static conditions up to 96 hours. Controls were maintained for the same period as the experimental snails. Mortality was defined as a complete immobilization and failure to respond probing. Dead snails were removed daily from each concentration. The concentration of a detergent which caused 50% mortality to test organisms during a specified time expressed in terms of LC_{50}. The lethal concentrations were calculated using probit analysis[16].

Histopathologic Study

Mortal animals were removed promptly. For histopathology studies both the control group and those of experimental groups that survived at the end of 96 hrs. exposure were fixed in Susa, dehydrated in alcohol grades and were embedded in paraffin wax. The animals were cut at 6 - 8µ and take serial sections of the animal and stained with Heidenhain's Azan and PAS (Periodic acid-Schiff). Sections were examined for abnormality under a light microscope.

RESULTS

Results were expressed in LC_{50} values for 24, 48, 72 and 96hrs. Acute toxicity tests were performed under static conditions to determine the toxicity.

The behaviour of the control snails was normal. After the introduction of detergent in different aquaria at different concentration levels, avoidance behaviour is clearly observed as the snails tended to move to the walls of the glass troughs and secrete excess of mucous. After sometime, they become weak and mortality was recorded when the animals became detached from the walls of the troughs and showed no reaction when gently probed by a glass rod. From the mortality data LC_{50} values have been determined for 96 hrs. The average percent of mortality at selected time interval is presented in table 2.1 (Fig. 2.1). The LC_{50} values along with standard error, 95% fiducial limits of the snail, *B. bengalensis*for 24, 48, 72 and 96 hrs have been calculated and shown in table 2.2 (Fig. 2.2). The LC_{50} values obtained with the snails exposed to detergent (Tide) are 213.7 ppm for 24 hrs., 134.896 ppm for 48 hrs., 104.71 ppm for 72 hrs. and 69.18 ppm for 96 hrs. According to this data, it is clear that there was linear relationship between percent or probit mortality and detergent concentration. Thus the percent or probit mortality increased with the increasing detergent concentration. The data also reveal that mortality to the pollutant increases with increase in time of exposure period. To have reproducible results and to increase the accuracy of experiment, the bioassay experiments were conducted in triplicates.

The LC_{50} values obtained have shown that the detergent Tide has affected the foot, mantle, digestive gland and neurosecretory cells of *B.bengalensis* when compared with their respective controls. The foot considered to be the strongest part of the animal is also not spared by the detergents.The normal foot in control experimental snail consists of dorsal and ventral ciliated columnar epithelium, epidermal mucocytes, mucous gland cells, muscle fibres and connective tissue. The epithelium of the foot directly in contact with the polluted water shows desquamation at different concentrations of detergent. The foot shows severe damage at highest concentrations and congestion was severe at 213.7, 263, 316.2 mg. Disruption of muscle fibres and desquamation of epithelial layers can be seen at 69.18 mg. (96 hrs.). The glandular cells were affected after 96 hrs. exposure and different parts of foot were affected severely i.e damaged connective tissue, shrunken epidermal cells, broken basement membrane and faintly stained degenerated cells (Figs. 2.3 - 2.6).

The mantle is a thin surface which lines the shell and forms the roof of the body cavity. The normal mantle consists of outer and inner columnar epithelial layers, muscle fibres, connective tissue, aggregates of glandular cells and epithelial mucocytes. These cells are damaged after exposure to acute toxicity of detergent (Tide).The mantle edge being directly in contact with the polluted waters accumulated considerable amounts of surfactants in their cells and produce toxic effects like hypertrophy of the epithelial cells with vacuolation and disorganisation of cell walls leading to necrosis. After

96 hrs exposure the tissue of mantle showed the desquamation of epithelial cells, atrophy of muscle fibres, necrosis and disruption of shell glands (Figs. 2.7 & 2.8).

Table 2.1: Tolerance of *B. bengalensis* Exposed to Different Concentrations of Detergent (Tide) at 24, 48, 72 and 96 hrs. Interval. Each Value Represents the Mean ± Standard Deviation of Ten Experiments

Concentration of Detergent (ppm)	No. of Snails Exposed	Per cent Mortality ± SD			
		24 hrs.	48 hrs.	72 hrs.	96 hrs.
40	10	1 ± 0.22	2.3 ± 0.34	10 ± 1.3	18 ± 2.52
80	10	3 ± 0.45	14 ± 2.1	32 ± 4.472	46 ± 5.4
120	10	10 ± 1.4	30 ± 4.2	50 ± 6.5	52 ± 7.8
160	10	22 ± 3.3	58 ± 7.54	76 ± 9.12	100 ± 11.5

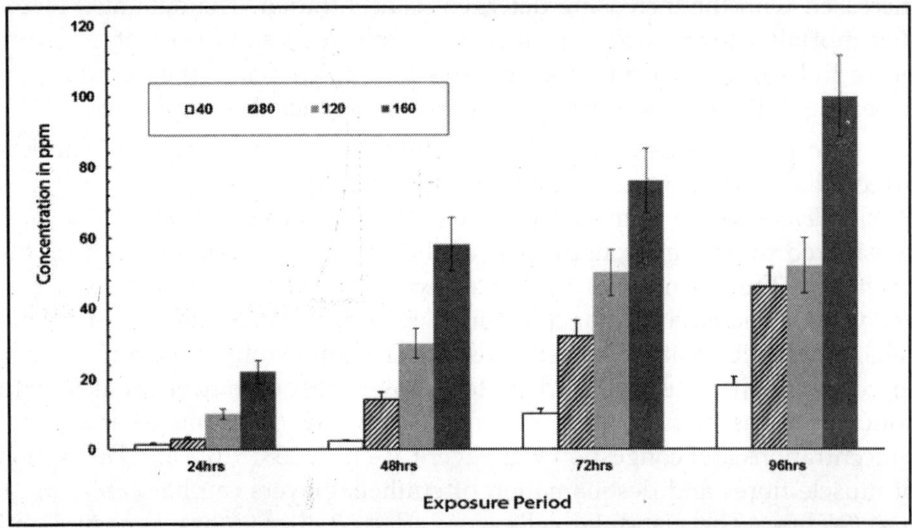

Fig. 2.1: Mortality of *B. bengalensis* Exposed to Different Concentrations of Detergent (Tide) at 24, 48, 72 and 96 hrs. Vertical Lines Represent Standard Deviation

The normal histological structure of digestive gland of *B. bengalensis* is showing large number of round tubules called as acini. Each acinus consists of two types of cells *i.e* digestive absorptive cells and calciferous or excretory cells are lined with epithelium. An empty space, lumen is present in the center of acinus.In the present study the microscopic observations of digestive gland showed histopathological changes due to the stress caused by detergent tide in *Bellamyabengalensis*. Degeneration of cells is gradually increased in the snails*B. bengalensis* which are exposed to detergent tide at 24, 48, 72 and 96 hrs respectively. Snails exposed at 24 hrs, showing shrinkage in the tubules or acini.

Table 2.2: Lethal Concentration of Detergent (Tide) of *B. bengalensis* at 24, 48, 72 and 96 hrs. Each Value Represents the Concentration ± Standard Error. The Values in the Parentheses Represent 95% Fiducial Limits

Lethal Concentration	Concentration (ppm) ± SE			
	24 hrs.	48 hrs.	72 hrs.	96 hrs.
LC_5	132.4 ± 4.755 (137.15-127.64)	87.096 ± 2.159 (89.255-84.937)	39.84 ± 6.77 (46.61-33.07)	35.15 ± 2.83 (37.98-32.32)
LC_{10}	147.9 ± 5.845 (153.74-142.05)	95.49 ± 2.338 (97.82-93.15)	47.68 ± 8.606 (56.286-39.074)	41.11 ± 1.719 (42.82-39.39)
LC_{25}	177.8 ± 8.735 (186.53-169.065)	112.201 ± 2.8 (115.001-109.401)	64.56 ± 12.59 (77.15-51.97)	52.48 ± 0.827 (53.3-51.65)
LC_{50}	213.7 ± 13.085 (226.78-200.61)	134.896 ± 3.635 (138.531-131.261)	104.71 ± 19.21 (123.92-85.5)	69.18 ± 2.568 (71.74-66.61)
LC_{75}	263.0 ± 20.08 (283.08-242.92)	162.181 ± 4.925 (167.106-157.256)	123.78 ± 29.49 (153.27-94.29)	93.54 ± 3.915 (97.45-89.62)
LC_{90}	316.2 ± 36.219 (352.41-279.98)	190.546 ± 6.507 (197.053-184.039)	169.15 ± 42.85 (212-126.3)	121.059 ± 6.66 (127.71-114.39)

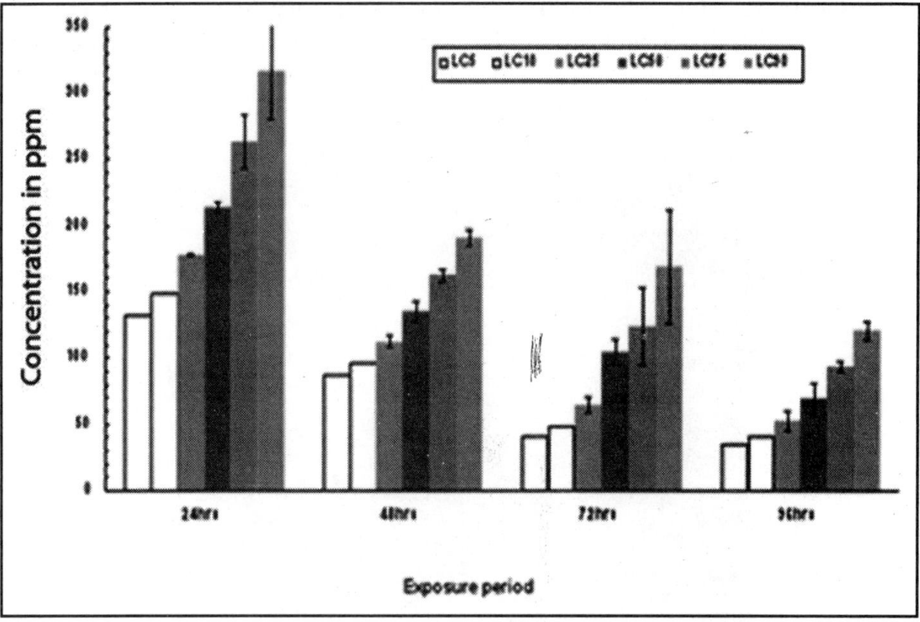

Fig. 2.2: Regression Line Representing the Relation Between Probit Values and Detergent (Tide) Concentrations in *B. bengalensis* at 24, 48, 72 and 96 hrs.

After 48 and 72 hrs., disintegration of basement membrane due to damaged epithelial cells, vacuolization, disappearance of cellular integrity, increase in the lumen of tubules, disorganisation of individual cells, peripheral thickening of hepatocytes are observed. Both the absorptive cells and calciferous cells are ruptured. At the end of 96 hrs., damage is highly pronounced in hepatic tubules resulting in elongated hepatic cells or inflammation of hepatic tubules, hypertrophy of muscles, disintegration of cellular boundaries appears like cellular mass and the luminal space is filled by cell debris (Figs. 2.9 - 2.11). The major part of tubules is damaged beyond any possibility of recovery.

The normal histological structure of neurosecretory cells showed three types of cells arranged at the peripheral region of ganglion and their axons running centrally in to the neuropile. NS cells differ from the ordinary neurons in their large size, large nuclei with abundant cytoplasm and distinct nucleoli. The cytoplasm is filled with small granules which are characteristically stained intensely pink with Heidenhain's Azan. On the basis of difference in size, number of nuclei, three cell types could be identified. These are designated as 'A', 'B' and 'C'. *B. bengalensis* exposed to different concentrations of detergent Tide showed discoloration of the neurosecretory cells. After 24 and 48 hrs of exposure, the neurosecretory cells exhibited mild congestion, lysis of chromation and less vacuolation. Whereas snails exposed to 104.71 and 69.18 ppm concentration of detergent Tide for 72 and 96 hrs showed cytological alterations observed in the neurosecretory cells is shrinkage and disruption of the NS cells, the enlargement of vacuoles in the cytoplasm, disorientation of nerve fibres or neuropile, eccentric nuclei and severe chromatolysis (Figs. 2.12 - 2.14).

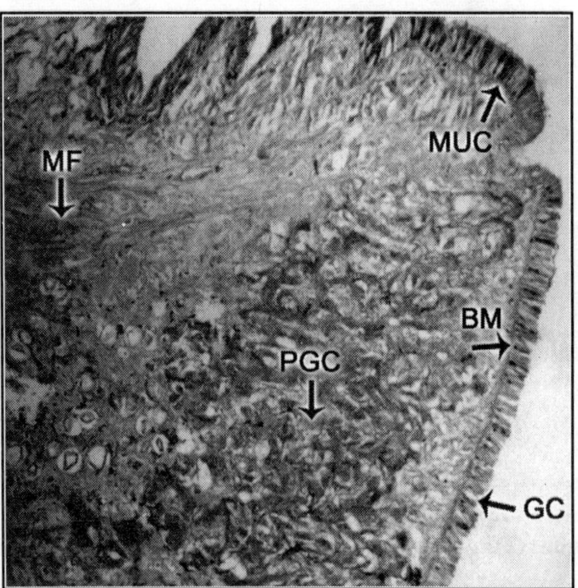

Fig. 2.3: Sagittal Section of Foot (PAS) Normal

PGC - Pedal Gland Cells, MF - Muscle Fibres, MUC – Mucocytes, EC - Epithelial Cells

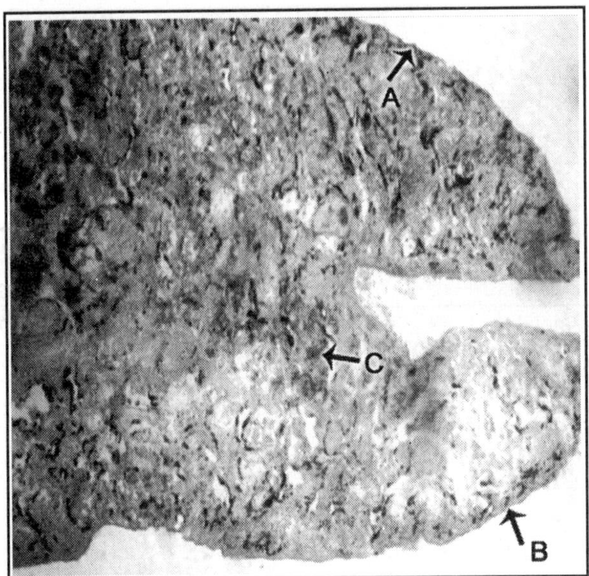

Fig. 2.4: Foot of *B. bengalensis* Exposed to 104.71 ppm Detergent (Tide) for 72 hrs. (PAS)

(A) Broken basement membrane

(B) Epithelial mucocytes appearing empty with collapsed walls

(C) Decreased staining ability

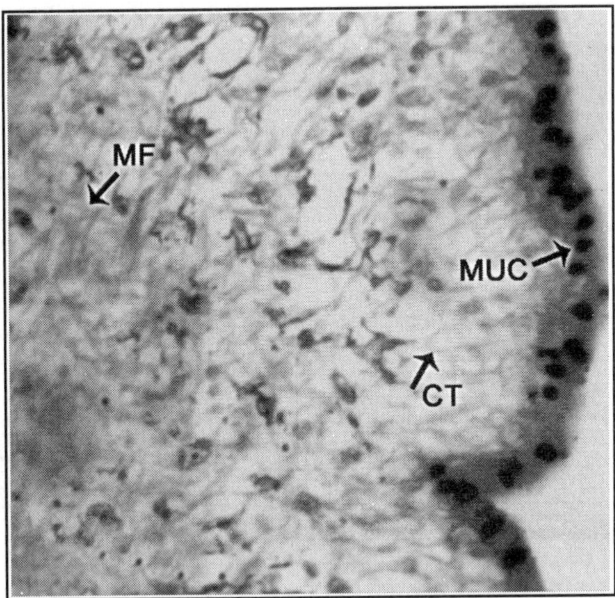

Fig. 2.5: Enlarged View of Foot (Control) of *B. bengalensis* Showing Epithelial Mucocytes (PAS)

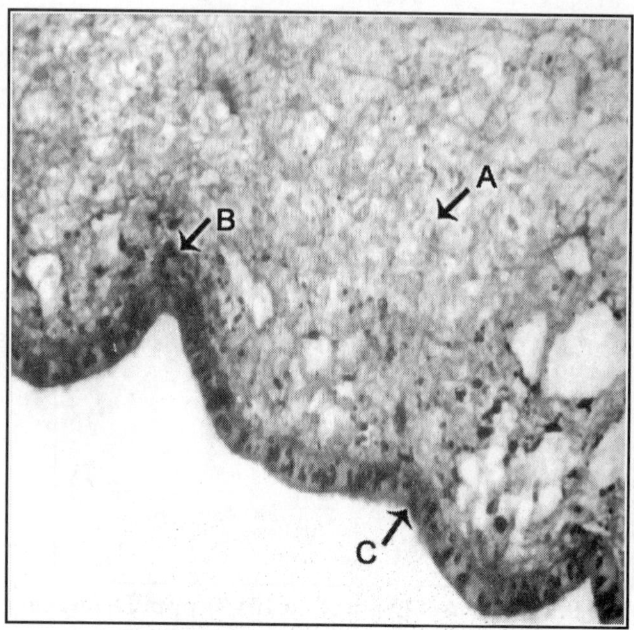

Fig. 2.6: 96 hrs. of foot (PAS) showing
(A) Desquamation of epithelial cells
(B) Broken basement membrane
(C) Shrunken pedal gland cells

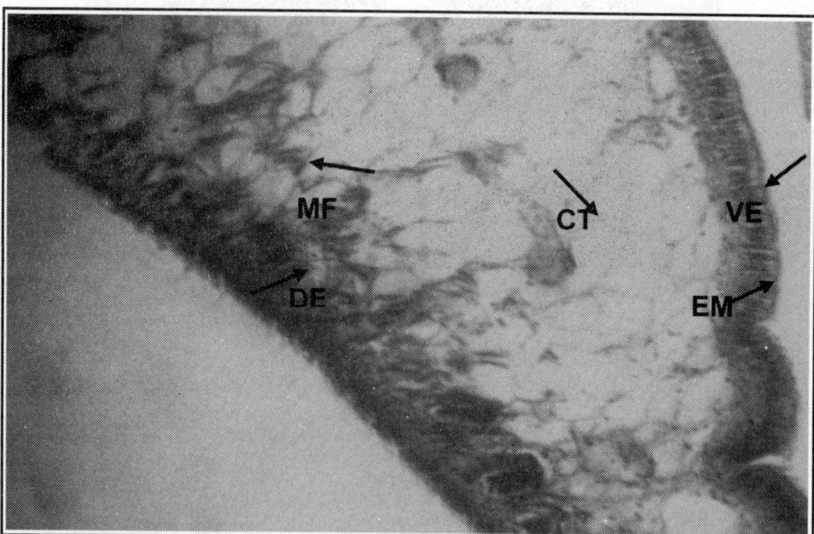

Fig. 2.7: Sagittal Section of Mantle (Azan) Normal
DE- Dorsal Epithelium, VE - Ventral Epithelium, MF - Muscle Fibres
CT - Connective Tissue, EM - epithelial mucocytes

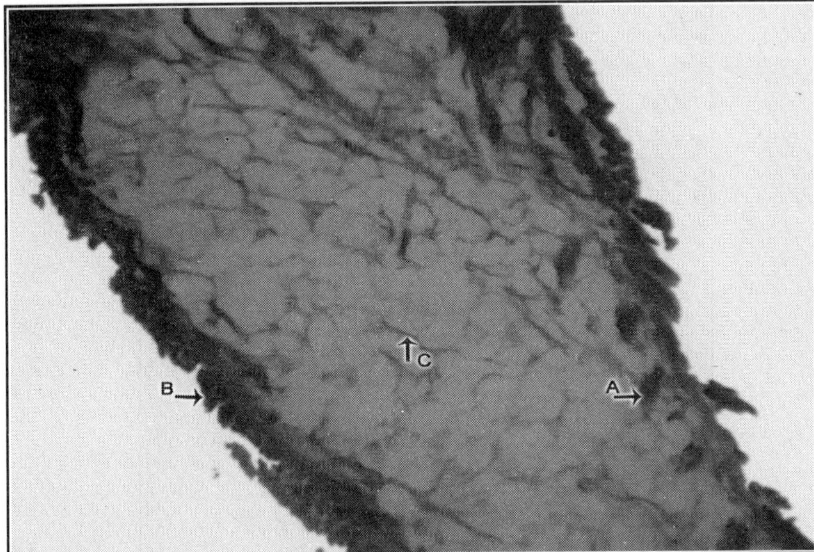

Fig. 2.8: 96 Hours Mantle Showing
(A) Epithelial mucocytes appeared empty with collapsed cell walls
(B) Desquamation of epithelial cells
(C) Atrophy of muscle fibres

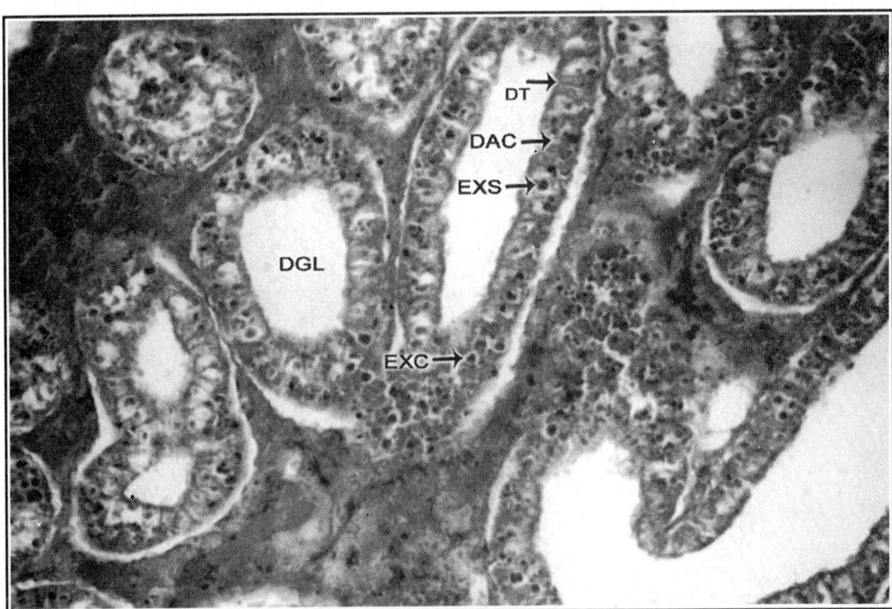

Fig. 2.9: Section of Digestive Gland (PAS) Normal
CT- Connective Tissue, DT- Digestive Tubule, EC- Excretory Cells
DGL - Digestive Gland Lumen, DAC-Digestive Absorptive cells

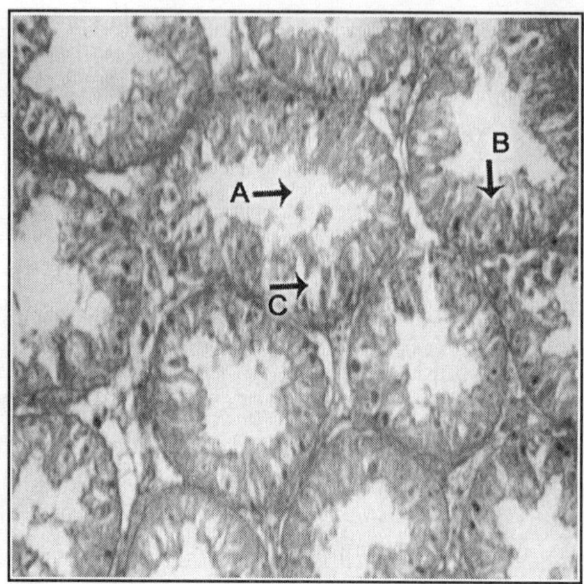

Fig. 2.10: Digestive Gland of *B. bengalensis* Exposed to 134.896 ppm Detergent (Tide) for 48 hrs. (PAS)

(A) Exudation in the lumen of tubules.

(B) Degeneration of hepatic cells

(C) Increased Vacuolization

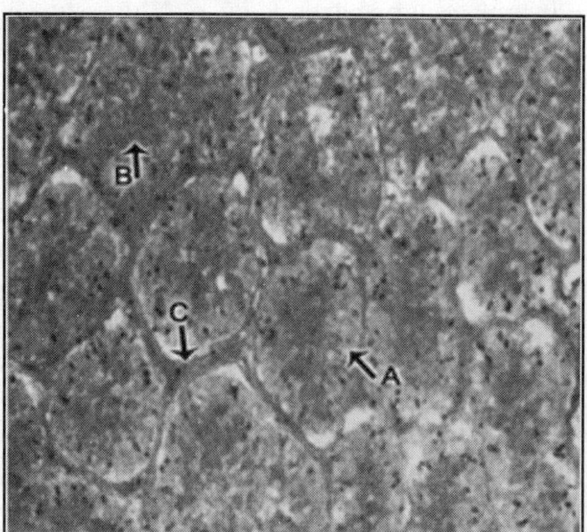

Fig. 2.11: Digestive Gland of *B. bengalensis* exposed to 69.18 ppm Detergent (Tide) for 96 hrs (PAS)

(A) Disintegration of cellular boundaries appears like cellular mass

(B) Luminal space filled with cell debris

(C) Peripheral thickening of hepatocytes

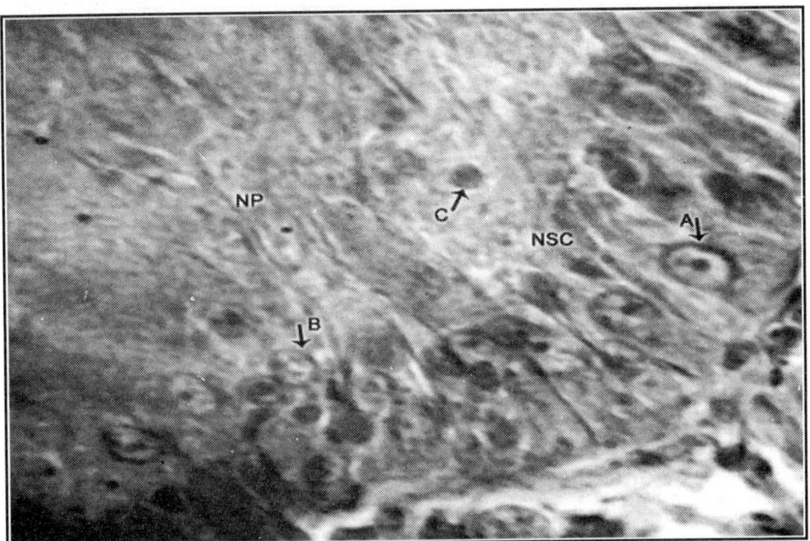

Fig. 2.12: Enlarged view of NS cells (A, B & C) – Azan.

(A) NSC-Neurosecretory cells

(B) 'A'- Large cells

(C) 'B'- Medium cells

(D) 'C'- Small cells

(E) NP - Neuro Pile

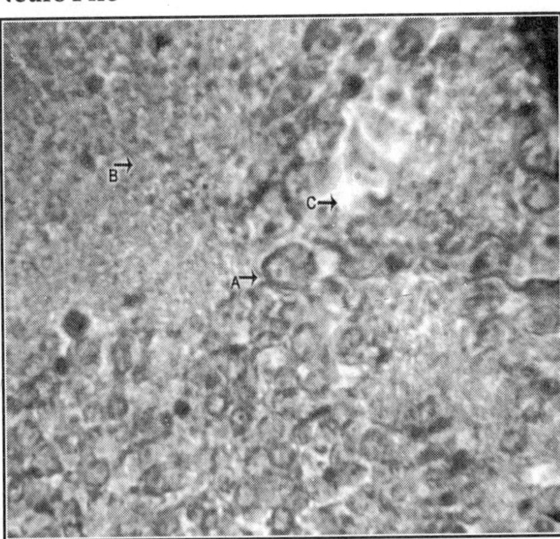

Fig. 2.13: Enlarged View of NS Cells Exposed to 134.896 ppm Detergent (Tide) for 48 hrs (Azan)

(A) Mild congestion of cells

(B) Degenerated neuropile

(C) Vacuolation in perineurium

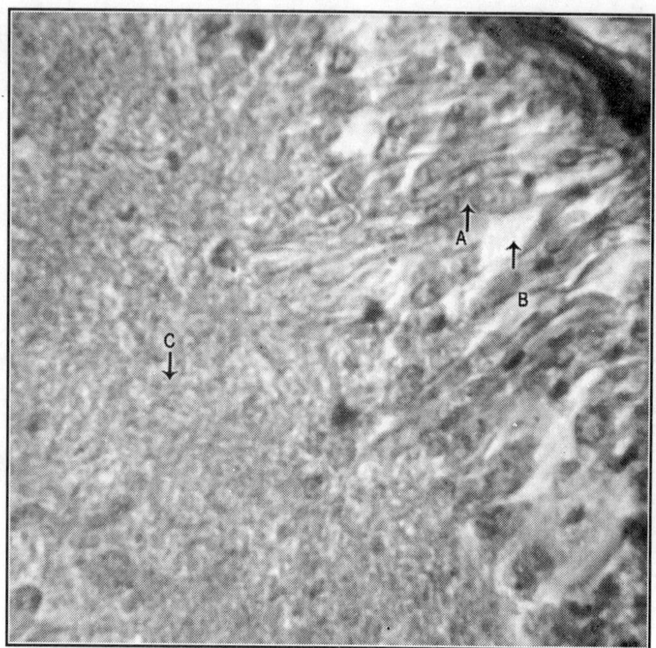

Fig. 2.14: Enlarged View of NS Cells Exposed to 69.18 ppm Detergent (Tide) for 96 hrs. (Azan)

(A) Shrinkage and disruption of NS cells

(B) Enlargement of vacuolation

(C) Disorientation of nerve fibres

DISCUSSION

Pollution is the chief wrecker of the declining of molluscan population. At the banks of the rivers, lakes, canals and streams washer men are active. Much of the detergent thus let into the water make a study of the sub-lethal effects on *Bellamyabengalensis*. *Bellamyabengalensis* is exposed to sub-lethal concentrations of detergent (Tide) for different periods of time for a histological study. The morphological effects of the detergents are clearly seen as the abnormal behaviour of snails and changes in histopathology of the various tissues like foot, mantle, digestive gland and nervous system. This gives a clue to understand the effect of pollutants on the aquatic organisms. Excess of mucous produced at the time of exposure is one of the reactions of stress; chemical irritation is also caused by molluscicidal chemicals (Triebskorn*et al*., 1998). Generally prosobranch snails have opercula to protect themselves when surrounding water becomes hazardous to them. Hence they are more tolerant to pollutants than opisthobranchs and pulmonates. When *B. bengalensis* are exposed to detergent at various concentrations, they showed abnormal behaviour. They moved slowly, then did not move, closed their opercula and secreted large amount of mucous. The present study has shown the LC_{50} values in various exposure periods and several degeneration changes in the histological structure of the foot, mantle, digestive gland and neurosecretory cells of *B. bengalensis* exposed to 96 hrs LC_{50} of the detergents.

The acute toxicity of detergent to freshwater invertebrates is generally less than that of metals and pesticides. Acute toxic effects of lead have been recorded at concentrations between 10.50 - 30.00 mg/L in *Babylonia areolata* (Supanopas et al., 2005). The median lethal cadmium concentration (LC_{50}) and 95% confidence limits in *Babylonia areolata* at 24, 48, 72 and 96 hrs were 0, 13.86, 4.39 and 3.35 mg/L respectively. The LC_{50} of cadmium in *B. areolata* progressively decreased as the exposure time was increased. The highest accumulation of cadmium was found in the digestive gland than foot (Tanhan et al., 2005). Based on theseLC_{50} values, *B. bengalensis* seemed to have a high tolerance to detergent because their LC_{50} values for 24, 48, 72 and 96 hrs were 213.7, 134.896, 104.71 and 69.18 ppm respectively. Another marine prosobranch, *Neritasaxitilis*, an efficient biologic monitor to heavy metal pollution in the Red sea had much higher LC_{50} values (300.35μg/L) Abd Allah and Moustafa (2002). Comparatively the freshwater prosobranch, *Filopaludinamartensimartensi* also had a high 96 hrs. LC_{50} value of (191. 69 mg/ L) Jantataemeet al (1996). Generally prosobranch snails have opercula to protect themselves when surrounding water becomes hazardous to them. Hence, they are more tolerant to pollutants than opisthobranchs and pulmonates. Kamble and potdar (2010) reported the histopathological changes after the exposure of *Bellamyabengalensis* to lead acetate up to 96 hrs are swelling and rupturing of digestive absorptive cells, degeneration of calciferous cells, atrophy in the muscular layer, and hypertrophy in cells in digestive gland of snail. Similar reports were observed in the digestive gland of *Gafrariumdivaricatum*exposed to xylene, benzene and gear oil-WSF (Agwuocha et al., 2011).

The snails, *Galba truncatula*were exposed to sub-lethal concentration of pesticide (Thiodon) at 0.33% and 0.65% in glass jar for short term exposure (96 hrs) caused significant histopathological changes in the tissues of digestive gland and foot (Cengiz et al., 2005). The snails were exposed to two sub-lethal concentration of endosulfan (0.4 and 0.8 mg/l) for period of 10 days effects the foot, mantle and digestive gland of great ramshorn snail *Planorbariuscorneus* revealed the similar histopathological examinations like desqumation of the epithelial cells, change in the number of mucocytes and atrophy of the columnar muscle fibres were observed which were observed in *B. bengalensis* exposed to detergent (Otludil et al., 2004). The terrestrial snail, *Eobaniavermiculata* exposed to sub lethal doses and concentration of two carbamatemolluscicides for 1, 3, 5, 7, 14 days of treatment showed the histopathological alterations in the digestive gland (Sherifa et al., 2007). Similar results were observed in *B. bengalensis*. Pathological disturbances in freshwater snail, *Bellamyadissimilis* due to pesticide toxicity is well documented by Jonnalagadda and Rao (1996). The LC_{50} concentrations of endosulfan, metacid, quinalphas and nuvan at 96 hrs are 1.8, 4.7, 1.9, 20.89g/L respectively. These four pesticides have affected the digestive gland and foot of *B. dissimilis*. BalajagannadhaRao and Kishore (2007) reported the effect of detergent Rin on the frog *Ranacyanophlyctis*. The values found being 267.1468, 193.7314, 177.0109 and 160.7681ppm for 24, 48, 72 and 96hrs of exposure to detergent in a static medium. These results indicate that the survival rate decreased as the exposure increased, at the time the LC_{50} values were determined through probit analysis.

In the present study it is interesting to note that histopathological changes induced by detergent are more intense. But there is no information on the histopathological effects of detergents on the tissues of molluscans. The present results are comparable with the findings in various gastropod snails by many scientists. The mantle of *Viviparusbengalensis* was exposed to sub lethal concentrations of pentachlorophenol and sodium pentachlorophenate resulting in the formation of intercellular spaces, the shrinkage and elongation of epithelial cells, enlargement of nuclei, shrinkage of the basement membrane and loss of shape of polygonal cells of connective tissue (Gupta and Durve, 2006). Heng and Rusin (2004) reported the cellular histological alterations in the digestive gland showing rupturing of hepatopancreatic luminal cells, cellular hypertrophy in snail *Turritella sp.* due to acute toxicity of zinc and copper. There was a prevalence of hepatocellular foci of cellular alterations (FCA), peripheral thickening and inflammation of hepatic tubules of the hepatocytes are observed in the digestive gland of giant land snail, *Archachatinamarginata* exposed to the sub-lethal concentrations of copper and lead (Otilojuet al., 2009). Hanumanteet al. (1979) observed the depletion of neurosecretory material in the neurohaemal areas and large number of vacuoles in the perikarya of both the cells after $CuSO_4$ treatment. Cytological alterations of NS cells observed in the *Indoplanorbisexustus*intoxicated with niclosamide are the enlargement of vacuoles in the cytoplasm. Essawyet al. (2009)investigated the neuropathological effect of the two carbamate pesticides; methomyl and methiocarb on the neurons of the buccal ganglia in the land snail *Eobaniavermiculata*. These alterations included shrinkage of the perikarya of neurons, increased cytoplasmic basophilia, and extreme indentation of the plasma membrane. In addition, the nuclei appeared karyolitic, eccentric, and highly shrunken with an irregular nuclear envelope.

Taking into consideration the curious accommodating abilities and successful survival of *B. bengalensis* in the pollutant waters of river Godavari, the animal has been selected for toxicological studies. Though there is every possibility of calling this an indicator species, we still hesitate to give this species that status because of its selectivity in its free distribution. The detergent 'Tide' has been selected for the study as this forms the main pollutant of the waters they inhabit.

The long lasting use of detergent causes the excess deposition of detergent compounds in the waterways which is toxic to freshwater snails. This leads not only to tissue damage in snail organs but also responsible for death which ultimately results in decrease in snail population. Therefore indiscriminate use of detergent by washer men should be discouraged particularly in an area where snails are abundant.

REFERENCES

Abd Allah, A.T., and Moustafa, M.A. (2002): Accumulation of Lead and Cadmium in the Marine Prosobranch Neritasaxtilis, Chemical Analysis, Light and Electron Microscopy, Environ Pollut, 116: 185.

Agwuocha, S., Kulkarni, B.G. and Pandey, A.K. (2011). Histopathological Alterations in Hepatopancreas of Gafrariumdivaricatum Exposed to Xylene, Benzene and Gear oil-WSF. Journal of Environmental Biology, 32(1): 35-38.

Balajagannadha Rao, K. and Kishore, B. (2007): Observations on the Effects of the Detergent Rin on the Frog Ranacyanophlyctis Schneider (Amphibia: Anura). J. of TheEkol, 7 (1-2): 107-112.

Belanger, S., Davidson, D., Cherry, D., Farris, J. and Reed, D. (1993): Effects of Cationic Surfactant Exposure to a Bivalve Mollusc in Streamesocosms. Environmental Toxicology and Chemistry, 12(10): 1789-1802.

Boer, H.H., Moorer-van Delft, C.M., Müller, L.J., Kiburg, B.,Vermorken, J.B. and Heimans, J.J.(1995): Ultra Structural and Neuropathological Effects of Taxol on Neurons of the Freshwater Snail Lymnaeastagnalis. J Neuro-Oncol, 25: 49-57.

Carpenter, K.E.(1924): A Study of the Fauna of Rivers Polluted by Lead Mining in the Aberystwyth District of Cardiganshire. Annal.Applied Biol, 11(1): 1-23.

Cengiz, E.I., Yildirim, M.Z., Otludil, B. and Unlu, E.(2005): Histopathological Effects of Thiodan on the Freshwater Snail Galba truncatula (Gastropoda: pulmonata). J. Applied Toxicol, 25 (8): 484-489.

Chellan, B., Ramesh, M. and Manavala Ramanujam, R. (2003): Lethal and Sub-lethal Effects of the Synthetic Detergents on Liver, Muscle and Branchial Na+, K+ ATPase Enzyme Activity in Labeorohita. Indian J. of. Fish, 50(3): 405-408.

Essawy, A.E., Abdelmeguied, N.E., Radwan, M.A., Hamed, S.S. and Hegazy, A.E.(2009): Neuropathological Effect of Carbamate Molluscicides on the Land Snail, Eobaniavermiculata. Cell. Biol. Toxicol, 25: 275-290.

Finney, D.J. (1971): Probit Analysis. 3rd ed., Cambridge University Press, London, pp. 333.

Glaister, J.R. (1986): In Principles of Toxicological Pathology. Taylor & Francis, London Philadelphia.

Gupta, P.K. and Durve, V.S. (2006): Histopathological Changes Induced by Pentachlorophenol and Sodium Pentachlorophenate in the Mantle of the Freshwater Snail Viviparusbengalensis (L). ActaHydrochem.Hydrobiol, 14: 433-437.

Gupta, P.K., Kangarot, B.S. and Durve, V. S.(1981): The Temperature Dependence of the Acute Toxicity of Copper to a Freshwater Pond Snail, Viviparusbengalensis, L. Hydrobiologia, 83 (3): 461-464.

Hanumante, M.M., Nagabhushanam, R. and Vaidya, D.P. (1979): Aberrations in the Neurosecretory Cells of a Fresh Water Pulmonate, Indoplanorbisexustus, Chronically Exposed to Sub-lethal Concentration of Two Molluscicides, $Bacl_2$ and CuSO4. Bull. Environm.Contam.Toxicol, 23: 070-072.

Henderson, C., Pickering, Q.H. and Cohen, J.M.(1959): The Toxicity of Synthetic Detergents and Soaps to Fish, Sewage ind. Wastes, 31: 295-306.

Heng, L.Y. and Rusin, S. (2004): The Bioaccumulation of Trace Essential Metals by the Freshwater Snail Turritellasp. Found in the Rivers of Borneo East Malaysia. J. Biol. Sci, 4 (4): 441-444.

Hinton, D.E., Kendall, M.W. and Silver, B.B. (1973): Use of Histologic and Histochemical Assessment in the Prognosis of the Effects of Aquatic Pollutants. Biological Methods for the Assessment for Water Quality. American Society for Testing and Materials, 194-208.

Jantataeme, S., Kruatrachue, M., Kaewsawangsap, S., Chitramvong, Y., Sretarugsa, P. and Upatham, E.S.(1996): Acute Toxicity and Bioaccumulation of Lead in the Snail Filopaludina (Siamopaludina) Martensimartensi (Frauenfeldt). J. Sci. Soc.Thailand, 22: 237-247.

John, W. A.(1970): Chronic Effects of Linear Alkylate Sulfonate Detergent on Gammaruspseudolimnaeus, Campelomadecisum and Physaintegra. Water Research, 4(3): 251-257.

Jonnalagadda, P.R. and Rao, B.P. (1996): Histopathological Changes Induced by Specific Pesticides on Some Tissues of the Fresh Water Snail, Bellamyadissimilis (Muller) Bull. Environ. Contam.Toxicol, 57: 648-654.

Jose, V.T. and Oliva Nunez. (1987): Effect of Sodium lauryl Sulfate on Limnaeaperegra Shells. Bull. Environm. Contam.oxicol, 39: 1036-1040.

Kamble, N.A. and Potdar, V.V. (2010): Hepatopancreatic Damage in Snail Bellamyabengalensis (L) Tested Against Lead Acetate Toxicity. Indian Journal of Comparative Animal Physiology, Vol. 28 (1): 7-10.

Lloyd, R. (1977): The LC_{50} Values Derived from Acute Toxicity Tests are Best Used to Assess the Margins of Safety. Aston, 102-109.

Muley, D.V. and Mane, U.H. (1990): Histopathological Changes in Body Parts of the Freshwater Gastropod, Viviparusbengalensis Lam. due to Pesticides. J. Environ. Biol, 11: 413-425.

Otitoloju, A.A., Ajikobi, D. O. and Egonmwan, R. I. (2009): Histopathology of Bioaccumulation of Heavy Metals (Cu & Pb) in the Giant land Snail, Archachatinamarginata (Swainson). The Open Environmental Pollution & Toxicology Journal, 1: 79-88.

Otludil, B., Cengiz, E.I., Yildirim, M.Z., Unver, O. and Unlu, E. (2004): The Effect of Endosulfan on the Great Ramshorn Snail Planorbariuscorneus (Gastropoda: Pulmonata): A Histological Study. Chemosphere, 56: 707-716.

Palanichamy, R. and Murugan, V.(1991): Acute Toxicity of House Hold Detergents to a Weed Fish, Rasboraelonga. J. Environ. Biol, 12(2): 143-148.

Panwar, R.S., Gupta, R.A., Joshi, H.C. and Kapoor, D. (1982): Toxicity of Some Chlorinated Hydrocarbon and Organophosphorous Insecticides to Gastropod, Viviparusbengalensis Swainson. J. Environ. Biol, 3 (1): 31-36.

Radwan, M.A., El-Wakil, H .B. and Osman, K. A.(1992): Toxicity and Biochemical Impact of Certain Oximecarbamate Pesticides Against Terrestrial Snail, Thebapisana (Muller). J. Environ. Sci. Health, 27: 759-773.

Radwan, M.A., Essawy, A.E., Abdelmeguied, N.E., Hamed, S. S. and Hegazy, A. E.(2008): Biochemical and Histochemical Studies on the Digestive Gland of Eobaniavermiculata Snails Treated with Carbamate Pesticides. Pesticide BiochemPhysiol, 90: 154-167.

Sherifa, S.H., Nabila, E.A., Essawy, A.E., Radwan, M.A. and Hegazy A.E. (2007): Histological and Ultrastructural Changes Induced by Two Carbamatemolluscicides on the Digestive Gland of Eobaniavermiculata. Journal of Biological Sciences, 7(6): 1017-1037.

Sprague, J. B.(1969): Measurement of Pollutant Toxicity to Fish. I: Bioassay Methods for Acute Toxicity. Water Research, 3: 793-821.

Supanopas, P., Sretarugsa, P., Kruatrachue, M., Pokethitiyook, P. and Upatham, E.S.(2005): Acute and Sub-chronic Toxicity of Lead to the Spotted Babylon, Babylonia areolata (Neogastropoda: Buccinidae). Journal of Shellfish Research, 24 (1): 91-98.

Tanhan, P., Sretarugsa, P., Pokethitiyook, P., Kruatrachue, M.and Upatham, E.S. (2005): Histopathological Alterations in the Edible Snail, Babylonia Areolata (Spotted Babylon) in Acute and Subchronic Cadmium Poisoning, Environ. Toxicol, 20: 142.

Tarazona, J.V., Munoz, M.J. and Ortiz, J.A.(1983): Introduccion al estudio. Ecotoxicologico de la cuence del rio Tajo. In: Res II Cong EspLimnd, Murcia, Spain.

Triebskorn, R., Christensen, K. and Heim, I. (1998): Effects of Orally and Dermally Applied Metaldehyde on Mucus Cells of Slugs (*Derocerasreticulatum*) Depending on Temperature and duration of Exposure. J. Moll. Stud, 64: 355-375.

Viant, M.R., J.H. Walton, P.L. TenBrook and Tjeerdema, R.S. (2002): Sublethal Actions of Copper in Abalone (Haliotisrufescens) as Characterized by in Vivo 31P-NMR. Aquat.Toxicol, 57: 139-151.

Warner, R.E. (1967): Bioassays for Microchemical Environmental Contaminants. Bull. W.H.O, 36: 181.

Abundance and Diversity of Ephemeroptera and its Correlation with Physico-chemical Properties of River Narmada Madhya Pradesh, India

Shailendra Sharma*; Anis Siddiqui**
Imtiyaz Tali; Zahoor Pir*****

* Department of Biotechnology, Adarsh Institute of Management & Science Damnod (M.P.), India
** Department of Zoology, Govt. Holkar Science College, Indore (M.P.), India
*** Department of Zoology, Govt. PG Girls College Motitabela, Indore (M.P.), India

ABSTRACT

Limnological studies on various stations of river Narmada was carried out from June 2010 to December 2010.The present investigation was carried out to enumerate the biodiversity of ephemeroptera fauna and to analyze water qualities parameters throughout various stations of river Narmada. Water samples and insects were collected monthly from August 2010 to July 2011. Mayflies were sampled using standard entomological methods, while water samples were analyzed using APHA methods to determine the Physico- chemical properties. The physico-chemical parameters showed wide variations throughout the study period. During present investigation, 17 species comprising of 6 families were recorded including Baetidae, Caenidae, Ephemeridae, Ephemerellidae, Heptageniidae and Leptophtebiidae. The dominant family was Baetidae of which Baetis simplex was the most common species. The value of Shannon and Weaver Index was found within the range between 0 and 2.597.

Keywords: *Physico-chemical parameters, ephemeroptera fauna, diversity, Pollution, narmada river.*

INTRODUCTION

Insects are the most diverse group of organisms in freshwater. Estimates on the global number of aquatic insect species derived from the fauna of

North America, Australia and Europe is about 45,000, of this about 5,000 species are estimated to inhabit inland wetlands of India. Aquatic insects of inland wetlands comprise some well- known groups like mayflies (Ephemeroptera), dragonflies (Odonata) and caddiesflies (Trichoptera).

Among the MacroinvertebratesEpemeroptera (Mayflies) are truly the 'ballerians' of the insect world. Mayflies are an ancient order of insects that are globally distributed in both northern and southern hemispheres. Mayfly is the common name for any of the insects that belong to the order Ephemeroptera. Other common names for Mayflies include 'day fly', 'june bug', 'shad fly', 'canandian solider' and 'fish fly' (Staneff-Cline and Neff 2007).

Mayflies have a complex life cycle, involving both aquatic and terrestrial phases. Such life cycles create evolutionary dichotomy with selection pressures operating in two, more or less independent environments (Wilbur 1980). This dichotomy will lead to the reduction of one of these phases. This is clearly seen in the extremely short-lived adult stages of the Ephemeroptera whose sole, but crucial roles are reproduction and dispersal. They are the only insects to have two flying stages and can be recognized by their three caudal filaments (tails) at the tip of the abdomen, and a single claw on each leg. This differentiates them from the closely related stoneflies which have two tarsal claws. The flying stages are characterized by relatively large forewings, which are usually kept upright, and reduced or nonexistent hind wings.

Ephemeroptera nymphs are usually microhabitat specialists. Each species survives best on a specific substrate at a certain depth under water with a certain amount of wave action. For example, Rithrogena generally live in medium to large trout streams. Ephemeridae burrow into soft areas where flow is slower, or in areas of lakes and rivers where deposits occur; the particular substrate and burrow depends on the genus. The primitive habitat of schistonate mayflies is still water even though most extant mayflies live in running water (Mccafferty 1990). In some areas, succession occurs by different species. For example, in Utah *Epeoruslongimanus* is followed by *E. deceptivus*. Some species dominate in the spring while others dominate in autumn (Edmunds *et al.*, 1976). Some mayfly nymphs are quite sensitive to pollution and are used to evaluate water pollution and stream health.

A number of factors influence Ephemeroptera species distributions. It has been reported in a number of studies that environmental variables such as stream size, velocity, pH, conductivity, nutrients, amount of dissolved oxygen, riparian forest, and presence of impoundments are associated with Ephemeroptera distribution (Ogbogu and Akinya 2001, Ogbeibu and Oribhabor 2002, Rueda *et al.*, 2002, Buss and Salles 2007).

Deforestation is one of the primary threats to mayfly biodiversity and conservation in the tropics (Bensteadet *al*., 2003, Benstead and Pringle 2004, Dudgeon 2000a, 2000b) whereas pollution (Rosenberg and Resh 1993) and building and reshaping of the banks leading to a lack of connectivity with the floodplain (Buijse et *al*., 2002) or habitat fragmentation (Zwick 1992) are the main causes in temperate areas.

Mayflies are extremely important in the ecology of fresh water streams. Both immature and adult mayflies are an important part of the food web, particularly for carnivorous fish such as trout in cold water streams or bass and catfish in warm water streams. Their presence is an indication of good water quality given their sensitivity to pollution (PSERIE 2003). Mayflies are highly susceptible to pollution and thus are important indicators of water quality. Most mayfly species are known as sensitive to pollution (Bauernfeind and Moog 2000). Mayflies requires high quality water for their existence, thus biologists have used their presence or absence, in conjunction with the numbers present at a particular location in a stream or river, to develop several indices of water quality.

MATERIALS AND METHODS

Study Site

The Narmada, also called Rewa is a river in central India and the fifth largest river in the Indian subcontinent. It is the third largest river that completely flows within India after Ganges and Godavari. It forms the traditional boundary between North India and South India and flows westwards over a length of 1,312 km before draining through the Gulf of Cambey (Khambat) into the Arabian Sea, 30 km west of Bharuch city of Gujarat (NVDA). It is one of only three major rivers in peninsular India that runs from east to west (largest west flowing river) along with the Tapti River and the Mahi River. It is the only river in India that flows in a rift valley flowing west between the Satpura and Vindhya ranges although the Tapti River and Mahi River also flow through rift valleys but between different ranges.

The Narmada basin, hemmed between Vindya and Satpuda ranges, extends over an area of 98,796 km^2 and lies between east longitudes 72 degrees 32′ to 81 degrees 45′ and north latitudes 21 degrees 20′ to 23 degrees 45′ lying on the northern extremity of the Deccan Plateau. The basin covers large areas in the states of Madhya Pradesh (86%), Gujarat (12%) and a comparatively smaller area (2%) in Maharashtra. The river Narmada receives 41 principal tributaries (Alvares and Ramesh 1988), each with a catchments area exceeding 500 sq. kms. Out of these 22 (21 in MP and 1 in Gujarat) joins the river from left bank and 19 (18 in MP and 1 in Gujarat) from right bank (Ghoshet *al*., 2004). The total length of these principal tributaries is 3387 Kms.

Sampling Stations

The present study was conducted for the period of one year from August 2010 to July 2011. The water and biological samples were collected from the various selected sampling stations in the river Narmada which are as under. A reconnaissance visit to the proposed study stations was made to select sampling locations, design sampling protocol and work out the logistics.

(A) Omkareshwar (S1)

Omkareshwar is a famous place of pilgrimage located in Khandwa District of Madhya Pradesh, on the Mandhata hill on the banks of the Narmada river. The river Narmada branches into two and forms an island Mandhata or Shivapuri in the center. The shape of the island resembles that of the visual representation of the Omkara sound, OM. There are two temples here, one to Omkareshwar and one to Amareshwar. Millions of pilgrims of both local and foreigners visit the place every year. There are steamboats across the Narmada river and also two connecting bridges to reach the temple.

It's Latitude is 22° 15′ 1″ N and Longitude is 76° 8′ 48″E.

(B) Khalghat (S2)

Khalghat is a small town and a Municipality in Dhar district in the state of Madhya Pradesh, India. It is located on the banks of Narmada River and national Highway 3 Agra- Indore – Dhule – Mumbai. It is 76 km away from Indore.

Its latitude is 22° 10′ O″ N and longitude is 75° 27′O″ E.

(C) Koteshwer (S3)

Koteshwer is a holy place in Barwani District Madhya Pradesh in Central India. It is located 17 km from Barwani District and 160 km from indore.

Its latitude is 22° 1′ 60″N and longitude is 75° 54′ 0″ E.

Physico-chemical Analysis

The analysis of the Physico-chemical properties of water was performed by standard method prescribed in limnological literature. The Physico-chemical parameters were determined by standard methods of APHA (2002).

Biological Analysis

Collection of Samples: Different methods were employed to sample aquatic insects from the target habitats. The samples were collected with various types of nets, surber sampler at shallow profundal zone, Ekman grab at deeper profundal zone and by random sampling. Supportive qualitative sampling was done by a hand net, D-net and by handpicking the zoo-benthos from different substrata in similar habitats. The substrate was disturbed in front of the D-net to collect the benthos. Artificial substrates, woods and other detritus were also looked upon for insects. The stones were also turned and observed.

Preservation and Further Investigation

The samples were preserved in 75% alcohol solution and transported to the laboratory for further investigation. In the laboratory, the samples were rinsed thoroughly with pure water to remove preservative through a sieve (100 ìm mesh size). The samples were then poured in a white-bottomed tray of the appropriate size for good visualisation and the sorted mayflies were then identified.

Identification of Samples: Collected samples were examined under a standard microscope and identified using standard taxonomic literature. Samples were assigned to a family or genus using taxonomic keys like Dudgeon (1999), Soldan and Landa (1999), Barber-James and Lugoortiz (2003).

Diversity Index

The numerical relationship between the species population and whole communities often provides better reliable indications of pollution than single species (Datta and Datta 1995). These relationships are represented by "Diversity Indices". In the present study Shannon and Weaver diversity index (H) were used.

RESULTS

The result of the physico-chemical parameters of river Narmada water is presented in Table 3.1. The spatial trend in the pattern of each physical and chemical characteristic was similar along the river. During the present study, the physico-chemical parameters showed wide variations throughout the study period. The water temperature varied between 18-35°c. The minimum water temperature was recorded in the month of January and the maximum water temperature was recorded in the month of May. The value of pH varied from 7.1 to 8.9 and the Dissolved oxygen fluctuated between 7.1 mg/l to 8.9 mg/l . The biological oxygen demand varied between 0.31 mg/l to 1.3 mg/l with minimum in January and maximum in the month of May. Alkanity of the river Narmada varied between 95- 235. Minimum alkanity was recorded at Station I & III and maximum alkanity was recorded at Station I. The value of total hardness during the present study varied between 85 mg/l to 190 mg/l. Minimum total hardness value was recorded in October and maximum total hardness was recorded in the month of June.

Ephemeropterans were present at all sampling stations during the study period but at Station III (Koteshwer), the abundance of Ephemeroptera was low. A combined total of 17 taxa of Ephemeropterain six families were present along the whole system. The dominant family was Baetidae of which Baetis simplex was the most common species. Maximum biodiversity of ephemeroptera were noted in post monsoon and summer season.

At Station I, seventeen species of Ephemeroptera (Mayflies) belonging to six families were recorded. The dominant species recorded were *Baetiellaladakae*and *Baetis simplex* belonging to family Baetidae, while the species *Heptageniasolangensis* belonging to family Heptageniidae was less dominant throughout the study period. At station II, the most dominant species recorded were *Baetiellaladakae, Baetis simplex, Thraulusgopalani* belonging to family Baetidae and Leptophtebiidae and species *Heptagenianubila* belonging to family Heptageniidae was less dominant as compered to other species. In the present study, sixteen species of Ephemeroptera (Mayflies) belonging to six families were recorded. The most dominant species recorded was *Baetis simplex* belonging to family Baetidae and *Heptagenianubila* belonging to family Heptageniidae was totally absent throughout the study period at this sampling station. The diversity and distribution of Ephemeroptera species at this station was very low as compared to other selected sampling stations.

Table 3.1: Range of Variation, Mean and Standard Deviation of Water Quality Parameters of River Narmada during August 2009 to July 2010

Parameters	Station I	Station II	Station III
Temperature	27.08 ± 0.707 (22-33)	25.33 ± 1.414 (18-32)	28.25 ± 1.414 (22-35)
pH	8.6 ± 0.919 (7.6-9.3)	7.8 ± 0.2828 (7.4-8.5)	8.8 ± 0.141 (7.3-8.8)
Dissolved Oxygen	7.87 ± 0.070 (7.2-8.7)	8.1 ± 0.070 (7.1-8.9)	7.9 ± 0.141 (7.2-8.8)
Biochemical Oxygen Demand	0.66 ± 0.098 (0.31-1.05)	0.75 ± 0.056 (0.37-1.25)	0.72 ±0.084 (0.35-1.30)
Alkanity	154.41 ± 21.21 (95-235)	169 ± 10.60 (110-222)	158.92 ± 9.89 (95-225)
Total Hardness	122.83 ± 14.14 (85-190)	132.25 ± 14.14 (98-170)	128.25 ± 17.67 (90-160)

The value of Shannon and Weaver Index during the study period was found within the range between 0 to 2.597. This indicates that river Narmada has moderate water quality except during monsoon season in which water gets polluted due to heavy floods. The minimum value of Shannon and Weaver Index was recorded at Station III.

DISCUSSION

The physico-chemical parameters are important for assessing the water quality. Physico-chemical properties of a natural water body (like river), their spatial distribution and variation in time provide a lot of information about the ecosystem. The physico-chemical characteristics of the water body have direct influence over its flora and fauna. It is difficult to understand biological phenomena fully without the knowledge of water chemistry as the metabolism of the ecosystem and hydro biological interactions may be understood in relation to water chemistry (Kulahresth 2005). Study of physico-chemical characteristics of the river Narmada depict that the various physical and chemical characteristics show monthly and spatial changes.

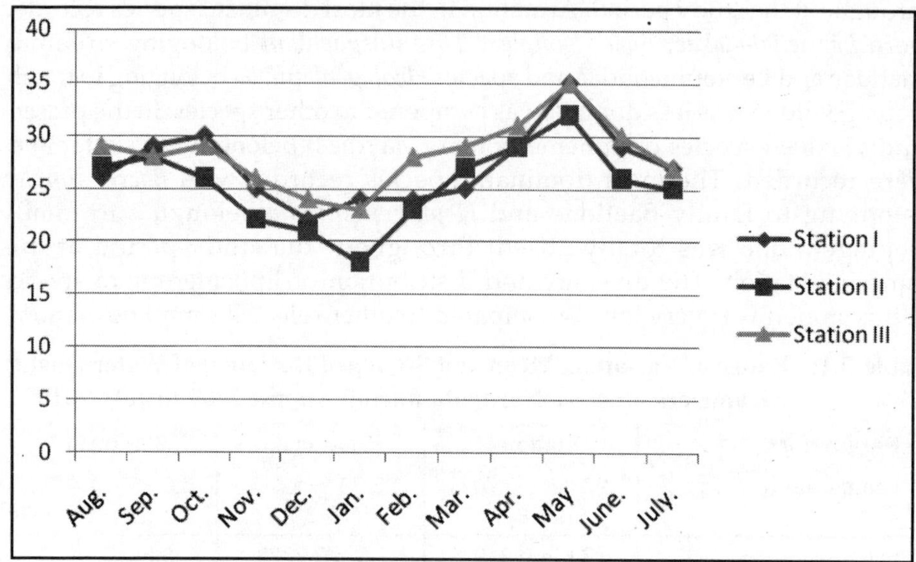

Fig. 3.1: Monthly Flunctuation in Temperature (°C) in River Narmada from August 2010 to July 2011

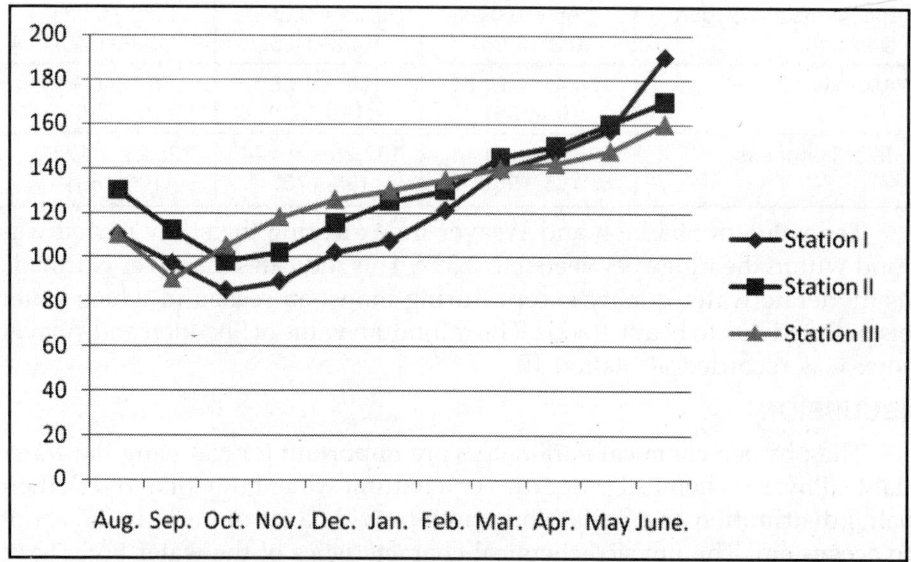

Fig. 3.2: Monthly Flunctuation in pH in River Narmada from August 2010 to July 2011

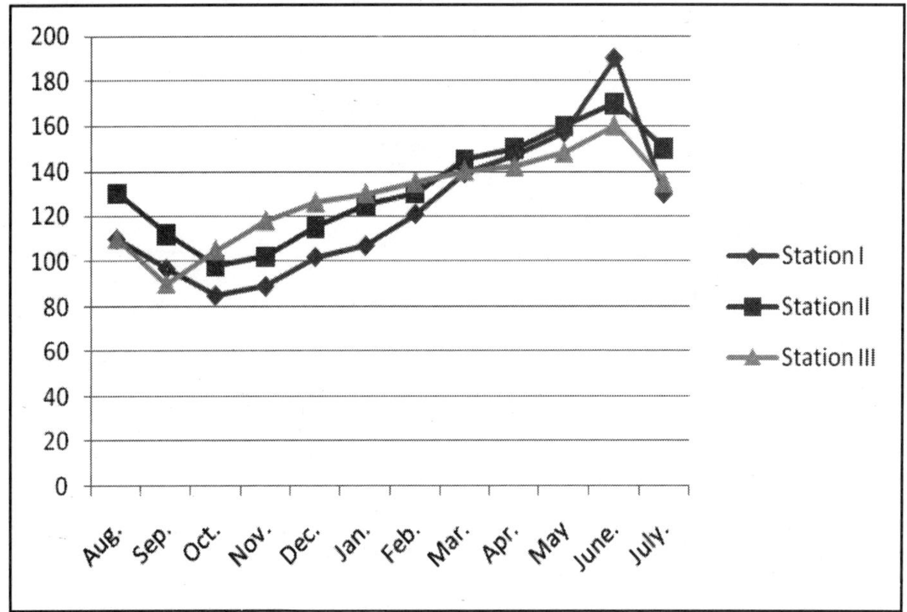

Fig. 3.3: **Monthly Flunctuation in Dissolved Oxygen in Narmada River from August 2010 to July 2011**

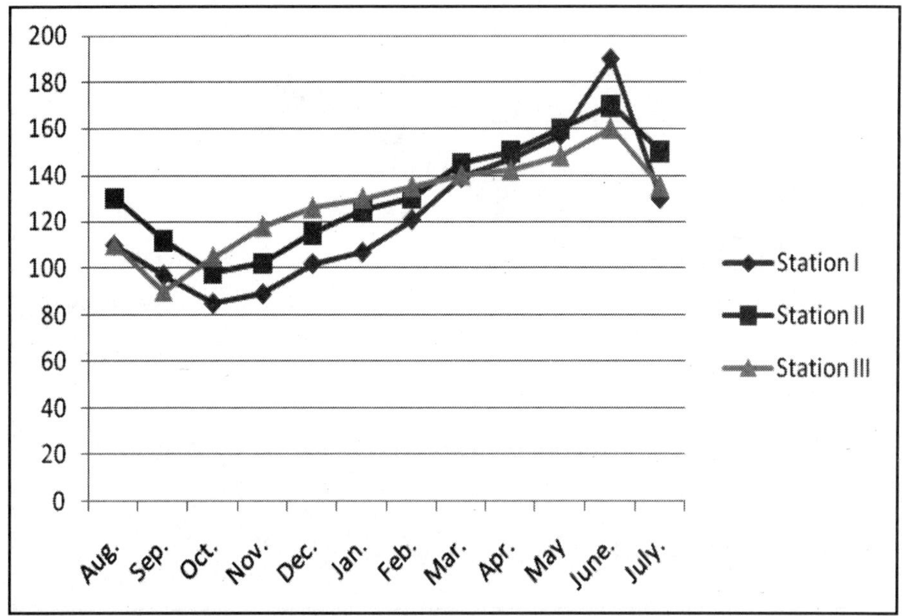

Fig. 3.4: **Monthly Flunctuation in Biological Oxygen Demand in Narmada River from August 2010 to July 2011**

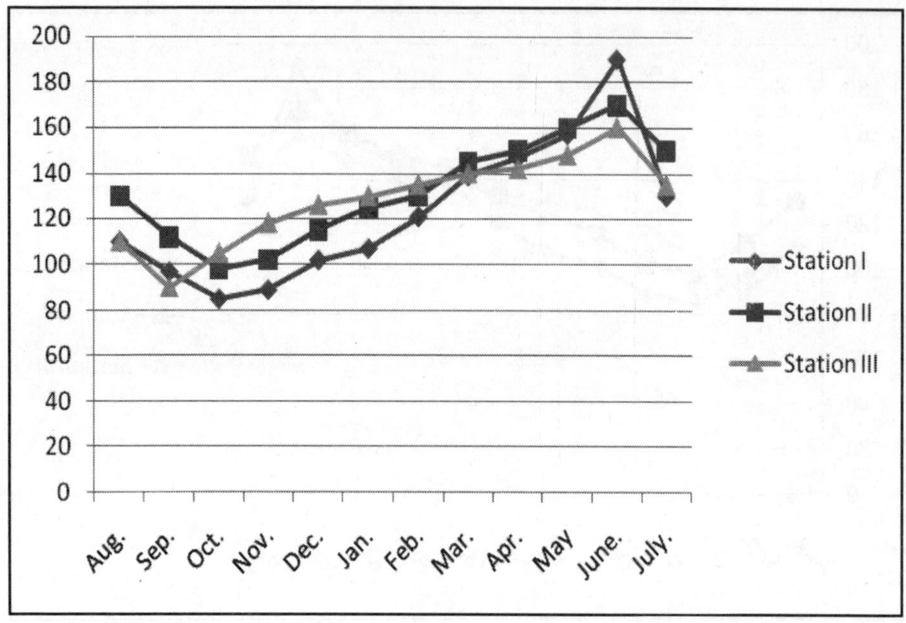

Fig. 3.5: Monthly Flunctuation in Alkanity in Narmada River from August 2010 to July 2011

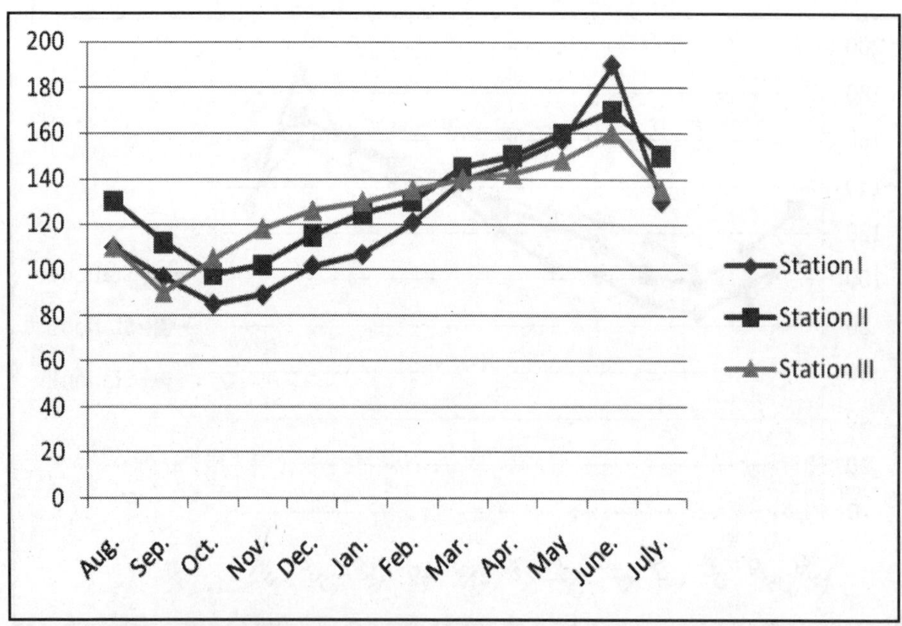

Fig. 3.6: Monthly Flunctuation in Total Hardness in Narmada River from August 2010 to July 2011

In present study the temperature of water ranged between 18°c to 35°c.These types of observations in river Narmada have also reported by Yodha (2004), Verma (2006), Bakawle (2008) and Sharma *et al.*, (2011).Highest values of pH in summer may be due to the reduction in water volume and increase in photosynthetic activities and lower values of pH in rainy season may be attributed due to the dilution of water by rain. The present study records of DO values resemble the general trend as reported from other Indian rivers. As per the IST the minimum DO recommended is 3.00 mg/l. In the present study, the DO values were above 3.00 mg/l at all the study stations and hence river Narmada is not polluted respect to dissolved oxygen.During the present study the BOD values fluctuated between the ranges of 0.31 mg/l– 1.30mg/l at all sampling stations.Similar observations were confirmed by many other workers such as Pathak and Mudgal (2005), Mishra and Joshi (2003).In the present study total alkanity values resemble the general trend as reported by various workers from other Indian water bodies. Seasonal variation in total alkanity in the river Narmada seems to be controlled by several factors such as rain fall, sewage inputs and water temperature, but higher photosynthesis at the surface also has profound importance. The huge alkaline condition in river Narmada may be due to high photosynthesis activity of phytoplankton.In the present study the values of the total hardness varied between 85- 190 mg/l. These observations indicate that the Narmada water is neither hard nor very soft. The lower values of total hardness in post monsoon might be due to settlement of anions and cations.

Ephemeroptera is an important group of insects used in the bioassessment and monitoring of freshwater bodies worldwide because of their relative abundance in a wide variety of substrates and their increasing chances of detecting pollution impacts. They are often the most abundant and recognizable freshwater insects' especially in riffles, runs, and marginal vegetation and form an important component of fish diets (Miserendino and Pizzolon 2001, Barber-James *et al.*, 2008).

In the present study 17 species of Ephemeroptera (Mayflies) belonging to 6 families were recorded from river Narmada. The population of mayflies fluctuated from season to season. The mayfly diversity was maximum in post monsoon season and during summer and was very low in monsoon season. This is consistent with the observations made by Arimoro and Ikomi (2009) that numbers of taxa and the mean abundance of mayflies increased in the dry season and decreased in the wet season in the upper reaches of river Warri, Niger Delta.

During the present study the diversity of mayfly nymphs was very low in monsoon season due to the heavy floods and poor water quality in the river. Pupilli and Puig (2003) also reported that floods especially those with a long return time can have a catastrophic effect on mayfly communities. Maldonado *et al*., (2001) while studying four non- Andean streams in central Venezuela reported that the rainfall to be a determining factor in the temporal fluctuation of density and composition of mayfly communities.

In the present study the diversity of mayflies was very low in monsoon season due to pollution inputs by runoff waters, lower values of dissolved oxygen and disturbed ecological condition by high water current, which were directly responsible for reduction of mayfly species. Similar trend was observed by Kaushik*et al*., (1991) and Shukla and Shrivastava (2011),who showed the Ephemeroptera population was very low during rainy season due to high water discharge, which destroys habitats.

REFERENCES

Alvares C. and Billorey R. (1988): Damming the Narmada. Published by Third World Network, Malaysia. 1-196.

APHA (2002): Standard Method for Examination of Water and Waste Water, American Public Health Association Inc. New York 22nd Ed.

Arimoro F. O. and Ikomi R. B. (2009): Ecological Integrity of Upper Warri River, Niger Delta Using Aquatic Insects as Bioindicators. *Ecological Indicators*, 9: 455-461.

Bakawle S. (2008): Effect of Impoundment on Fish Population Dynamics & Socio-economic Status of Fishermen Ph.D. Thesis, Devi Ahilya University, Indore (M.P.): 1-231.

Barber-James H.M. and Lugoortiz C.R. (2003): Ephemeroptera. In I.J. de Moor, J.A. Day, & F.C. de Moor (Eds.), Guides to the Freshwater Invertebrates of Southern Africa South Africa: *Water Resource Commission Pretoria*. 7(1): 16-159.

Barber-James H.M., Gattolliat J., Sartori M. and Hubbard M.D. (2008): Global Diversity of Mayflies (Ephemeroptera, Insecta) in Freshwater. *Hydrobiologia*, 595: 339-350.

Bauernfeind E. and Moog O. (2000): Mayflies (Insecta: Ephemeroptera) and the Assessment of Ecological Integrity: A Methodological Approach. *Hydrobiologia*, 422: 71-83.

Benstead J.P. and Pringle C.M. (2004): Deforestation Alters the Resource Base and Biomass of Endemic Stream Insects in Eastern Madagascar. *Freshwater Biology*, 49: 490-501.

Benstead J.P., Rham P.H., Gattolliat J.L., Gibon F.M., Loiselle P.V., Sartori M. and Sparks J.S. (2003): Conserving Madagascar's Freshwater Biodiversity. *Bioscience*, 53: 1101-1111.

Buijse A.D., Coops H., Staras M., Jans L.H., Van Geest G.J. Grift R.E. and Ibelings B.W. (2002): Restoration Strategies for River Floodplains Along Large Low Land Rivers in Europe. *Freshwater Biology*, 47: 889-907.

Buss D.F. and Salles F.F. (2007): Using Baetidae Species as Biological Indicators of Environmental Degradation in a Brazilian River Basin. *Environmental Monitoringand Assessment*, 130: 365-372.

Datta M.J. and Datta J.S. (1995): Fundamentals of Freshwater Biology. Narendra Publishing House. Delhi (India). 1-222.

Dudgeon D. (1999): Tropical Asian Streams-zoobenthos, Ecology and Conservation. *Hongkong University Press*. Hongkong. 828.

Dudgeon D. (2000a): The Ecology of Tropical Asian Rivers and Streams in Relation to Biodiversity Conservation. *Annual Review of Ecology and Systematics*, 31: 239-263.

Dudgeon D. (2000b): Riverine Biodiversity in Asia: A Challenge for Conservation Biology. *Hydrobiologia*, 418: 1-13.

Edmunds G.F., Steven J., Jensen L. and Lewis B. (1976): The Mayflies of North and Central America. University of Minnesota Press, Minneapolis.

Ghosh T.K., Shakila B. and Kaul S.N. (2004): Protection of Ecologicaliy Sensitive Areas: Origin of Rivers and Upper Catchment Areas. *J. of Indian Association for Enviro.Management*, 31: 59-64.

Kaushik S., Sharma S. and Saksena D.N. (1991): Ecological Studies on Certain Polluted Lentic Waters of Gwalior Region with Reference to Aquatic Insect Communities. *Current Trends of Limnology*, 1: 185-200.

Kulshrestha S.K. (2005): Biodiversity of Tropical Aquatic Ecosystems Anmol Publ. New Delhi. pp: 1-438.

Maldonado V., Perez B. and Cressa C. (2001): Seasonal Variation of Ephemeroptera in Four Streams of Guatopo National Park, Venezuela. In: Dominguez E. (Eds.) Trends in Research in Ephemeroptera and Plecoptera. Kluwe Academic/Plenum Publishers. New York.

Mccafferty W.P. (1990): Ephemeroptera. Bulletin of the Amercian Museum of Natural History, No. 195.

Miserendino M.L. and Pizzolon L.A. (2001): Abundance and Altitudinal Distribution of Ephemeroptera in an Andean-Patagonean River System (Argentina). In E. Dominguez (Ed.), *Trends in Research in Ephemeroptera & Plecoptera* The Netherlands: Kluwer Academic. pp: 135-142.

Mishra S. and Joshi B.D. (2003): Assessment of Water Quality with Few Selected Parameters of River Ganga at Haridwar. *J. Env. Zool*, 17(2): 113-122.

Ogbeibu A.E. and Oribhabor B.J. (2002): Ecological Impact of River Impoundment Using Benthic Macroinvertebrates as Indicator. *Water Research*, 36: 2427-2436.

Ogbogu S.S. and Akinya T.O. (2001): Distribution and Abundance of Insect Orders in Relation to Habitat Types in Opa Stream Reservoir, Nigeria. *Journal of Aquatic Science*, 16(1): 7-12.

Pathak S.K. and Mudgal L.K. (2005): Limnology and Biodiversity of Fish Fauna in Virla Reservoir, MP India. *J. Comp. Toxicol. Physiol.* 2(1) 86-90.

Pennsylvania State University at Erie (PSERIE) (2003): Return of the Mayfly: An Indicator of an Improving Habitat Penn State at Erie. Retrieved January 15, 2008.

Pupilli E. and Puig M.A. (2003): Effects of a Major Flood on the Mayfly and Stonefly Populations in a Mediterranean Stream (Matarranye Stream. Ebro River Basin, North East Spain). in E. Gaino, Editor Research Update on Ephemeroptera and Plecoptera. University of Perugia, Italy. 381-389.

Rosenberg D.M. and Resh V. (1993): Freshwater Biomonitoring and Benthic Macroinvertebrates. Chapman & Hall, New York, 1-488.

Rueda J., Camacho A., Mezquita F., Hernanadez R. and Roca J. R. (2002): Effect of Episodic and Regular Sewage Discharge on Water Chemistry and Macroinvertebrate Fauna of a Mediteranean Stream. *Water Airand Soil Pollution, 140*(34): 425-444.

Sharma S., Rakesh V., Savita D. and Praveen J. (2011): Evaluation of Water Quality of Narmada River with Reference to Physico-chemical Parameters at Hoshangabad City, MP, India. *Res. J. Chem. Sci,* 1(3): 40-48.

Shukla A. and Shrivastava S. (2004): Species Diversity of Macrozoobenthos: A Tool for Bio Monitoring Water Pollution of Gandhisagar Reservoir, M.P. India. *Bio. Memoirs,* 30(1): 7-13.

Soldan T. and Landa V. (1999): A Key to the Central European Species of the Genus *Rhithrogena* (Ephemeroptera: Heptageniidae). *Klapalekiana,* 35: 25-37.

Staneff-Cline D. and Neff W. (2007): Born to Swarm The Plain Dealer. Retrieved January 15, 2008.

Verma D. (2006): Studies of Water Pollution of the River Narmada in Western Zone Ph.D. Thesis, Devi Ahilya University, Indore (M.P.)

Wilbur H.M. (1980): Compex Life Cycles. *Annual Review of Ecology and Systematics,* 11: 165-169.

Yodha R.K. (2004): Limno-chemistry of River Narmada (Khedighat Barwaha M.P) and a Distillery Effluent. M.Phil. Thesis, Devi Alihya Vishvavidyalaya, Indore, M.P.

Zwick P. (1992): Stream Habitat Fragmentation - A Threat to Biodiversity. Biodiversity and Conservation 1: 80-97.

Polychaete Diversity of Digha Coast of West Bengal, India

Santanu Mitra*; Amales Misra**

* Zoological Survey of India, Fire Proof Spirit Building, 27, J.L. Nehru Road, Kolkata - 700 016, West Bengal, India

** Paribesh Unnayan Parishad, Sagar Island, 24 Parganas (S), West Bengal, India

INTRODUCTION

Among all the marine benthic organisms, polychaetes constitute a most important component of the benthic macro-invertebrates. They are multi-segmented annelids with parapodia bearing numerous setae in distinct fascicles; generally with anterior appendages of various sorts - antennae, palps, tentacular cirri, etc.; dioecious and have simple exit ducts from the gonads. They are usually marine, more rarely freshwater and only rarely terrestrial or parasitic in habit.

Abundance of polychaetes, in both density and diversity, command their importance in the marine environment as they enter into and form an essential component of the complex food chain, both in adult as well as in larval forms. The variety and abundance of polychaete species present can often be used as an indication of the cleanliness of the environment in which they live (Jones, 1969; Moore, 1972). Considering the importance of polychaetes in marine ecosystems, Reish (1979) opined that all marine benthic studies whether for academic pursuit or for environmental studies, should include polychaetes and these must be adequately identified.

Studies on Polychaete fauna was initiated by Willey (1908); later Southern (1921) and Fauvel (1932, 1953) documented only 30 species from the gangetic delta. Subsequently Misra et al (1984), Misra (1999) listed 72 species of polychaete from the streatch of West Bengal coast belongs to 50 genera and 27 families.

Studies on the polychaetous annelids of Digha Coast, West Bengal, based on the material collected by Zoological Survey of India parties, led to the identification of 40 species under 29 genera and 18 families. This is nearly 60% of the total polychaete fauna of the marine and estuarine habitats of West Bengal. Very recently Mitra and Misra (2010) recorded a taotal 74 species of polychaetes belongs to 51 genera under 28 families.

In the present chapter, attempt has been made to include a taxonomic key to the species in addition to diagnostic features and short habitat data wherever possible. This key and habitat data will be of immense help to the students and future research workers in getting the desired polychaete species in right place at right time, and also to get the specimens identified at their own level.

TAXONOMIC CHARACTERS WITH TERMINOLOGY

(a) **External characters**: The body is generally elongated with numerous segments. It consists of a cephalic lobe or prostomium, a segmented body or metastomium and a tail end or pygidium.

(b) **Prostomium**: This is an anterior-most, pre-segmental part of the body anterior to the mouth, enclosing at least the anterior part of the brain, often with antennae, palps and eyes. In some families like Nereididae the distal part of the palps or palpostyle is separated from the prostomial part or palpophore by a deep groove. All the prostomial appendages are best developed in Polychaeta Errantia, while in Polychaeta Sedentaria these are reduced or lost. The presence of either one or all categories of appendages is of great taxonomic importance.

The position of the palp varies from dorsal to ventral, from frontal to occipital. The position and function of the palps furnish important taxonomic characters.

(c) **Peristomium:** This is the first distinct post-postomial region; strictly including only the region around the mouth, in practice including also segments fused to this structure, forming the posterior part of the recognisable head. It usually carries a single pair of dorsal cirri called peristomial cirri, while the fused segments may carry parapodial remnants called tentacular cirri. The number of tentacular cirri may vary from family to family.

(d) **Eversible pharynx:** Most of the errantiate polychaetes are provided with an eversible proboscis - pharynx armed with strong horny jaws or with papillae or with chitinous denticles called paragnaths. Usually, each family has a characteristic kind of pharynx. The detailed structure of the pharynx, specially the equipment of jaws, teeth or other chitinised structures are very important characters at the generic and specific level.

(e) **Parapodia:** These are segmentally arranged projections carrying setae, can be biramous with both noto - and neuropodia developed or uniramous with only the neuropodia developed. The detailed development of each ramus with the varied parapodial lobes and cirri is verry important at the generic and specific level. The cirri are the sensory projections usually slender and cylindrical arise from the superior part of the parapodia or from the inferior part of neuropodia. The presence of branchiae associated with the parapodia is of variable taxonomic importance.

(f) **Setae:** These are chitinous bristles commencing out of parapodia, and are very important taxonomic characters. Numerous kinds of setae have been described – limbate setae, pectinate setae, sub-acicular hooks, composite spinigers and falcigers, uncini etc. The detailed construction of the setae is impoprtant at the specific level. The simplest forms are slender tapering hair-like stuctures called capillaries, simple setae with flattened margin or wing called limbate setae may be jointed so that the base articulates with distal blades called the compound seate.

(g) **Branchiae:** These are extensions of the body wall with a loop of the vascular system or which well-equiped with capillary blood-vessels. They may occur on any part of the body but are commonly dorsal in region either on the dorsum itself or associated with the notopodium. In filter-feeding fan worms the branchial crown on the head serves both as a respiratory organ and a food-gathering apparatus but in the deposit-feeders the branchiae are separate from the buccal tentacles and occur on a few segments behind the head.

METHOD OF COLLECTION AND PRESERVATION

Collections are to be made during the low tide periods when sufficient exposure is available. Qualitative samples of polychaete fauna are collected on the intertidal regions down the shore starting from high water mark to low water mark as well as along the shore. Soft substratum is generally dug out in small blocks using a hand shovel and placed in large container. The sample is then broken up by hand and visible organisms are collected. After hand sorting, the samples are screened through 1 mm seive. But seiving of the mud sample is not advantageous because the sticky mud does not facilitate this process. Only silty sand samples thus sieved produced good results. Tube-dwelling polychaetes are very carefully collected by digging the soil following the course of the tubes. Burrowing samples are detected first by carefully ovserving their castings, if any, then tried to collect by digging the soil. All the samples are preserved in 10% neutral sea water farmalin after necessary narcotization. Preserved samples are sorted out very carefully using a low power stereo microscope.

After the collection, the material is placed in natural sea water and then allowed to relax in 7% magnesium chloride prepared in sea water for about half an hour to avoid twisting or breaking of the specimens. Narcotization is done by addition of 70% alcohol drop by drop, slowly. Before fixation, polychaetes of the family Phyllodocidae, Nereididae and glyceridae are treated with sudden addition of strong alcohol for everting their pharynx. Standard fixating agent for polychaetes is 10% neutralised formalin in sea water. The most commonly used neutralising agent is borax ($Na_2B_4O_7$). Sample are kept in more or less stretched condition in formalin for 24 hours and then transferred to 70% alcohol after proper washing in fresh water for preservation.

DESCRIPTION OF STUDY AREA

The coastal stretch of West Bengal with a length of about 350 km comprises the two districts- Purba Medinipur (East Midnapur) and Dakshin Chabbisparagana (South 24 Paraganas). The coastal belt of Midnapore district represents 27% of West Bengal of coastal tract (60 km) extending along the west bank of Hooghly estuary from New Digha and then curving around Junput, Dadanpatrabarh, Khejuri and Haldia on the east to the further north east upto Tamluk or even on the bank of Rupnarayan. Digha beach situated close to the Gangetic mouth facing Bay of Bengal, Digha – Sankarpur area is a part of Contai coastal area of Purba Medinipur district, West Bengal. This area lies in the coastal tract of adjoining Bay of Bengal and boarder of West Bengal and Orissa. The extents of the study area is between latitudes -21036 "50" N and 21030 "00" N and longitudes 87029 "40" E and 87037 "00" E. (Fig. 4.1)

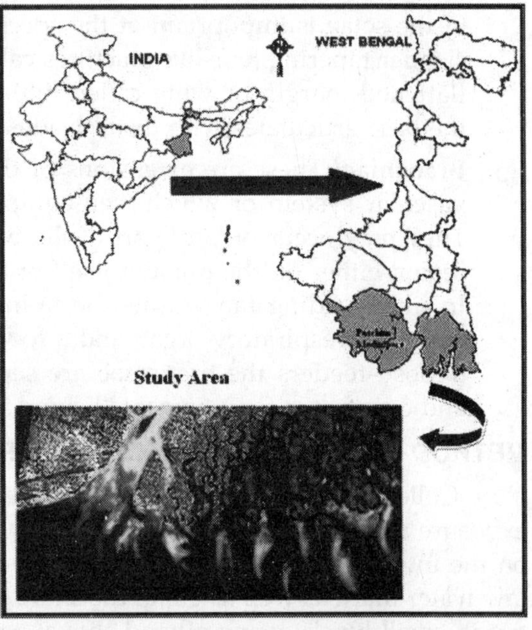

Fig. 4.1: Map of Digha Coastal Belt

SYSTEMATIC LIST OF THE SPECIES

Family: POLYODONTIDAE

1. *Eupanthalis edriophthalma* (Potts, 1910)*

Family: SIGALIONIDAE

2. *Sigalion capense* Day, 1960
3. *Thalenessa djiboutiensis* Gravier, 1902

Family: AMPHINOMIDAE

4. *Chloeia parva* Baird, 1870
5. *Chloeia rosea* Potts, 1909

Family: PHYLLODOCIDAE

6. *Eteone barantollae* Fauvel, 1932
7. *E. (Mysta) ornata* Grube, 1878

Family: TALEHSAPIIDAE

8. *Talehsapia annandalei* Fauvel, 1932

Family: NEREIDIDAE

9. *Ceratonereis burmensis* Monro, 1937
10. *Dendronereides gangetica* Misra, 1998
11. *Dendronereides heteropoda* Southern, 1921
12. *Dendronereis dayi* Misra, 1998
13. *Lycastonereis indica* Rao, 1981
14. *Namalycastis fauveli* Rao, 1981
15. *Neanthes meggitti* (Monro, 1931)
16. *Perinereis cultrifera* (Grube, 1840)

Family: NEPHTYIDAE

17. *Nephtys oligobranchia* Southern, 1921
18. *Nephtys polybranchia* Southern, 1921

Family: GLYCERIDAE

19. *Glycera convoluta* Keferstein, 1862
20. *Glycera lancadivae* Schmarda, 1861
21. *Glycera longipinnis* Grube, 1878
22. *Glycera rouxii*, Audouin & Milne Edwards, 1833
23. *Glycera tesselata* Grube, 1863

Family: GONIADIDAE

24. *Glycinde oligodon* Southern, 1921

Family: ONUPHIDAE

25. *Diopatra cuprea* (Bosc, 1802)
26. *Onuphis eremita* Audouin & Milne Edwards, 1833

Family: EUNICIDAE

27. *Marphysa mossambica* (Peters, 1854)

Family: LUMBRINERIDAE

28. *Lumbrineris notocirrata* (Fauvel, 1932)
29. *Lumbrineris simplex* (Southern, 1921)
30. *Lumbrineris polydesma* (Southern, 1921)

Family: ORBINIDAE

31. *Scoloplos marsupialis* Southern, 1921

Family: SPIONIDAE

32. *Prionospio cirrobranchiata* Day, 1961
33. *Prionospio krusadensis* Fauvel, 1929
34. *Pseudopolydora kempi* (Southern, 1921)
35. *Scolelepis squamata* (Muller, 1806)

Family: MLDANIDAE

36. *Euclymene annandalei* Southern, 1921

Family: OWENIIDAE

37. *Owenia fusiformis* delle Chiaje, 1844

Family: TEREBELLIDAE

38. *Loimia medusa* (Savigny, 1818)

Family: SABELLIDAE

39. *Potamilla leptochaeta* Southern, 1921
40. *Laonome indica* Southern, 1921

TAXONOMIC DESCRIPTION

I. Family: POLYODONTIDAE

Genus: *Eupanthalis* McIntosh, 1876

1. *Eupanthalis edriophthalma* (Potts, 1910)

1910. *Panthalis edriophthalma* Potts, *Trans. Linn. Soc.*, Lond. (Zool), 13: 345: 56-57.

Material: 4 ex., Digha beach, 24.02.1986, A.K.Das

Diagnosis: Prostomium spherical with 2 pairs of small, sessile eyes, 3 antennae; notosetae few, serrated capillaries, neurosetae of 3 kinds, i.e. spinulose setae, aristate seate and curved spinulose setae.

Habitat: Prefer sandy soil in the mid-tidal zone.

Distribution: India: Digha coast (West Bengal)

Abroad: Sri Lanka; Myanmar (Burma)

II. Family: SIGALIONIDAE

Key to genera

Tentacular segments with two bundles of setae; two lateral antennae ...... *Sigalion*

Tentacular segments with one bundle of setae; three small antennae ...... *Thalenessa*

Genus *Sigalion* Audouin and Milne Edwards, 1832.

2. *Sigalion capense* Day, 1960

1960. *Sigalion capense* Day, *Ann. S. Afr. Mus.*, 45: 291.

Material: 3ex, Lykani khal, Digha, 21.2.1988, R.K.Chakraborty.

Diagnosis: Prostomium oblong, rounded posteriorly; antennae small; tentacular cirri sub-equal; branchiae cirriform, arise from the medial sides from setiger 5; notosetae long and fine with hair like tips, neurosetae 3 to 6 simple bipinnate setae supiriorly.

Habitat: Burrowing worms living in sandy mud.

Distribution: India: Digha (West Bengal).

Abroad: South Africa.

Remarks: This species is recorded for the first time from the coast of West Bengal.

Genus *Thalenessa* Baird, 1868

3. *Thalenessa djiboutiensis* (Gravier, 1902)

1902. *Thalenessa djiboutiensis* Gravier, *Nouv.Archs.Mus. Hist. Nat.*, Paris (sr. 4), 3: 231.

Material: 1 ex., Digha Beach, 15.2.87, A.K.Mandal; 1 ex., Digha Beach, 14.5.87, A.K.Mandal; 1 ex., Digha, 29.4.1987, Mandal & Misra ; 1 ex., Digha; 14.5.1987, A.K.Mandal; 1 ex., 1.5.1989, A.K. Das.

Diagnosis: prostomium with three pairs of eyes and 3 small antennae; elytra reniform, with long digitiform multifid papillae on the external margin; notopodia with ciliated ctenidial ridge; notosetae slender, tuft of spinolose capillaries, neurosetae composite with simple blades.

Habitat: prefer sandy mud in the mid tidal zone.

Distribution: India: Digha coast (West Bengal); Orissa (Off Puri); Madras Coast.

Abroad: Persian Gulf; Sri Lanka; Mergui; Pedro Shoal; Australia; Red Sea.

III. Family: AMPHINOMIDAE

Genus: *Chloea* Savigny, 1818

Key to species

Back with 'T' or 'Y'-shaped median purple spots ...... *Chloea parva*

Uniformly reddish pink, without any dorsal spots ...... *Chloea rosea*

4. *Chloeia parva* Baird, 1870

1870. Chloeia parva Baird, *J. Proc. Linn. Soc. London (Zool),* 10: 233.

Material: 3 ex., Lykani khal, Digha, 21.2.1988, R.K.Chakraborty; 6 ex., Talsari, 26.5.94. S.Talukdar.

Diagnosis: A mid-dorsal row of dark marks in the form of roman 'T'; carancle with crest surmounted by a black wavy line extending up to setiger 6, branchiae from setiger 4; notosetae short and serrated , neurosetae long and smooth.

Habitat: Pelagic, comes with fishing nets.

Distribution: India: Digha coast and Mouth of Hooghly estuary (West Bengal), Chandipur (Orissa), Vishakhapattanam (Andhra Pradesh), Andamans; west coast of India.

Abroad: Gulf of Oman; Sri Lanka; Malay; Mergui; Sumatra; Jave, New Guinea.

5. *Chloeia rosea* Potts,1909

1909. *Chloeia rosea* Potts, *Trans. Linn. Soc. Lond* (Sr. 2) 12: 357.

Material: 1 ex., Digha Mohana, 21.11.1991, S.Talukdar; 1 ex., Digha Mohana, 26.03.1992, S.Talukdar.

Diagnosis: Uniformly reddish pink without any dorsal pattern; branchiae well-developed and overlap the middle line.

Habitat: Pelagic, comes with fishing nets.

Distribution: Digha coast of West Bengal, Tamil Nadu, Karnataka.

Abroad: Arabian Sea; Persian Gulf.

Remarks: This species is recorded for the first time from the coast of West Bengal.

IV. Family: PHYLLODOCIDAE

Genus: *Eteone* Savigny, 1820

Key to species

Body yellowish white, pharynx with 5 rows of distal swollen papillae ...... *E. barantollae.*

Body with three rows of dark spots, pharynx with 3 to 4 rows of swollen Papillae ...... *E. ornata*

6. *Eteone barantollae* Fauvel, 1932

1932. *Eteone barantollae Fauvel, Mem. India Mus.,* 12: 72.

Material: 4 ex., Baratala ghat, 26.6.1991, S.Talukdar; 1 ex., Udipurghat, 29.12.1992; 3 ex., Digha, 30.10.1991, S.Talukdar; 6 ex., 24.10.1991, S.Talukdar; 7 ex., 27.2.1992,

Diagnosis: Yellowish white in live condition, brown in spirit; prostomium oval with 2 pairs of short antennae; tentacular cirri 2 pairs, subulate,; pharynx eversible, smooth at base and with 5 longitudinal rows of ridges distally.

Habitat: Crawl on the surface of the soil during low tide at mid-littoral zone.

Distribution: India: Digha coast, Salt Lake, mouth of Hooghly river (West Bengal); Baitarani estuary (Orissa); Pulikat Lake (Tamil Nadu).

7. *Eteone (Mysta) ornata* Grube, 1878

1878. *Eteone (Mysta) ornata* Grube, *Mem. Acad. Sci., S. Peterb.,* 25: 106.

Material: 16ex. Digha, 1979, A. Misra.

Diagnosis: Body elongated with 3 striking longitudinal rows of violet pigment spots upon a pale yellowish colour towards the middle part of body, becomes gradually smaller and blend into a single streak, disappear completely posteriorly; proboscis with lateral rows of soft papillae and small spinous tubercles.

Habitat: Lives in crevices under stones.

Distribution: India: Digha, Mouth of Hooghly eastuary (West Bengal); Mozambique; Philippines; N. Japan Sea.

V. Family: TALEHSAPIIDAE

Genus *Talehsapia* Fauvel, 1932

8. *Talehsapia annandalei* Fauvel, 1932

1932. *Talehsapia annandalei* Fauvel, *Mem. Indian Mus.* 12: 251.

Material: 8 ex., Duttapur Ghat (Digha), 29.12,1992, T.K. Chatterjee

Diagnosis: Body slender; prostomium small conical without eyes, antennae and palps. Tentacular cirri absent; parapodia sub-biramous; notopodia reduced with 1 or 2 smooth capillaries; neuropodia blunt, cylindrical lobe with straight capillaries with several transverse rows of spines.

Habitat: solid clayey soil in the upper tidal zone.

Distribution: Digha coast, Hooghly-Matla estuary (West Bengal); Baitarani estuary (Orissa); Thailand.

VI. Family: NEREIDIDAE

Key to genera

1. Some notopodia with branchiae 2

   - Notopodia without branchiae 3

2. Branchiae arise form dorsal cirri, setae composite spinigers throughout ...... *Dendronereis*

   - Branchiae arise form notopodial lobes, setae composite spinigers and falcigers ...... *Dendronereides*

3. Parapodia sub-biramous throughout without ligules ...... *Namalycastis*

   - Parapodia bi-ramous from 3rd segments onwards, with well-developed ligules 4

4. Tentacular cirri 3 pairs, chitinous paragnaths absent ...... *Lycastonereis*

   - Tentacular cirri 4 pairs, chitinous paragnaths present 5

5. Paragnaths of group VI of transverse bars ...... *Perinereis*

   - Paragnaths all separate and conical 6

6. Chitinous paragnaths present on all groups of both the basal & maxillary rings ...... *Neanthes*

   - Basal ring of proboscis smooth; notosetae include homogomph spinigers and Heterogomph spinigers only ...... *Ceratonereis*

   Genus *Ceratonereis* Kinberg, 1866.

9. *Ceratonereis burmensis* Monro, 1937

   1937. *Nereis (Ceratonereis) burmensis* Monro, Ann. Mag. Nat. Hist. London, Sr. 10, 19: 532.

Material: 2ex., Digha Coast, 7.2.88. A. Chakraborty; 10 ex., Digha Mohana, 20.1.1994, S.Talukdar.

Diagnosis: Prostomium not incised, with small palpostyles and 4 small black eyes; notoseate spinigers and neurioseate spinigers and falcigers.

Habitat: Clayey or sandy soil towards low water zone.

Distribution: India: Sundarbans (West Bengal); Off Bombay (Mahastra). Abroad: Myanmar.

Genus: *Dendronereides* Southern,1921

Key to the species

Branchiae formed as clusters of branched filaments; neuropodia with three digitate lobes ...... *D. heteropoda*

Branchiae formed as whorls of several simple filaments; neuropodia with bilobed anterior processes and a short rounded posterior lobe ...... *D. gangetica*

10. *Dendronereides gangetica* Misra, 1998.

    1998. *Dendronereides gangetica* Misra, *State Fauna Series 3: Fauna of West Bengal,* Part 10: 150

Material: 2 ex., 26.06.1983, A. Misra.

Diagnosis:Prostomium deeply indented anteriorly with two short tapered antennae; tentacular cirri 4 pairs; branchiae commensing from setiger 10 and extending up to 38, first in the form of simple filaments, then gradually forming a whorl involving 2 superior notopodial ligules; notosetae homogomph spinigers with long and short blades , neurosetae of 3 kinds – homo- and hemigomph spinigers and homogomph falcigers.

Habitat: Soft mud in the low tidal zone.

Distribution: India: Hooghly estuary, Champa River, near Digha coast (West Bengal).

11. *Dendronereides heteropoda* Southern, 1921.

1921. *Dendronereides heteropoda* Southern, *Mem.Indian Mus.*, 5: 603.

Material: 15 ex. Champa river, Ramnagar, Midnapur, 25.6.1983, A. Misra.

Diagnosis: Prostomium broad, slightly indented in front; branchiae in the form of branched bunches of filaments arising below dorsal cirrus, commencing from setiger 7 or 8 extending up to the setiger 25 –35; notosetae homogomph spinigers, neurosetae of 4 kinds – homo- and heterogomph spinigers and homo and hetrogomph falcigers.

Habitat: Burrows in soft silty mud from mid-tidal level to low water line.

Distribution: India: Hooghly estuiary, Champa river, (W.B).; Burhabalang estuary, Chandipur, (Orissa); Tarapur, Bombay (Maharashtra); Vellarpadan (Kerala)

Genus *Dendronereis* Peters, 1854

12. *Dendronereis dayi* Misra, 1998

1998. *Dendronereis dayi* Misra, *State Fauna Series 3: Fauna of West Bengal,* Part 10: 153.

Material: 7 ex., Champa river, Ramnagar, 25.6.1983, A. Misra; 1 ex., Digha beach, 3.1.1989, A.K. Barua.

Diagnosis: Prostomium deeply cleft anteriorly, antennae short, slender originating from the base of the palps, eyes 3 pairs; branchiae in the form of simple filaments initially, then a row of two lateral simple divisions and latter 2 rows of uni-pinnate division; notosetae homogomph spinigers, neurosetae of 2 kinds – homogomph and hemigomph spinigers.

Habitat: Soft mud in the low water zone.

Distribution: India: Endemic in the North-east coast of India – Hooghly estuary, West Bengal and Baitarani estuary, Bhitarkanika estuary(Orissa); Vishakhapatnam (Andhra Pradesh).

Remarks: This species is Endemic in the North-east coast of India.

Genus *Lycastonereis* Rao, 1981

13. *Lycastonereis indica* Rao, 1981

1981. *Lycastonereis indica* Rao, *Bull. Zool.Surv. India,* 3 (3): 213.

Material: 4 ex., Champa river, Ramnagar, 25.06.1986, A. Misra

Diagnosis: Prostomium with dark brown spots forming a definite pattern, extending in 3 rows up to setiger 24/26, a pair of short antennae; tentacular cirri 3 pairs; notosetae homogomph spiniger with minute serrations, neurosetae of 3 kinds- homo- and hemigomph spinigers and heterogomph falcigers.

Habitat: Soft black mud near the mid-tidal zone, particularly abundant in sewage outfall areas.

Distribution: Endemic in north-east coast of India – lower reaches of Hooghly estuary, Champa river, West Bengal; Baitarani river (Orissa).

Genus *Namalycastis* Hartman, 1959

14. *Namalycastis fauveli* Rao, 1981

1981. *Namalycastis fauveli* Rao, *Bull. Zool. Surv. India,* 3(3) : 215.

Material: 1 ex., Joshipur khal, 22.04.1992, Ramakrishna.

Diagnosis: Porstomium wider than long, anterior border straight, no median groove, palps short and broad, tentacular cirri 4 pairs,short, sub-equal, hardly reaching beyond setiger 1; parapodia sub-biramous throughout; notosetae hemigomph spinigers, neuroseate of 2 kinds- heterogomph spinigers and heterogomph falcigers.

Habitat: Soft clayey soil in the zone between high water line and mid tidal line.

Distribution: India: upper and middle reaches of Hooghly estuary (West Bengal); Subarnarekha estuary, Baitarani river, (Orissa).

Remarks: This species is Endemic in the North-east coast of India.

Genus Neanthes Kinberg,1866

15. *Neanthes meggitti* (Monro, 1931)

1931. Nereis (*Neanthes) meggitti* Monro, *Ann. Mag. nat. Hist.*, (Sr. 10), 8: 580.

Material: 11ex. Digha mohona, 20.1.94. S. Talukder.

Diagnosis: Prostomium short, quadrangular, as broad as long; Paragnath arranged as follows: I = 3-4 large cones, II = 11-12 small cones in irregular oblique rows; III= several large and small cones in 3-4 irregular rows, IV = several small cones in cresentic cluster. V = 4-5 cones in oblique lines; VI = 5-6 cones in round clusters , VII & VIII = several large and small cones in 3-4 irregular rows. Notosetae homogomph spinigers and neurosetae homo- and heterogomph spinigers and heterogomph falcigers.

Habitat: Soft mud under brick stones in the zone at mid-tidal level.

Distribution: India: Upper & middle reaches of Hooghly estuary (West Bengal).

Abroad: Myanmar.

Genus *Perinereis* Kinberg,1866

16. *Perinereis cultrifera* (Grube, 1840)

1840. Nereis *cultrifera* Grube, *Actinien Echinodermen und wurmen Description Adriatischen und mittelmeeres*, p. 74.

Material: 2ex., Digha beach, 30.4.1983, A.K. Mandal

Diagnosis: Prostomium sub-ptyriform with dark longitudinal bands of pigments between anterior pair of eyes; paragnaths arranged as follows : I = 2 cones in vertical line; II = 10-12 cones in curved rows, III = 12-16 cones in oval patch; IV = 20-25 cones about three oblique rows forming a wedge, V = 3 cones in triangle, VI = a single transeverse bar on each side, VII-VIII = 2-3 continuous transverse rows of cones reducing to single row at both sides; notosetae homogomph spinigers only, neurosetae homo- and heterogomph spinigers and heterogomph falcigers.

Habitat: Soft mud at low water zone.

Distribution: India: Hooghly estuary (West Bengal); Gulf of Mannar; Andamans; Maharashtra.

VII. Family: NEPHTYIDAE

Genus *Nephtys* Cuvier 1817 in Audouin and Milne Edwards 1833.

Key to species

Interramal cirri commencing on setiger 5, absent after setiger 23-25 ...... *N. oligobranchia.*

Interramal cirri commencing on setiger 2, extending up to posterior end ...... *N. polybranchia*

17. *Nephtys oligobranchia* Southern, 1921

1921. *Nephtys oligobranchia* Southern, *Mem. Indian Mus.*, 5: 610.

Material: 7ex., Digha Ghat Sea beach, 27.2.92, Ramakrishna.

Diagnosis: Pharynx eversible, divisible, into short muscular distal region and inflated proximal region; interramal cirri commencing on setiger 5 absent after setiger 23-24; setae simple and of three types – barred, spinulose and capillaries.

Habitat: Soft mud or silty mud in ther zone near and below low water line.

Distribution: India: Hooghly estuary (upper reaches), Port Canning, (W.B.); Baitarani river, Chilka Lake (Orissa), Vishakhapatnam, Godabari estuary, Cochin backwater (Kerala).

18. *Nephtys polybranchia* Southern, 1921

1921. *Nephtys polybranchia* Southern, *Mem. Indian Mus.*, 5: 607.

Material: 4 ex., 13.5.1987, A.K.Mandal; New Digha beach.

Diagnosis: Pharynx eversible, divisible into short muscular distal region and inflated proximal region; interramal cirri commencing on setiger 2, extending up to posterior end; setae simple and of three types – barred, spinulose and smooth capillaries.

Habitat: Soft silty sediments, muddy sands in the zone near the low water line.

Distribution: India: Upper & middle reaches of Hooghly estuary (W.B.); Chilka Lake (Orissa); Adyar estuary (Madras); Cochin backwater (Kerala); Umbargoan (Gujarat).

VIII. Family: GLYCERIDAE

Genus *Glycera* Savigny, 1818

Key to species

1. Branchiae absent 2

   - Branchiae present 3

2. Post-setal lobe single ...... *G. lancadivae*

   - Post-setal lobe double ...... *G. tesselata*

3. One posterior lobe on parapodia ...... *G. longipinnis*

   - Two posterior lobes on parapodia 4

4. Branchial filaments start from the dorsal edge pf setiger 35-40 ...... *G.convoluta*

   - Branchial filaments start from the anterior surface of setiger 22-24 ...... *G.rouxi*

19. *Glycera convoluta* Keferstein, 1862

1862. *Glycera convoluta* Keferstein, *Z. Wiss.zool.*, 12:106.

Material: 7ex, Digha, 3.2.79. A. Misra; 6ex. Digha, 16.7.82. A. Misra.;13ex. Digha Beach, 2.9.64. Dr. S.K. Dutta

Diagnosis: prostomium with 10-12 rings, 2 small eyes, and 4 small tentacles distally; branchiae simple appear as short stumpy lobes above the dorsal edge of setiger 35 to 40; notosetae capillaries, neurosetae composite homogomph spinigers.

Habitat: Silty mud in the zone between mid tidal level and low tidal level.

Distribution: Lower reaches of Hooghly estuary (W.B.); Gangam coast, Puri, Konarak (Orissa); Cochin backwater (Kerala); Ghogha (Gujarat), Coast of Maharashtra; Marmagaon Bay (Goa).

20. *Glycera lancadivae* Schmarda, 1861.

1861. *Glycera lancadivae* Schmarda, *Neue Wirbellose Thiere... und Annelida,* p. 95.

Material: 3ex. Digha; March,1983; A. Misra.

Diagnosis: Pharyngeal papillae of two kinds– slender and triangular, and rounded, both with medial ducts, without any rings; branchiae absent; presetal ligules sub-equal, post-setal lobe single.

Habitat: Silty sediments near low water level.

Distribution: Hooghly estuary (lower reaches) (West Bengal). Chandipur, Konarak, Puri, Gopalpur, (Orissa); Godavari estuary (A.P.), Madras coast, Lakshadweep.

21. *Glycera longipinnis* Grube, 1878

1878. *Glycera longipinnis* Grube, *Acad. Sci. S.peterb,* 25:182.

Material: 1ex. Digha, March,'83. A. Misra. 1ex. Digha coast, 7.2.88, A. Chakraborty.

Diagnosis: Pharyngeal papillae of two kinds; parapodia biramous with 2 subequal, cirriform presetal ligules, and a single postsetal lobe; branchial filaments simple, longer than presetal ligules, commencing from the dorsal surface of setiger 20-22.

Habitat: Silty muds towards the low water zone.

Distribution: India: Hooghly estuary (West Bengal)

22. *Glycera rouxii* Aud. & Milne Edward, 1833

1833. *Glycera rouxii* Aud.& Milne Edward, *Annls. Sci. nat.*, 29: 264.

Material: 1ex, Digha Beach, Aug.,1978. A. Misra.

Diagnosis: Pharygeal papillae in the form of smooth conical globular processes; branchiae simple slender, retractile and start from the anterior surface of setiger 22-24; pre-setal ligules sub-equal and short, post-setal lobe rounded.

Habitat: Soft silty sediments near or below low water level.

Distribution India: Hooghly estuary (lower reaches), Canning (W.B.); Chandipur (Orissa); Vishakha patnam (A.P.), Vellar estuary, Gulf of Maanar, Pamban backwater (Tamil Nadu); Andamans; Kerala Coast; Lakshadweep.

23. *Glycera tesselata* Grube, 1863.

1863. *Glycera tesselata* Grube, *Arch. Naturgesch.*, 29: 41.

Material: 5 ex., Digha, 24.2.1986, A. Misra; 1 ex., Lykani khal, Digha, 22.2.1988, R.K.Chakraborty; 26ex. Digha beach, March,' 83. A. Misra.

Diagnosis: Pharyngeal papillae uniform, very long and grooved without rings; pre-setal ligule sub-equal and 2 shorter rounded sub-equal post setal lobes; branchiae absent.

Habitat: Sandy upper tidal area of the beaches.

Distribution: India: Sundarbans (West Bengal); Chandipur, Gopalpur (Orissa); Godavari estuary (A.P.); Andamans; Nani Daman (Daman).

IX. Family: GONIADIDAE

Genus *Glycinde* Muller,1858

24. *Glycinde oligodon* Southern, 1921

1921. *Glycinde oligodon* Southern, *Mem. Indian Mus*., 5: 629.

Material: 10. ex., Digha, 24.2.1986, A.Misra

Diagnosis: Pharynx eversible without 'V'–shaped paragnaths; pre-setal lobe long, a short rounded post-setal lobe; notosetae simple acicular, neurosetae compound.

Habitat: Soft mud towards low water level.

Distribution: India: Hooghly estuary (West Bengal); Vishakhapatnam, Kakinara (A.P.); off Santapalli, Vellar estuary (Chennai).

Remarks: Endemic in east coast of India.

X. Family: ONUPHIDAE

Key to genus

Branchial filaments arranged spirally ...... *Diopatra*

Branchiae as pectinate filaments ...... *Onuphis*

Genus *Diopatra* Audouin and Milne Edwards, 1833

Diopatra cuprea (Bosc, 1802)

1802. *Nereis cuprea* Bosc, *Histoire. Naturele...Nat. Paris*, 1: 143.

Material: 1ex. Digha mohona Sea beach, 23.12.92.; 14ex. Digha, 28.2.79. A. Misra.

4ex. Digha Beach, 24.6.87. A. K. Mondal

Diagnosis: Prostomium with a pair of short,subulate frontal antennae, a pair of oval cushion-like palps, and five occipital antennae; tentacular cirri present; branchiae commencing from setiger 4 to 5, extending up to setiger 50-61, branchial filaments arranged in 10-12 whorls; setae include limbate seate, pseudocomposite hooks, pectinate setae and sub-acicular hooks.

Habitat: Lives in tough tubes made of fine sands, projected part decorated with shell fragments, leaves, and embedded in stiff mud towards the low water zone.

Distribution: India: Hooghly estuary, Matla river(West Bengal); Chandipur (Orissa); Ratnagiri (Maharashtra)

XI. Family : EUNICIDAE

Genus *Onuphis* Audouin & Milne Edwards, 1833

Onuphis eremita Audouin & Milne Edwards, 1833

1833. *Onuphis eremita* Audouin & Milne Edwards, *Faune de France*, 5: 414.

Material: 1 ex., Digha Beach, 24.2. 1986, A.K. Das; 1 ex., Digha Beach, 8.7.1986, A.K. Das.

Diagnosis: Median occipital antennae shorter than the inner laterals; tentacular cirri inserted dorso-laterally and longer than the peristomial segments; branchiae from the first setiger with simple filaments, with 2 filaments from 22-24 setigers, reaching maximum with 4-5 filaments and then decrease posteriorly; setae include anterior hooded pseudocomposite hooks, posterior winged capillaries, pectinate setae and bidentate acicular setae with guard.

Habitat: Lives in thin tubes encruasted with sand towards the low-water zone.

Distribution: India: Digah Coast (West Bengal); Chennai coast.

Abroad: Sri Lanka; Madagascar, Mergui Archipelago; Maynamar

Genus *Marphysa* Quatrefages, 1865

Marphysa mosambica (Peters, 1854)

1854. *Marphysa mosambica* Peters, *Acad. wiss. Berlin*,: 612.

Material: 1ex., Digha beach and Junput beach, 5.9.64., A.K. Dutta

Diagnosis: prostomium wider than long, with a deep anetrior notch and 5 smooth occiopital antennae; branchiae commencing form setiger 15-30, extending up to posterior end, with a maximum of ten filaments; setae include capillaries and pectinate setae only.

Habitat: Lives in deep burrows in soft mud towards low-water zone.

Distribution: Hooghly estuary, Sundarbans (West Bengal); Pondichery; Krusadai Island, Killakarai, Nicobar Island; Maharastra.

XII. Family : LUMBRINERIDAE

Genus *Lumbrineris* Blainville, 1828

Key to species

1. All setae simple capillaries, no hooks; dorsal cirri absent ...... *L. simplex*

   - Simple capillary setae and hooded hooks present; dorsal cirri may be present 2

2. Dorsal cirri present ...... *L. notocirrata*

   Dorsal ciri absent ...... *L. polydesma*

Lumbrineris notocirrata Fauvel (1932)

1932. *Lumbrcoineris notocirrata* Fauvel, *Mem. Indian Mus.*, 12: 156.

Material: 2 ex., Talsari, 26.5.1994, S.Talukdar; 1 ex., Digha, 21. 3. 1980, A. Misra.

Diagnosis: Prostomium bluntly conical without eyesand antenna; parapodia biramous with dorsal cirri reduced to small knobs in anterior feet, and long and strap-like in middle and posterior ends; Capillaries in all feet and simple hooded hooks from setiger 40-45.

Habitat: Occurring in sandy muds at mid-littoral zone.

Distribution: India: Hooghly estuary, Sudarbans (West Bengal); Chandipur, Orissa coast, Vishakhapatna backwater (A.P.)

Lumbrineris simplex Southern (1921)

1921. *Lumbriconeris simplex* Southern , *Mem. Indian Mus.*, 5: 625.

Material: 1 ex., Digha beach, 11.5.1987, A.K.Mandal

Diagnosis: Prostomium triangular with round edges; anterior lobe of parapodia rounded, and posterior lobe blunt and conical; all setae simple capillaries, hook absent.

Habitat: Soft mud towards lower zone.

Distribution: Digha Coast (West Bengak); Chilka Lake (Orissa).

Lumbrineris polydesma (Southern, 1921)

1921. *Lumbriconeris polydesma* Southern,mem. Indian Mus., 5:622.

Material: 1 ex., Digha, 7.7.1986, A.K. Das; 1 ex., Digha Beach, 21.1. 1988, A.K. Mandal.

Diagnosis: Prostomium bluntly conical without eyes and any other appendages; parapodia uniramous, postsetal lobe short, narrow, conical and longer that presetal lobes in posterior setigers; setae of 2 kinds, limbate and simple hooks.

Habitat: Soft mud towards lower zone.

Distribution: India: Hooghly estuary (West Bengal); Chandipur Talichua, Chilka Lake, (Orissa), Vellar Estuary, Adyar Estuary, Pulikat lake (T.N.), Nani Daman, Davka (Daman)

Family: ORBINIIDAE

Genus *Scoloplos* Blainville, 1828

Scoloplos marsupialis Southern 1921

1921. *Scoloplos marsupialis* Southern, Mem. Indian Mus., 5: 632.

Material: 1 ex., 15.5.1987, A.K.Mandal;

Diagnosis: prostomium conical, narrow and pointed; eye spot absent; thoracic setigers 18 or 19; branchiae simple, commencing from setiger 14; abdominal segments with membranous pockets between adjacent neuropodia.

Habitat: low-water zone with fine sandy and silty mud.

Distribution: India: Digha coast, Hooghly estuary (West Bengal); Chilka Lagoon (Odisha); Gulf of Mannar, Krusadai Island, Tuticorin (Tamil Nadu)

Family: SPINOIDAE

Key to genera

1. Setiger 5 with strongly modified setae ...... *Pseudopolydora*

   Setae change gradually along the body; no segment with remarkable setae 2

2. Prostomium blunt, without lateral wings; branchiae 4 pairs starting from setiger 2, not fused with the notopodial post-setal lobes ...... *Prionospio*

   Prostomium usually poited, with lateral wings; branchiae more than 4 pairs, starting from setiger 2, partially fused to the notopodial post-setal lobes in anterior segments ...... *Scolelepis*

Genus *Prionospio* Malmgren,1867

Key to the species

Branchiae 3 pairs, on 2nd, 3rd & 4th setigerous segment, all pinnate ...... *P. krusadensis*

Branchiae 11-12 pairs, starting from setiger 2, all simple ...... *P. cirrobranchiata*

Prionospio cirrobranchiata Day, 1961

1961. *Prionospio cirrobranchiata* Day, J. Linn. Soc. zool. 44: 488.

Material: 1 ex., Digha beach, 21.1.1988, A.K.Mandal

Diagnosis: Prostomium depressed, square in front and produced back as an inconspicuous plate but not keeled posteriorly; branchiae smooth, starting setiger 2, 11-12 pairs, uniform in length and about equal to the notopodial lamellae; about 5 hooded hooks in neuropodia from setiger 18-19 onwards, each hook with a single tooth above the main fang.

Habitat: Fine sandy mud, within slimy mucous tube.

Distribution: India: Digha Beach (West Bengal) Chilka Lagoon (Odisha)

Prionospio krusadensis Fauvel, 1929

1929. *Prionospio krusadensis* Fauvel, Bull. Soc.zool. France, Paris, 14: 182.

Material: 1 ex., Digha beach, 16.12.1986, A.Misra; 1 ex., Digha Beach, 18.2.1986, A.K.Das.

Diagnosis: Prostomium short-rounded, frontal peaks and occipital tentacles absent, eyes present; branchiae 3 pairs, pinnate, on 2nd 3rd and 4th setigerous segments; lamellae large, oval or sub-triangular; dorsal hooks from 40-42 segments; without genital pouches.

Habitat: Fine sandy mud, within slimy mucous tube.

Distribution: India: Digha Coast (West Bengal); Gulf of Mannar, Krusadai Island (Tamil Nadu).

Genus *Pseudopolydora* Czerniavsky, 1881.

Pseudopolydora kempi (Southern, 1921).

1921. *Polydora kempi* Southern, Mem. Indian Mus., 5: 636.

Material: 6 ex., Digha beach, 22.10.1987, A.K. Mandal

Diagnosis: Prostomium faintly notched anteriorly with a posterior occipital papillae,eyes 2 pairs; first setiger without notosetae; branchiae 10-11 pairs from setiger 7; setiger 5 with normal notopodia capillaries; abnormal setae of the 5th setigerous segment with curved blunt teeth.

Habitat: Occur in silty mud towards low-water zone.

Distribution: India: Digha coast, Hooghly estuary (West Bengal); Godavari estuary, Adyar estuary, Vembanad Lake (Tamil Nadu).

Genus *Scolelepis* Blainville, 1828

Scolelepis squamata (Muller, 1806)

1806. *Lumbricus squamata* Muller, *Zoologica Danica. Prodromus Senanimalian Danice ...... Notorum Description et Historia, Atlas*: 39.

Material: 14 ex., Digha beach, 6.8.1980; A. Misra

Diagnosis: Prostomium pointed anteriorly with 6 eyes in a row and a well-developed occipital ridge extending up to setiger 2; notopodial lamellae fused with branchiae anteriorly, but acicular and mainly free posteriorly; bidentade neuropodial hooded hooks from setiger 30-35 onwards, notopodia hooks appearing more posteriorly.

Habitat: Occur in fine sand, towards low–water zone.

Distribution: India: Digha coast, Hooghly estuary (West Bengal); Vishakhapatnam (Andhra Pradesh) Lakshadweep.

Family: MALDANIDAE

Genus *Euclymene* Verrill, 1900

Euclymene annandalei Southern, 1921

1921. *Euclymene annandalei* Southern, Mem. Indian Mus. 5: 648.

Material: 7ex. Digha Ghat sea beach, 27.2.92, Ramakrishna; 4 ex., Digha beach, 27.2.1992, S.K. Talukdar.

Diagnosis: Body cylindrical with long segments, 21 setigers; Prostomium bluntly triangular with numerous ocelli; cephalic rim crenulate posteriorly; a dorsal glandular streak from setiger 9; notosetae mainly with narrow winged capillaries anteriorly, include feathered forms posteriorly; setigers 1-3 with a single acicular spine with a smooth bent teeth; neurosetae with numerous hooks each with a vertical series of 5-6 teeth above the main fang.

Habitat: Lives in burrows in open sandy bed forming fragile tubes.

Distribution: India: Hooghly estuary, Digha Coast (West Bengal); Chilka Lake (Odisha) Camorta and Nicobar Island, Andaman Sea.

Family: OWENNIDAE

Genus *Owenia* delle Chiaje, 1841

Owenia fusiformis delle Chiaje, 1844

1844. *Owenia fusiformis* delle Chiaje, Descrizione ... neglianni 1842-30: 31.

Material: 3ex., Old Digha beach; 22.2. 1988, R.K. Chakraborty.

Diagnosis: Body elongated and cylindrical with few segments; tube cartilaginous strengthened by imbricating shell fragments or sand grains; head with a frilly feeding membrane; thoracic region with 3 short setigers bearing capillary setae; first five abdominal setigers longer, abdomen with notopodial capillaries and neuropodial rows of minute long-shaft hooks.

Habitat: Lives in tough tubes in muddy sand on midilitoral zone.

Distribution: India: digha coast, Hooghly estuary (West Bengal); Orissa Coast, Tuticorin (Tamil Nadu) Lakshadweep; Andamans.

Family: TEREBELLIDAE

Genus *Loimia* Malmgren, 1866

38. *Loimia medusa* (Savigny, 1818)

1818. T*erebella medusa* (Savigny), Histoire naturalle Description animaxces Sans Vertebres; p. 95.

Material: 1ex. Digha, 28.2.79. A. Misra.

Diagnosis: Tentacular lobe short with several eye-spots; lateral lobe membranous, horizontally placed over segment 2 and 3; branchiae 3 pairs, first often longer than other two; uncini pectiniform with a single vertical series of 5-6 teeth, in double rows, set back to back on posterior thorax; abdominal uncini on square pinnules.

Habitat: Live in tubes made of sand grains and build in open beaches.

Distribution: India: Hooghly eastuary (West Bengal); Gulf of Mannar (Tamil Nadu);Vembanad Lake (Kerala); Ratnagiri (Maharashtra); Beyt Island (Gujarat); Lakshadweep; Andamans.

Family: SABELLIDAE

Key to genera

Thoracic neurosetae include a row of avicular uncinii and a row of pick-axe seate (paleae) ...... *Potamilla*

Thoracic neurosetae are a simple row of avicular uncini only ...... *Laonome*

Genus *Potamilla* Malmgren, 1866

39. *Potamilla leptochaeta* Southern, 1921

1921. *Potamilla leptochaeta* Southern, Mem. Indian Mus., 5: 615.

Material: 1ex, Digha beach, 22.10.1987, A.K.Mandal

Diagnosis: Head with a tentacular crown of 7-9 pairs of radioles, each with 10-14 branchial filaments; thoracic notosetae on 2 types - narrow winged capillaries having long filiform tips, and baynet-shaped spatulate setae; thoracic neurosetae include an anterior row of companion setae, and a posterior row of avicular uncini; abdominal notosetae include avicular uncini and neurosetae all capillaries.

Habitat: Lives in muddy tube made of mucous.

Distribution: India: Digha coast, Hooghly eastuary, Matla river (West Bengal), Vishakhapatnam (Andhra Pradesh) Adyar estuary, Pulicat Lake (Tamil Nadu); Malvan coast, Miramar (Goa)

Abroad: Sri Lanka, Malay.

Genus Laonome Malmgren,1866

40. *Laonome indica* Southern, 1921

1921. *Laonome indica* Southern, Mem.Indian Mus, 5: 652.

Material: 4 ex., Digha beach, 13.5.1987, A.K. Mandal; 3 ex., Digha beach, 24.10.1987, A. Misra.

Diagnosis: Branchial lobes symmetrical, semi-circular; thoracic segments 6 with dorsal long capillaries having narrow wings and long tapering tips, and setae with spatulate tips terminating in a long fine point; uncini with a stout rounded base and 4-5 rows of teeth above the main fang.

Habitat: Lives in tubes made of fine silt mixed with mucous.

Distribution: India: Hooghly estuary (West Bengal) Chilka Lake (Orissa).

DISCUSSION

West Bengal has got very limited coastline which includes Digha, a well known place of tourist interst. This place not only attracts the tourist, but also frequently visited by the biology students and researchers for the collection of intertidal fauna. Polychaetes constitute one of the most important components of the intertidal macro-invertebrates. It appears that these worms remain mostly unidentified, if not send to polychaete taxonomists. The existing literature does not always include suitable taxonomic keys and most of the species expected to be available at Digha coast, West Bengal.

The prsent report is based on a large number of collections made by several parties from Zoological Survey of India since 1979. The present authors have got opportunities for visiting the area three times for the purpose of collection of polychaete worms. As a result more than 500 examples of worm were collected and identified. Ther report includes 40 species of polychaetes under 29 genera and 18 families. Moreover, an easy key is provided which is expeted to help the future workers in getting the worms identified at least up to certain level.

Considering the present trends of environmental degradation, particularly, in coastal areas, this diversity of poychaete fauna is expected to be diminished. Therefore, proper steps may be taken by demarcating certain portions, at least, of the beach as the Conservation Zone.

SUMMARY

Studies on the polychaetous annelids of Digha Coast, West Bengal, led to the identification of 40 species under 29 genera and 18 families. Keys for the identification of most of the species are included along with a short account of taxonomic characters and habitat data. A general account of the morphological characters along with collection and preservation techniques is also included.

REFERENCES

Day, J.H.1967. A Monograph on the Polychaeta of South Africa. Parts I & II, British Museum (Nat. Hist.), London, Publ. No. 656: XXXVIII + 878.

Fauvel, P. 1953. The Fauna of India including Pakisthan, Ceylon, Burma & Malay., Annelida, Polychaete.XII + 507 pp., Indian Press Ltd., Allahabad.

Jones, D. 1969. The Fauna of the Kelp Holdfast. Rep.Underwat. Ass., 4: 75-80.

Misra, A. 1998. Polychaeta. In: State Fauna Series 3 Fauna of West Bengal, pt. 10: 125-225. Zool. Surv. India.

Misra, A., Soota T.D. & Choudhury, A. 1984. On Some Polychaetes from Gangetic Delta, West Bengal, India, Rec. zool. Surv. India, 81: 41-54.

Misra, A. 1999. Polychaete, Zool. Surv. India. State Fauna Series 3: Fauna of West Bengal , Part 10: 125-225, 1998.

Moore, P.G. 1972. Particular Matter in the Sub-litoral Zone of an Exposed Coast and its Ecological Significance with Special Reference to the Fauna Inhabiting Kelp Holdfast. J. Exp. Mar. Biol. Ecol., 10: 59-80.

Rao, C.A.N. 1981. On Two New Polychaetes from Estuarine Waters of India. Bull. Zool. Survey India, 3(3): 213-217.

Reish, P.J. 1979. Bristle Worms (Annelida: Polychaeta). In: C.W. Hart (Jr.). and S.L.H. Fuller (Eds.). Pollution Ecology of Estuarine Invertebrates, pp. 78-125. Academic Press, N.Y.

Southern, R. 1921. Polychaeta of Chilka Lake and also of Fresh and Brackish Water in Other Parts of India. Mem. Indian Mus. 5: 563-659.

Willey, A.1908. The Fauna of Brackish Ponds at Port Canning, Lower Bengal XII. Description of a New Species of Polychaete Worm of the Genus Spio. Rec. Indian Mus. 2 (4): 389-390.

Fly Ash from Thermal Power Plants
A Structural Material

Manas Ranjan Senapati*

* Dept of Chemistry, Trident Academy of Technology, Bhubaneswar - 751 024, Odisha, India

ABSTRACT

Energy requirements for the developing countries in particular are met from coal based thermal power plants. The disposal of the increasing amounts of solid wastes from coal fired thermal power plants is becoming a serious concern to the environmentalists. The coal ash, 80% of which are very fine in nature and thus known as fly ash is collected by electrostatic precipitators in the stacks. In India nearly 90 million tones of fly ash are generated per annum at present and largely responsible for environmental pollution. In developed countries like Germany, 80% of the fly ash generated is being utilized, whereas in India only 3% of fly ash is being consumed.

This is an attempt to highlight the morphological study & management of fly ash to make use of this solid waste, in order to save our environment. The utilization of fly ash in construction, embankment, mine back fill and road sub-base is discussed.

Key Words: Fly Ash, Pozzolan, Colosseum & Embankment.

INTRODUCTION

Coal based thermal power plants have been major source of power generation in India. In India 75% of the total power obtained, is from coal based thermal power plants. The coal reserve of India is about 200 billion tons and its annual production reaches 250 million tons approximately. Coal is a dominant commercial fuel in India, where 565 mines are operated by Coal India and other subsidiaries. In 2003, production of hard coal was 358.4 Mt.; while utilization was 407.33 Mt. India is the sixth largest electricity generating and consuming country in the world. About 70% of this is used in power sector. In India, unlike in most of the developed countries, the ash content in the coal used for power generation is 30-40%. High ash coal means more wear and tear of plant and machinery, low thermal efficiency of boiler, slogging, choking and scaling of furnace and most serious of all generation of large amount of fly ash. India is the fourth in the world to produce coal ash as the byproduct waste after USSR, USA and China in order. Fly ash is defined in Cement and Concrete Terminology (ACI Committee 116) as the "finely divided residue resulting from the combustion of ground or powdered coal, which is transported from the fire box through the boiler by flue gases." Fly ash is fine, glass powder the particles of which are generally spherical in shape and range in size from 0.5 mm to 100mm. Fly ash is classified into two types according to the type of coal used. Anthracite and bituminous coal produces fly ash classified as class F. Class C fly ash is produced by burning lignite or sub-bituminous coal. Class C fly ash has self cementing properties. The estimated thermal power generation, coal consumption and ash generation in India is given in Table 5.1 & 5.2.

Table 5.1: Thermal Power Generation, Coal Consumption and Ash Generation in India

Year	Thermal Power Generation (MW)	Coal Consumption (Million Tones)	Ash Generation (Million Tones)
1995	54,000.00	200	75
2000	70,000.00	250	90
2010	98,000.00	300	110
2020	1,37,000.00	350	140

ENGINEERING PROPERTIES OF FLY ASH

Some of the engineering properties of fly ash that are of particular interest when fly ash is used as an embankment or fill material are its moisture-density relationship, particle size distribution, shear strength, consolidation characteristics, bearing strength, and permeability.

Moisture-Density Relationship: Fly ash has a relatively low compacted density, thereby reducing the applied loading and resultant settlement to the supporting sub grade. Conditioned fly ash tailgated over the slope of an embankment can have a loose dry density as low as 650 to 810 kg/m^3 (40 to 50 lb/ft^3). However, when it has been well compacted at an optimum moisture content (usually between 20 and 35%), the dry unit weight of fly ash may be greater than 1380 kg/m^3 (85 lb/ft^3), possibly even as high as 1620 kg/m^3 (100 lb/ft^3).

Table 5.2: Details of NTPC Power Plants in India

Sl. No.	Power Station	Location	District	State	Region	Installed Capacity (MW)
1.	Badarpur TPP	Badarpur	New Delhi	NCT Delhi	Northern	705.00
2.	Singrauli TPP	Shakti Nagar	Sonebhadra	U.P	Northern	2000.00
3.	Rihand TPP	Rihand Nagar	Sonebhadra	U.P	Northern	2000.0
4.	Feroz Gandhi Unchahar	Unchahar	Raebarelii	U.P	Northern	1050.00
5.	Tanda TPP	Vidyutnagar	Ambedaknagar	U.P	Northern	440.00
6.	KorbaSTPP	Jamani palli	Korba	C.G	Western	2100
7.	Sipat TPP	Sipat	Bilaspur	C.G	Western	1000
8.	Vindhyachal STPS	Vidhya nagar	Sidhi	U.P	Northern	3260
9.	Ramagundam STPS	Jyothi nagar	Karimnagar	A.P	Southern	2600
10.	Simhadri STPS	Simhadri	Visakhapatnam	A.P	Southern	1000
11.	Farakka STPS	Nagarun	Mushidabad	W.B	Eastern	1600
12.	Kahalgaon STPS	Kahalgaon	Bhagalpur	Bihar	Eastern	2340
13.	Talcher STPS	Kaniha	Angul	Odisha	Eastern	3000
14.	Talcher TPP	Talcher	Angul	Odisha	Eastern	460

Particle Size Distribution: Fly ash is predominantly a silt-sized nonplastic material. Between 60 and 90 percent of fly ash particles are finer than a 0.075 mm (No. 200) sieve.

As such, its particle size distribution falls essentially within the normally recognized limits for frost-susceptible soils. The potential for frost susceptibility of fly ash may account for the reluctance on the part of some geotechnical engineers to use fly ash as a fill material. The fine particle sizing of fly ash, together with the relative uniformity of the gradation in the coarse silt range, makes it imperative that the ash be handled with sufficient water to prevent dusting. Since fine-grained soils can be fairly easily eroded, enough moisture must also be present to support compaction equipment and to permit the material to be well densified, in order to prevent or minimize erodibility.

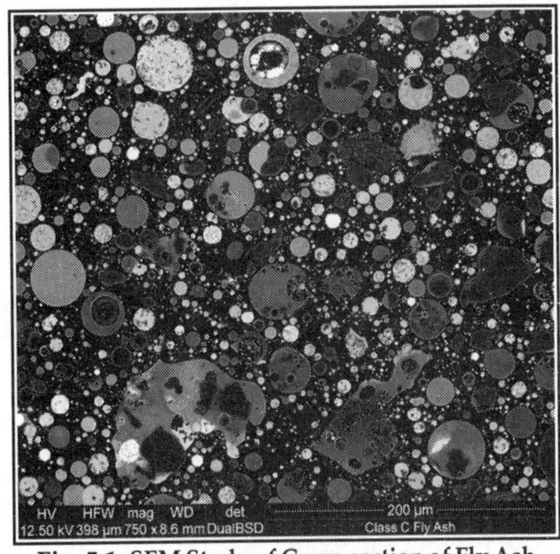

Fig. 5.1: SEM Study of Cross-section of Fly Ash

Shear Strength: Shear strength tests conducted on freshly compacted fly ash samples show that fly ash derives most of its shear strength from internal friction, although some apparent cohesion has been observed in certain bituminous (pozzolanic) fly ashes. The shear strength of fly ash is affected by the density and moisture content of the test sample, with maximum shear strength exhibited at the optimum moisture content. Bituminous fly ash has been determined to have a friction angle that is usually in the range of 26° to 42°. A test program involving shear strength testing for 51 different ash samples resulted in a mean friction angle value of 34°, with a fairly wide range.

Consolidation Characteristics: An embankment or structural backfill should possess low compressibility to minimize roadway settlements or differential settlements between structures and adjacent approaches. Consolidation has been shown to occur more rapidly in compacted fly ash than in silty clay soil because the fly ash has a higher void ratio and greater permeability than the soil. For fly ashes with age-hardening properties, including most "high lime" fly ashes from lignite or subbituminous coals, the age-hardening can reduce the time rate of consolidation, as well as the magnitude of the compressibility.

Bearing Strength: California bearing ratio (CBR) values for "low lime" fly ash from the burning of anthracite or bituminous coals have been found to range from 6.8 to 13.5 percent in the soaked condition (an optional procedure in the test method) to 10.8 to 15.4 percent in the unsoaked condition. For naturally occurring soils, CBR values normally range from 3 to 15 percent for fine-grained materials (silts and clays), from 10 to 40 percent for sand and sandy soils, and from 20 to 80 percent for gravels and gravelly soils.

Permeability: The permeability of well-compacted fly ash has been found to range from 10^{-4} to 10^{-6} cm/s, which is roughly equivalent to the normal range of permeability of a silty sand to silty clay soil. The permeability of a material is affected by its density or degree of compaction, its grain size distribution, and its internal pore structure. Since fly ash consists almost entirely of spherical shaped particles, the particles are able to be densely packed during compaction, resulting in comparatively low permeability values and minimizing seepage of water through a fly ash embankment.

FLYASH UTILIZATION

The ash generated from volcanoes was used extensively in the construction of Roman structures. Colosseum (constructed in the year 100 AD) is a classic example of durability achieved by using volcanic ash. Fly ash is generated in artificial volcanoes (coal fired). Volcanic ash acts just like fly ash obtained from coal fired thermal power plants.

During the last thirty years, extensive research has been carried out to utilize the fly ash in various sectors, as this is not considered as hazardous waste. Broadly fly ash utilization programmes can be viewed from two angles i.e. mitigating environmental effects and addressing disposal problems (Low value-High volume utilization).

Fly ash closely resembles volcanic ashes used in production of the earliest known hydraulic cements about 2,300 years ago. Those cements were made near the small Italian town of Pozzuoli - which later gave its name to the term "pozzolan".

Fig. 5.2: The Roman Colosseum

A pozzolan is a siliceous or siliceous/aluminous material that, when mixed with lime and water, forms a cementitious compound. Fly ash is the best known, and one of the most commonly used, pozzolans in the world.

Instead of volcanoes, today's fly ash comes primarily from coal-fired electricity generating power plants. These power plants grind coal to a powder fineness before it is burned. Fly ash - the mineral residue produced by burning coal - is captured from the power plant's exhaust gases and collected for use.

Fly ash is a fine, glass powder recovered from the gases of burning coal during the production of electricity. These micron-sized earth elements consist primarily of silica, alumina and iron. Fly ash is generally grey in color, abrasive, mostly alkaline, and refractory in nature.

The difference between fly ash and portland cement becomes apparent under a microscope. Fly ash particles are almost totally spherical in shape, allowing them to flow and blend freely in mixtures. That capability is one of the properties making fly ash a desirable admixture for concrete.

The principal components of bituminous coal fly ash are silica, alumina, iron oxide, and calcium, with varying amounts of carbon, as measured by the loss on ignition (LOI). Lignite and sub-bituminous coal fly ash is characterized by higher concentrations of calcium and magnesium oxide and reduced percentages of silica and iron oxide, as well as lower carbon content, compared with bituminous coal fly ash. Very little anthracite coal is burned in utility boilers, so there are only small amounts of anthracite coal fly ash. The chief difference between Class F and Class C fly ash is in the amount of calcium and the silica, alumina, and iron content in the ash. In Class F fly ash, total calcium typically ranges from 1 to 12%, mostly in the form of calcium hydroxide, calcium sulphate and glassy components, in combination with silica and alumina. In contrast, Class C fly ash may have reported calcium oxide contents as high as 30-40%. Another difference between Class F and Class C is that the amount of alkalis (combined sodium and potassium), and sulphates (SO_4), are generally higher in the Class C fly ash than in the Class F fly ash. Table 5.1 compares the normal range of the chemical constituents of bituminous coal fly ash with those of lignite coal fly ash and sub-bituminous coal fly ash.

From the Table 5.3, it is evident that lignite and sub-bituminous coal fly ash has a higher calcium oxide content and lower loss of ignition than fly ash from bituminous coals. Lignite and sub-bituminous coal fly ash may have a higher concentration of sulphate compounds than bituminous coal fly ash. According to the American Society for Testing Materials (ASTM C618), the ash containing more than 70 wt% $SiO_2 + Al_2O_3 + Fe_2O_3$ and being low in lime are defined as class F, while those with a $SiO_2 + Al_2O_3 + Fe_2O_3$ content between 50 and 70 wt% and high in lime are defined as class C. Briefly, the high-calcium Class C fly ash is normally produced from the burning of low-rank coals (lignite or sub-bituminous coals) and have cementitious properties (self-hardening when reacted with water). On the other hand, the low-calcium Class F fly ash is commonly produced from the burning of higher-rank coals (bituminous coals or anthracites) that are pozzolanic in nature (hardening when reacted with $Ca(OH)_2$ and water).

Table 5.3: Chemical Composition for Fly Ash Produced from Different Coal Types

Component (wt.%)	Bituminous	Sub-bituminous	Lignite
SiO_2	20-60	40-60	15-45
Al_2O_3	5-35	20-30	10-25
Fe_2O_3	10-40	4-10	4-15
CaO	1-12	5-30	15-40
MgO	0-5	1-6	3-10
SO_3	0-4	0-2	0-10
Na_2O	0-4	0-2	0-6
K_2O	0-3	0-4	0-4
LOI	0-15	0-3	0-5

Use of fly ash as a partial replacement for Portland cement is generally limited to Class C fly ashes. Class "F" fly ashes can have volatile effects on the entrained air content of concrete, causing reduced resistance to freeze/ thaw damage. Fly Ash often replaces up to 30% by mass of Portland cement, but can be used in higher dosages in certain applications. Fly ash can add to the concrete's final strength and increase its chemical resistance and durability. Fly ash can also significantly improve the workability of concrete. Recently concrete mix design for partial cement replacement with High Volume Fly Ash (50% cement replacement) has been developed.

For Roller Compacted Concrete (RCC) [used in dam construction] replacement values of 70% have been achieved with processed fly ash at the Ghatghar Dam project in Maharashtra, India.

Due to the spherical shape of fly ash particles, it can also increase workability of cement while reducing water demand.

The replacement of Portland cement with fly ash is considered by its promoters to reduce the greenhouse "footprint" of concrete, as the production of one ton of Portland cement produces approximately one ton of CO_2 as compared to zero CO_2 being produced using existing fly ash. New fly ash production, i.e., the burning of coal, produces approximately twenty to thirty tons of CO_2 per ton of fly ash. Since the worldwide production of Portland cement is expected to reach nearly 2 billion tons by 2010, replacement of any large portion of this cement by fly ash could significantly reduce carbon emissions. Fly ash has three effects in concrete, i.e., morphological, activated and micro aggregate effects. The three effects are relative each other. This shows that the morphological effect is the important aspect of fly ash effects.

Table 5.4: Comparison of Chemical and Physical Characteristics–Portland Cement, Fly Ash, Slag Cement and Silica Fume

Note that these are appropriate values. Values for a specific material may vary from what is shown (Note 1)

Property	Portland Cement	Class F Fly Ash	Class C Fly Ash	Slag Cement	Silica Fume
S_iO_2 content, %	21	52	35	35	85 to 97
Al_2O_3 content, %	5	23	18	12	
Fe_2O_3 content, %	3	11	6	1	
CaO content, %	62	5	21	40	<1
Fineness as surface area, m^1/kg (Note 2)	370	420	420	400	15,000 to 30,000
Specific gravity	3.15	2.38	2.65	2.94	2.22
General use in concrete	Primary binder	Cement replacement	Cement replacement	Cement replacement	Property enhancer

Note 1: Information from SFA and Kasmatka, Kerkoff and Panarese (2002)

Note 2: Surface area measurements for silica fume by nitrogen adsorption method. Others by air permeability method blaine.

In this chapter, it will be discussed emphatically. The morphological effect means that in concrete, mineral-powdered materials produce the effect due to the morphology, structure and surface property of the particle and the particle size distribution. From the influence of fly ash on the properties of cement-based materials, the morphology effect includes three aspects: filling, lubricating and well distributing. These roles depend on the shape, size distribution, etc., of fly ash and influence many properties of concrete. Flyash used in concrete is however a mature technology. Thirty percent of the flyash in the US is recycled into making concrete. The use of flyash concrete in structural applications such as wall-forms is standard technology. The use of recycled-content blocks, in particular fiber-cement, as part of a structural foundation system using flyash concrete is still early in development.

The geo-technical properties of fly ash (e.g., specific gravity, permeability, internal angular friction, and consolidation characteristics) make it suitable for use in construction of roads and embankments, structural fill etc. Coal fly ash has been successfully used as a structural fill or embankment material for highway construction projects in a number of different locations throughout the United States. Compared with conventional soils used to build embankments, fly ash is somewhat of a unique engineering material. When dry, fly ash is cohesionless and considered by many as a dusty nuisance. When saturated, fly ash becomes an unmanageable mess. But, as with most fine-grained soils, fly ash can be easily handled and compacted at more intermediate moisture contents, and does exhibit some cohesion.

Fig. 5.3: Upperdam of Ghatghar Constructed with RCC (65% Replacement of Cement with Fly Ash)

Nearly all of the fly ash used for embankment construction is anthracite or bituminous coal fly ash. Lignite or sub bituminous fly ashes, which are usually self-cementing, can harden prematurely when moisture is added, resulting in potential handling problems and inability to achieve the required degree of compaction. Fly ash use as a structural fill or embankment material was pioneered during the 1950's in Great Britain, where it is still bid as an alternate borrow material on roadway fill projects in areas where it is available. When used in structural fills or embankments, fly ash offers several advantages over natural soil or rock. Its relatively low unit weight makes it well suited for placement over soft or low bearing strength soils, and its high shear strength, compared with its unit weight, results in good bearing support and minimal settlement. The ease with which fly ash can be placed and compacted, especially when placed at the proper moisture content, can reduce construction time and equipment costs. In areas where fly ash is readily available in bulk quantities, costs for the purchase, permitting, and operation of a borrow pit can be reduced or eliminated.

There are some disadvantages of using fly ash in structural fills or embankments. Unless delivered to the project site within the proper moisture range, dust control measures may be needed. Also, since fly ash is a predominantly silt-size material, it is subject to erosion and, as a result; erosion control procedures may be needed.

Fig. 5.4: First Fly Ash Embankment in the Country (Okhla fly over, New Delhi)

OVERALL IMPACT – MANIFOLD INCREASE IN ASH UTILISATION

Wastes have always created a disposal problem. The problem of fly ash disposal has assumed such an alarming condition in the country that the Ministry of Environment & Forest (MoEF) issued a regulation on September 1999 specifying normative levels for progressive utilization of fly ash. According to the regulation, it is mandatory for the existing (Old) and new coal based thermal power plants to utilize 100% of the fly ash produced in a stipulated time of horizon. The new coal thermal power plants are required to use 100% of the fly ash produced within 9 years of commencing operation. The old power plants, however, are required to achieve 100% fly ash utilization goal within 15 years from the date of issue of the regulation.

During the last thirty years, extensive research has been carried out to utilize the fly ash in various sectors, as this is not considered as hazardous waste. Broadly fly ash utilization programmes can be viewed from two angles i.e. mitigating environmental effects and addressing disposal problems (Low value-High volume utilization).

Over a period of last ten years, the image of fly ash has completely been changed from a "Polluting Waste" to "Resource Material". The economic worth of fly ash has been understood by the people. It has now become a "sought after material". The utilisation of fly ash which was about one million tonne per year in 1994 (at the start of Mission) has now reached about 45 million tonne per year. As compared to 2-3 major areas of ash utilization about a decade back, now about 10 areas of ash utilization have been identified and fly ash has started being used in most of them. The focused thrust being provided by Fly Ash Mission (FAM) is still being continued through Fly Ash Utilisation Programme (FAUP), TIFAC and Department of Science & Technology (DST) with the help and support of all other stake holder agencies. With the significant progress made (45 times increase in ash utilization) during last 10 years, it seems that the flight of ash utilization is right at take-off stage, however, continued thrust and support of all stake holder agencies at much higher levels would still be required to sustain the pace to accelerate it further, especially, as our target (ash generation figure) is also rocketing high day by day.

CONCLUSION

It has been recognized worldwide that the utilization of an enormous amount of fossil fuel has created various adverse effects on the environment, including acid rain and global warming. An increase in average global temperatures of approximately 0.56 K has been measured over the past century. This increase is called global climate change or global warming. The gases with three or more atoms that have higher heat capacities than those of O_2 and N_2 cause the greenhouse effect. Carbon dioxide (CO_2) is a main greenhouse gas associated with global climate change. The disposal, management and proper utilization of waste products have become a concern for the scientists and environmentalists.

Proper management of solid waste fly ash from thermal power plants is necessary to safeguard our environment. Use of high volume fly ash concrete in construction is one big step in natural resource conservation and it needs to be promoted all over the world. In fact, it will not be wrong if we call high volume fly ash concrete as a green concrete, since it can protect the environment from global warming to a large extent. Fly ash use displaces cement use; it also reduces the need for cement production – a major energy user and source of "greenhouse gas" emissions. For every ton of cement manufactured, about 6.5 million BTUs of energy are consumed. For every ton of cement manufactured, about one ton of carbon dioxide is released. Replacing that ton of cement with fly ash would save enough electricity to power the average American home for 24 days, and reduce carbon dioxide emissions equal to two months use of an automobile. Because of high cost involved in road transportation for dumping of fly ash, it is advisable to explore all its possible applications.

Pradhan Mantri Gramya Sadak Yojana (PMGSY) would be a success and economically viable project by utilization of fly ash in road construction in remote & rural areas. Every village in India will have concrete roads and large portion of fly ash can be consumed in this process. Concentrated efforts are needed to utilize the fly ash to manufacture building bricks, cement and ceramics, mitigating the unemployment problem as well.

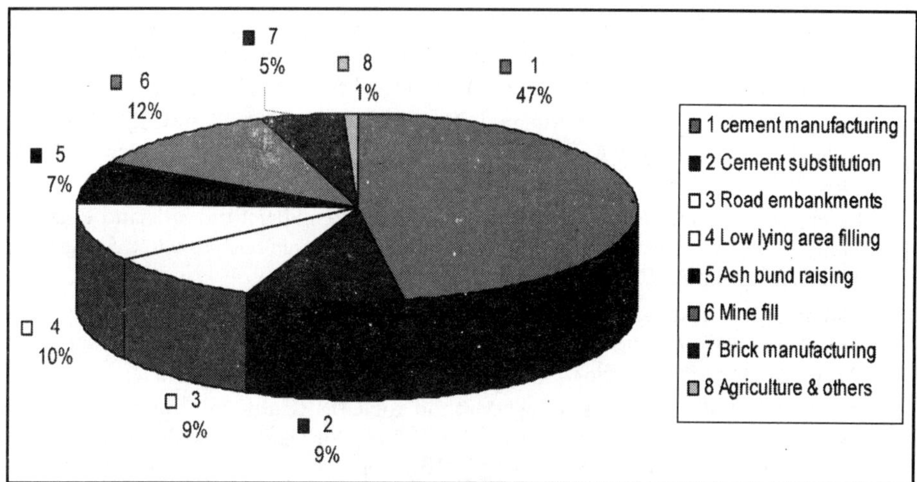

Fly Ash Utilization Status – 2012

REFERENCES

1. Clerk A.J., Disposal of Ash from U.K. Power Station Environmental Problems and Answers, June (1981).
2. Senapati M.R. & Banerjee J., Advances in Particulate Emissions Control, Paper Presented at Institution of Engineers (India) Odisha, November (1999).
3. Japans Environmental Agency Notification No. 13, 1973; Assay of Metals and Other Contaminants in Industrial Wastes.
4. Senapati M.R., The Times of India, June 5, 2009, Heal the World – Raising Mass Awareness will be the Key to Arrest Climate Change Globally (Special Article on World Environment Day).
5. Palit A., Coal Ash Utilization in India, Urja Journal, 32(3), 39-44 (1992).
6. Vimal Kumar, Fly ash Utilization, a Mission Mode Approach, TIDE Jr-6(1), 1726(1996).
7. Collins, Robert J. and Stanley K. Ciesielski. *Recycling and Use of Waste Materials and By-products in Highway Construction, Volume 2 – Technical Appendix*. National Cooperative Highway Research Program Synthesis of Highway Practice No. 199, Transportation Research Board, Washington, DC, 1994.
8. Patelunas, G.M. High Volume Fly Ash Utilization Projects in the United States and Canada. Electric Power Research Institute, Report No. CS-4446, Palo Alto, California, May, 1986.
9. Collins, R.J. and L. Srivastava. *Use of Ash in Highway Construction: Delaware Demonstration Project, Final Report*. Electric Power Research Institute, Report No. GS-6540, Palo Alto, California, November, 1989.
10. Brendel, G.F. and P.E. Glogowski. *Ash Utilization in Highways: Pennsylvania Demonstration Project*. Electric Power Research Institute, Report No. GS-6431, Palo Alto, California, June, 1989.
11. American Coal Ash Association. *Fly Ash Facts for Highway Engineers*. Federal Highway Administration, Report No. FHWA-SA-94-081, Washington, DC, December, 1995.

12. Gray, Donald H. and Yen-Kuang Lin. "Engineering Properties of Compacted Fly Ash," *Proceedings of the American Society of Civil Engineers National Water Resources Engineering Meeting*, Phoenix, Arizona, January, 1971.

13. DiGioia, Anthony M., Jr. and William L. Nuzzo. "Fly Ash as Structural Fill," *Proceedings of the American Society of Civil Engineers, Journal of the Power Division,* New York, NY, June, 1972.

14. Lamb, D. William, "Ash Disposal in Dams, Mounds, Structural Fills and Retaining Walls," *Proceedings of the Third International Ash Utilization Symposium*, U.S. Bureau of Mines, Information Circular No. 8640, Washington, DC, 1974.

15. McLaren, R.J. and A.M. DiGioia, Jr., "Typical Engineering Properties of Fly Ash," *Proceedings of Geotechnical Practice for Waste Disposal '87*, University of Michigan, Ann Arbor, Michigan, June, 1987.

16. ASTM D1883-87. "Standard Test Method for CBR (California Bearing Ratio) of Laboratory-Compacted Soils," American Society for Testing and Materials, *Annual Book of ASTM Standards,* Volume 04.08, West Conshohocken, Pennsylvania, 1994.

17. Martin, Joseph P., Robert J. Collins, John S. Browning, III, and Francis J. Biehl. "Properties and Use of Fly Ash for Embankments," Presented at the 22nd Annual Mid-Atlantic Industrial Waste Conference, Philadelphia, Pennsylvania, 1989.

18. Hough, B.K. *Basic Soils Engineering*. Ronald Press Company, New York, New York, 1969.

19. ASTM E1861-97. *Standard Guide for Use of Coal Combustion By-Products in Structural Fills*. American Society for Testing and Materials, West Conshohocken, Pennsylvania, 1997.

20. DiGioia, A.M., Jr., R.J. McLaren and L.R. Taylor. *Fly Ash Structural Fill Handbook*. Electric Power Research Institute, Report No. EA-1281, Palo Alto, California, December, 1979.

21. AASHTO *Guide for Design of Pavement Structures*. American Association of State Highway and Transportation Officials, Washington, DC, 1986.

22. Croney, D. and J.D. Jacobs. *The Frost Susceptibility of Soils and Road Materials*. British Ministry of Transport, Road Research Laboratory, RRL Report No. 90, Crowthorne, England, 1967.

23. Kinder, D.L. and R.E. Morrison. "An Engineering Approach for Using Power Plant Ash in a Structural Fill," *Proceedings of the Fifth International Ash Utilization Symposium*, U.S. Department of Energy, Report No. METC/SP-79-10, Atlanta, Georgia, February, 1979.

Immunogenic Activity of Chicken Antibodies Towards *Anopheles Dirus* Salivary Gland Antigen

Vemuri Praveen Kumar*

* Department of Biotechnology, K.L. University, Green Fields, Vaddeswaram, Guntur District, A.P. - 522 502 (India)

ABSTRACT

The growing diffusion of monoclonal and polyclonal antibodies in immunotherapy and immuno-diagnostics, and the strict standards for animal-care, has led to a renewed interest in the use of chickens for antibody production, as opposed to mammals. Egg yolk represents an economical source of polyclonal antibodies, since the amount of immunoglobulins (IgY) is similar or higher than in the serum of chickens or rabbits or humans reaching levels ranging from 15 to 25 mg IgY per ml of yolk in the case of hyper-immunized hen . In this study, we have examined the applicability for IgY and IgG, obtained from the screening of different kinds of hen eggs and serum sample respectively, for its capability to interact towards a novel antigenic protein. Due to the peculiar composition of the egg yolk, IgY are normally purified using complex and time consuming procedures involving a combination of precipitation and chromatographic steps . Soluble proteins were separated from the lipidic fraction of egg yolk by various methods and loaded onto PEG –column. High recovery and purity of IgY was obtained for normal and brown eggs by water dilution and chloroform methods. Similarly, IgG is also purified in extend of 90% with affinity chromatography. Immunogenic activity was tested for salivary gland antigens after various treatments.

INTRODUCTION

Immunology is a science that examines the structure and function of the immune system. It originates from medicine and early studies on the causes of immunity to disease. The earliest known mention of immunity was during the plague of Athens in 430 BC. Thucydides noted that people who had recovered from a previous bout of the disease could nurse the sick without contracting the illness a second time. In the 18th century, Pierre-Louis Moreau de Maupertuis made experiments with scorpion venom and observed that certain dogs and mice were immune to this venom. This and other observations of acquired immunity were later exploited by Louis Pasteur in his development of vaccination and his proposed germ theory of disease. Pasteur's theory was in direct opposition to contemporary theories of disease, such as the miasma theory. It was not until Robert Koch's 1891 proofs, for which he was awarded a Nobel Prize in 1905, that microorganisms were confirmed as the cause of infectious disease. Viruses were confirmed as human pathogens in 1901, with the discovery of the yellow fever virus by Walter Reed.

Immunology made a great advance towards the end of the 19th century, through rapid developments, in the study of humoral immunity and cellular immunity. Particularly important was the work of Paul Ehrlich, who proposed the side-chain theory to explain the specificity of the antigen-antibody reaction; his contributions to the understanding of humoral immunity were recognized by the award of a Nobel Prize in 1908, which was jointly awarded to the founder of cellular immunology, Elie Metchnikoff.

An **immune system** is a system of biological structures and processes within an organism that protects against disease by identifying and killing pathogens and tumor cells. It detects a wide variety of agents, from viruses to parasitic worms, and needs to distinguish them from the organism's own healthy cells and tissues in order to function properly. Detection is complicated as pathogens can evolve rapidly; producing adaptations that avoid the immune system and allow the pathogens to successfully infect their hosts.

To survive this challenge, multiple mechanisms evolved that recognize and neutralize pathogens. Even simple unicellular organisms such as bacteria possess enzyme systems that protect against viral infections. Other basic immune mechanisms evolved in ancient eukaryotes and remain in their modern descendants, such as plants and insects. These mechanisms include antimicrobial peptides called defensins, phagocytosis, and the complement system. Jawed vertebrates, including humans, have even more sophisticated defense mechanisms. The typical vertebrate immune system consists of many types of proteins, cells, organs, and tissues, which interact in an elaborate and dynamic network. As part of this more complex immune response, the human immune system adapts over time to recognize specific pathogens more efficiently. This adaptation process is referred to as "adaptive immunity" or "acquired immunity" and creates immunological memory. Immunological memory created from a primary response to a specific pathogen, provides an enhanced response to secondary encounters with that same, specific pathogen. This process of acquired immunity is the basis of vaccination.

Disorders in the immune system can result in disease. Immunodeficiency occurs when the immune system is less active than normal, resulting in recurring and life-threatening infections. Immunodeficiency can either be the result of a genetic disease, such as severe combined immunodeficiency, or be produced by pharmaceuticals or an infection, such as the acquired immune deficiency syndrome (AIDS) that is caused by the retrovirus HIV. In contrast, autoimmune diseases result from a hyperactive immune system attacking normal tissues as if they were foreign organisms. Common autoimmune diseases include Hashimoto's thyroiditis, rheumatoid arthritis, diabetes mellitus type 1 and lupus erythematosus. Immunology covers the study of all aspects of the immune system which has significant relevance to human health and diseases. Further investigation in this field is expected to play a serious role in promotion of health and treatment of diseases.

Immunogenicity is the ability of a particular substance, such as an antigen or epitope, to provoke an immune response. The ability to induce humoral and/or cell-mediated immune responses. The ability of antigen to elicit immune response is called "immunogenicity." Antigens that do provoke the immune response are "immunogens." Antigenicity is the ability of a chemical structure (referred to as an Antigen) to bind specifically with certain products of adaptive immunity: T cell receptors or Antibodies (a.k.a. B cell receptors). Antigenicity was more commonly used in the past to refer to what is now known as immunogenicity, and the two are still often used interchangeably. However, strictly speaking, immunogenicity refers to the ability of an antigen to Induce an adaptive immune response. Thus an antigen might bind specifically to a T or B cell receptor, but not induce an adaptive immune response. If the antigen does induce a response, it is an 'immunogeic antigen, which is referred to as an immunogen.

Immunogenic Potency of Antigens

Proteins are significantly more immunogenic than polysaccharides. Since lipids and nucleic acids are non-immunogenic haptens, they require conjugation with an epitope such as a protein or polysaccharide before they can evoke an immunologic response.

Cells of Immune System

An immune system is a collection of biological processes within an organism that protects against diseases, infections etc. The immune system is very complex. It's made up of several types of cells and proteins that have different jobs to do in fighting foreign invaders.

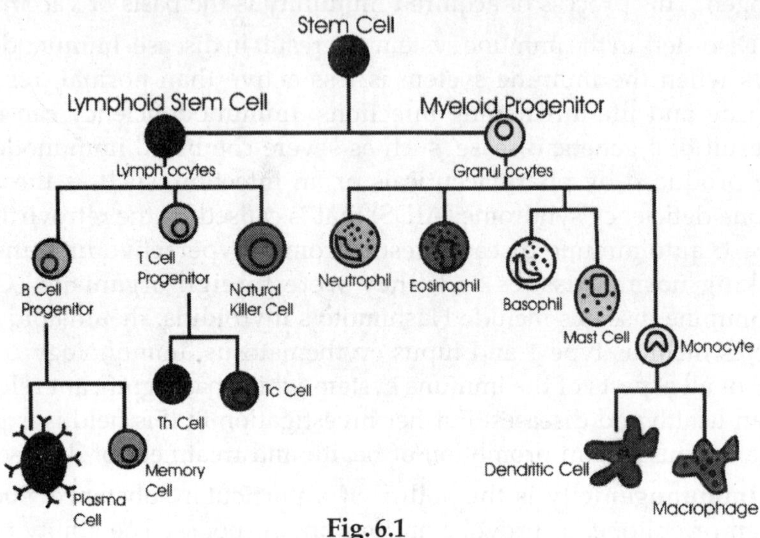

Fig. 6.1

Lymphocytes

Lymphocytes are the central cells of the immune system, responsible for adaptive immunity and the immunologic attributes of diversity, specificity, memory, and self/non self recognition. Lymphocytes constitute 20%-40% of the body's white blood cells and 99% of the cells in the lymph. These lymphocytes continually circulate in the blood and lymph and are capable of migrating into the tissue spaces and lymphoid organs, thereby integrating the immune system to a high degree. The lymphocytes can be broadly subdivided into three populations—B cells, T cells, and natural killer cells—on the basis of function and cell-membrane components.

B cells

These are lymphocytes that play a large role in the humoral immune response. The principal functions of B cells are to make antibodies against antigens, perform the role of Antigen Presenting Cells (APCs) and eventually develop into memory B cells after activation by antigen interaction. B cells are an essential component of the adaptive immune system. B cells recognize their cognate antigen in its native form. They recognize free (soluble) antigen in the blood or lymph using their BCR or membrane bound-immunoglobulin. Interaction between antigen and the membrane-bound antibody on a mature naive B cell, as well as interactions with T cells and macrophages, selectively induces the activation and differentiation of B-cell clones of corresponding specificity.

In this process, the B cell divides repeatedly and differentiates over a 4- to 5-day period, generating a population of plasma cells and memory cells. Plasma cells, which have lower levels of membrane-bound antibody than B cells, synthesize and secrete antibody. which assist in the destruction of microbes by binding to them and making them easier targets for phagocytes and activation of the complement system. Memory B cells live for a long time, and can respond quickly following a second exposure to the same antigen.

T cells

These play a central role in cell-mediated immunity. They can be distinguished from other lymphocytes by the presence of a special receptor on their cell surface called T cell receptors (TCR). To be recognized by most T cells, this antigen must be displayed together with MHC molecules on the surface of antigen-presenting cells or on virus-infected cells, cancer cells, and grafts. T cells are divided into two main sub populations based on the type of receptor it expressed. T cells expressing CD4 glycoproteins are called TH(T helper cells,class-2 restricted) and those expressing CD8 are called TC cells(T cytotoxic cells,class-1 restricted). TH cells are activated by recognition of an antigen–class II MHC complex on an antigen-presenting cell. After activation these TH cells secrete various cytokines, which play a central role in the activation of B cells, T cells, and other cells that participate in the immune response. Changes in the pattern of cytokines produced by TH cells can change the type of immune response that develops among other leukocytes. The TH1 response produces a cytokine profile that supports inflammation and activates mainly certain T cells and macrophages, whereas the TH2 response activates mainly B cells and immune responses that depend upon antibodies. TC cells are activated when they interact with an antigen–class I MHC complex on the surface of an altered self-cell (e.g., a virus-infected cell or a tumor cell) in the presence of appropriate cytokines. This activation, which results in proliferation, causes the TC cell to differentiate into an effector cell called a cytotoxic T lymphocyte (CTL). Incontrast to TH cells, most CTLs secrete few cytokines. Instead, CTLs acquire the ability to recognize and eliminate altered self-cells.

Natural Killer Cells

NK cells were subsequently shown to play an important role in host defense both against tumor cells and against cells infected with some, though not all, viruses. These cells constitute 5%-10% of lymphocytes in human peripheral blood. Although NK cells do not have T-cell receptors or immunoglobulin incorporated in their plasma membranes, they can recognize potential target cells in two different ways. In some cases, an NK cell employs NK cell receptors to distinguish abnormalities, notably a reduction inthe display of class I MHC molecules and the unusual profile of surface antigens displayed by some tumor cells and cells infected by some viruses. Another way in which NK cells recognize potential target cells depends upon the fact that some tumor cells and cells infected by certain viruses display antigens against which the immune system has made an antibody response, so that antitumor or antiviral antibodies are bound to their surfaces. Because NK cells express CD16, a membrane receptor for the carboxyl-terminal end of the Ig G molecule, called the Fc region, they can attach to these antibodies and subsequently destroy the targeted cells. This is an example of a process known as antibody-dependent cell mediated cytotoxicity (ADCC).

Granulocytic Cells

The granulocytes are classified as neutrophils, eosinophils, or basophils on the basis of cellular morphology and cytoplasmic staining characteristics . The neutrophil has a multilobed nucleus and a granulated cytoplasm it is often called a polymorphonuclear leukocyte (PMN) for its multilobed nucleus. The eosinophil has a bilobed nucleus and a granulated cytoplasm . The basophil has a lobed nucleus and heavily granulated cytoplasm .Both neutrophils and eosinophils are phagocytic, whereas basophils are not. Neutrophils, which constitute 50%-70%of the circulating white blood cells, are much more numerous than eosinophils (1%-3%) or basophils (1%).

Neutrophils

They are produced by hematopoiesis in the bone marrow. They are released into the peripheral blood and circulate for 7-10 h before migrating into the tissues, where they have a life span of only a few days. During the beginning phase of inflammation, particularly as a result of bacterial infection and some cancers, neutrophils are one of the first group of inflammatory cells to migrate toward the site of inflammation, firstly through the blood vessels, then through interstitial tissue, following chemical signals (such as Interleukin-8 (IL-8), Interferon-gamma (IFN-gamma), and C5a) in a process called chemotaxis. They are the predominant cells in pus, accounting for its whitish/yellowish appearance. Neutrophils are one of the first group of inflammatory cells to migrate toward the site of inflammation. Neutrophils are phagocytes, capable of ingesting microorganisms or particles. They can internalise and kill many microbes, each phagocytic event resulting in the formation of a phagosome into which reactive oxygen species and hydrolytic enzymes are secreted.

Eosinophils

Eosinophils, like neutrophils, are motile phagocytic cells that can migrate from the blood into the tissue spaces. Their phagocytic role is significantly less important than that of neutrophils, and it is thought that they play a role in the defense against parasitic organisms. The secreted contents of eosinophilic granules may damage the parasite membrane.

Basophils

These are nonphagocytic granulocytes that function by releasing pharmacologically active substances from their cytoplasmic granules. These substances play a major role in certain allergic responses.

Mast cells

Mast-cell precursors, which are formed in the bone marrow by hematopoiesis, are released into the blood as undifferentiated cells; they do not differentiate until they leave the blood and enter the tissues. Mast cells can be found in a wide variety of tissues, including the skin, connective tissues of various organs, and mucosal epithelial tissue of the respiratory, genitor urinary, and digestive tracts. Like circulating basophils, these cells have large numbers of cytoplasmic granules that contain histamine and other pharmacologically active substances. Mast cells, together with blood basophils, play an important role in the development of allergies.

Dendritic cells

There are many types of dendritic cells, although most mature dendritic cells have the same major function, the presentation of antigen to TH cells. Four types of dendritic cells are known: Langerhans cells, interstitial dendritic cells, myeloid cells, and lymphoid dendritic cells. Despite their differences, they all constitutively express high levels of both class II MHC molecules and members of the co-stimulatory B7 family. For this reason, they are more potent antigen-presenting cells than macrophages and B cells, both of which need to be activated before they can function as antigen-presenting cells (APCs). Immature or precursor forms of each of these types of dendritic cells acquire antigen by phagocytosis or endocytosis; the antigen is processed, and mature dendritic cells present it to TH cells. Following microbial invasion or during inflammation, mature and immature forms of Langerhans cells and interstitial dendritic cells migrate into draining lymph nodes, where they make the critical presentation of antigen to TH cells that is required for the initiation of responses by those key cells. Another type of dendritic cell, the follicular dendritic cell does not arise in bone marrow and has a different function from the antigen-presenting dendritic cells described above. Follicular dendritic cells do not express class II MHC molecules and therefore do not function as antigen presenting cells for TH-cell activation. These dendritic cells were named for their exclusive location in organized structures of the lymph node called lymph follicles, which are rich in B cells. Although they do not express class II molecules , follicular dendritic cells express high levels of membrane receptors for antibody, which allows the binding of antigen-antibody complexes. The interaction of B cells with this bound antigen can have important effects on B cell responses. Follicular dendritic cells do not express classII MHC molecules and therefore do not function as antigen presenting cells for TH-cell activation.

Macrophages

These are dispersed throughout the body. Some take up residence in particular tissues, becoming fixed macrophages, whereas others remain motile and are called free, or wandering, macrophages. Free macrophages travel by amoeboid movement throughout the tissues. Macrophage-like cells serve different functions indifferent tissues and are named according to their tissue location, eg: Alveolar macrophages in the lung Histiocytes in connective tissues, Kupffer cells in the liver, Mesangial cells in the kidney, Microglial cells in the brain, Osteoclasts in bone. Although normally in a resting state, macrophages are activated by a variety of stimuli in the course of an immune response. Phagocytosis of particulate antigens serves as an initial activating stimulus. However, macrophage activity can be further enhanced by cytokines secreted by activated TH cells, by mediators of the inflammatory response, and by components of bacterial cell walls. One of the most potent activators of macrophages is interferon gamma (IFN-γ) secreted by activated TH cells. Activated macrophages are more effective than resting ones in eliminating potential pathogens, because they exhibit greater phagocytic activity, an increased ability to kill ingested microbes, increased secretion of inflammatory mediators, and an increased ability to activate T cells. In addition, activated macrophages secrete various cytotoxic proteins that help them eliminate a broad range of pathogens, including virus-infected cells, tumor cells, and intracellular bacteria. Activated macrophages also express higher levels of class II MHC molecules, allowing them to function more effectively as antigen-presenting cells. Thus, macrophages and TH cells facilitate each other's activation during the immune response. The process of phagocytosis of particulate antigens serves as an initial activating stimulus. However, macrophage activity can be further enhanced by cytokines secreted by activated TH cells, by mediators of the inflammatory response, and by components of bacterial cell walls. One of the most potent activators of macrophages is interferon gamma (IFN-γ) secreted by activated TH cells. Activated macrophages are more effective than resting ones in eliminating potential pathogens, because they exhibit greater phagocytic activity, an increased ability to kill ingested microbes, increased secretion of inflammatory mediators, and an increased ability to activate T cells.

Immunoglobulins

Immunoglobulin, abbreviated Ig are gamma globulin proteins that are found in blood or other bodily fluids of vertebrates, and are used by the immune system to identify and neutralize foreign objects, such as bacteria and viruses. Also called as Antibodies, they are produced by a kind of white blood cell called a plasma cell. Once a B cell has identified an antigen, it starts replicating itself. These cloned cells mature into antibody-manufacturing plasma cells.

Structure

The structure carries heavy (~150kDa) globular plasma proteins having sugar chains added to some of their amino acid residues. In other words, they are glycoproein. The Ig monomer is a "Y"-shaped molecule that consists of four polypeptide chains; two identical heavy chains and two identical light chains . Each light chain is bound to a heavy chain by a disulfide bond, and by such non-covalent interactions as salt linkages, hydrogen bonds, and hydrophobic bonds, to form a heterodimer (H-L). Similar noncovalent interactions and disulfide bridges link the two identical heavy and light (H-L) chain combinations to each other to form the basic four-chain (H-L)2 antibody structure, a dimer of dimers the exact number and precise positions of these interchain disulfide bonds differs among antibody classes and subclasses.

Careful analysis of the amino acid sequences of immunoglobulin heavy and light chains showed that both chains contain several homologous units of about 110 amino acid residues. Within each unit, termed a domain, an intra-chain disulfide bond forms a loop of about 60 amino acids. Light chains contain one variable domain (VL), and one constant domain (CL); heavy chains contain one variable domain (VH), and either three or four constant domains (CH1, CH2, CH3, andCH4), depending on the antibody class.

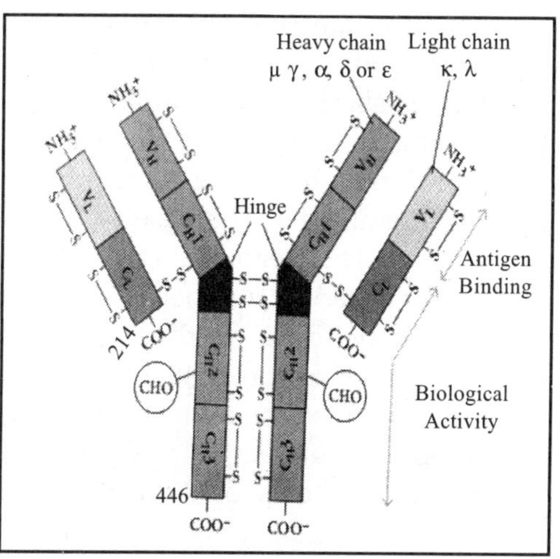

Fig. 6.2

VH and VL regions contain variable amino acids and constitute antigen binding site of the molecule. The sequence variation is concentrated in a few discrete regions of these variable domains. These regions were originally called hypervariable regions in recognition of their high variability. Hypervariable regions form the antigen binding site of the antibody molecule. Because the antigen binding site is complementary to the structure of the epitope, these areas are now more widely called complementarity determining regions (CDRs). The constant region domains are almost similar in a particular isotype. The heavy chains in IgA, IgD, and IgG contain three constant-region domains and a hinge region, whereas the heavy chains in IgE and IgM contain four constant-region domains and no hinge region. The corresponding domains of the two groups are as follows:

IgA, IgD, IgG	IgE, IgM
CH1/CH1	CH1/CH1
Hinge region	CH2/CH2
CH2/CH2	CH3/CH3
CH3/CH3	CH4/CH4

The carboxyl-terminal domain is designated CH3/CH3 in IgA, IgD, and IgG and CH4/CH4 in IgE and IgM. The heavy chains contain an extended peptide sequence between the CH1 and CH2 domains that has no homology with the other domains. This region, called the hinge region, is rich in proline residues and is flexible, giving IgG, IgD, and IgA segmental flexibility. The angle between the arms of the Y-shaped antibody molecules differs in the different complexes, reflecting the flexibility of the hinge region.

One constant and one variable domain from each heavy and light chain of the antibody constitute the Fab (fragment, antigen binding) region. The paratope is shaped at the amino terminal end of the antibody monomer by the variable domains from the heavy and light chains. The variable domain is also referred to as the F_V region and is the most important region for binding to antigens. The base of the Y plays a role in modulating immune cell activity. This region is called the Fc (Fragment, crystallizable) region, and is composed of two heavy chains that contribute two or three constant domains depending on the class of the antibody By binding to specific proteins the Fc region ensures that each antibody generates an appropriate immune response for a given antigen. The Fc region also binds to various cell receptors, such as Fc receptors, and other immune molecules, such as complement proteins. By doing this, it mediates different physiological effects including opsonization, cell lysis, and degranulation of mast cells, basophils and eosinophils

Types of Immunoglobulins:

A. IgG

1. Structure

The structures of the IgG subclasses are monomers (7S immunoglobulin). The subclasses differ in the number of disulfide bonds and length of the hinge region.

2. Properties

IgG is the most versatile immunoglobulin because it is capable of carrying out all of the functions of immunoglobulin molecules.

(a) IgG is the major Ig in serum - 75% of serum Ig is IgG

(b) IgG is the major Ig in extra vascular spaces

(c) Placental transfer - IgG is the only class of Ig that crosses the placenta. Transfer is mediated by a receptor on placental cells for the Fc region of IgG. Not all subclasses cross equally well; IgG2 does not cross well.

(d) Fixes complement - Not all subclasses fix equally well; IgG4 does not fix complement

(e) Binding to cells - Macrophages, monocytes, PMNs and some lymphocytes have Fc receptors for the Fc region of IgG. Not all subclasses bind equally well; IgG2 and IgG4 do not bind to Fc receptors. A consequence of binding to the Fc receptors on PMNs, monocytes and macrophages is that the cell can now internalize the antigen better. The antibody has prepared the antigen for eating by the phagocytic cells. The term opsonin is used to describe substances that enhance phagocytosis. IgG is a good opsonin. Binding of IgG to Fc receptors on other types of cells results in the activation of other functions. These antibodies are similar to those of IgY present in chickens in structure approximately and function. Hence IgY has become more important than IgG since it become easy to isolate chicken antibodies rather than human antibodies.

B. IgM

1. Structure

The structure of IgM exists as a pentamer (19S immunoglobulin) but it can also exist as a monomer. In the pentameric form all heavy chains are identical and all light chains are identical. Thus, the valence is theoretically 10. IgM has an extra domain on the mu chain (C_{H4}) and it has another protein covalently bound via a S-S bond called the J chain. This chain functions in polymerization of the molecule into a pentamer.

2. Properties

(a) IgM is the third most common serum Ig.

(b) IgM is the first Ig to be made by the fetus and the first Ig to be made by a virgin B cells when it is stimulated by antigen.

(c) As a consequence of its pentameric structure, IgM is a good complement fixing Ig. Thus, IgM antibodies are very efficient in leading to the lysis of microorganisms.

(d) As a consequence of its structure, IgM is also a good agglutinating Ig . Thus, IgM antibodies are very good in clumping microorganisms for eventual elimination from the body.

(e) IgM binds to some cells via Fc receptors.

(f) Surface IgM exists as a monomer and lacks J chain but it has an extra 20 amino acids at the C-terminus to anchor it into the membrane .Cell surface IgM functions as a receptor for antigen on B cells. Surface IgM is noncovalently associated with two additional proteins in the membrane of the B cell called Ig-alpha and Ig-beta. These additional proteins act as signal transducing molecules since the cytoplasmic tail of the Ig molecule itself is too short to transduce a signal. Contact between surface immunoglobulin and an antigen is required before a signal can be transduced by the Ig-alpha and Ig-beta chains. In the case of T-independent antigens, contact between the antigen and surface immunoglobulin is sufficient to activate B cells to differentiate into antibody secreting plasma cells. However, for T-dependent antigens, a second signal provided by helper T cells is required before B cells are activated.

C. IgA

1. Structure

Serum IgA is a monomer but IgA found in secretions is a dimer. When IgA exits as a dimer, a J chain is associated with it. When IgA is found in secretions is also has another protein associated with it called the secretory piece or T piece; sIgA is sometimes referred to as 11S immunoglobulin. Unlike the remainder of the IgA which is made in the plasma cell, the secretory piece is made in epithelial cells and is added to the IgA as it passes into the secretions. The secretory piece helps IgA to be transported across mucosa and also protects it from degradation in the secretions.

2. Properties

(a) IgA is the 2nd most common serum Ig.

(b) IgA is the major class of Ig in secretions - tears, saliva, colostrum, mucus. Since it is found in secretions secretory IgA is important in local (mucosal) immunity.

(c) Normally IgA does not fix complement, unless aggregated.

(d) IgA can binding to some cells - PMN's and some lymphocytes.

D. IgD

1. Structure

The structure of IgD exists only as a monomer.

2. Properties

(a) IgD is found in low levels in serum; its role in serum uncertain.

(b) IgD is primarily found on B cell surfaces where it functions as a receptor for antigen. IgD on the surface of B cells has extra amino acids at C-terminal end for anchoring to the membrane. It also associates with the Ig-alpha and Ig-beta chains. It does not bind to complement proteins.

E. IgE

1. Structure

   The structure of IgE exists as a monomer and has an extra domain in the constant region.

2. Properties

   (a) IgE is the least common serum Ig since it binds very tightly to Fc receptors on basophils and mast cells even before interacting with antigen.

   (b) Involved in allergic reactions - As a consequence of its binding to basophils an mast cells, IgE is involved in allergic reactions. Binding of the allergen to the IgE on the cells results in the release of various pharmacological mediators that result in allergic symptoms.

   (c) IgE also plays a role in parasitic helminth diseases. Since serum IgE levels rise in parasitic diseases, measuring IgE levels is helpful in diagnosing parasitic infections. Eosinophils have Fc receptors for IgE and binding of eosinophils to IgE-coated helminths results in killing of the parasite.

   (d) IgE does not fix complement.

Chicken IgY

IgY is an immunoglobulin first described in 1893 when Klemperer reported that immunized chickens produce antibodies detectable in their egg yolks as well as their blood. He noted that the concentrations of antibody were similar in both egg yolk and blood, although more recently, it's been reported that yolk concentrations of IgY are higher. When Klemperer described chicken immunoglobulins in the late 1800's, he didn't name them IgY. For the better part of the 20th century, the predominant immunoglobulin found in chicken blood and egg yolk was called IgG. It wasn't until more than 70 years later that the term IgY was coined by Leslie and Clem, not because the immunoglobulin was found in the yolk, but rather because the avian antibody was sufficiently different and antigenically distinct from the mammalian immunoglobulin counterpart (IgG). It's now known that IgY is the major immunoglobulin class in birds, reptiles, amphibia and lungfish.

Physicochemical Properties of IgY

It's easy to understand why IgY was first categorized as an immunoglobulin G – it's similar to mammalian IgG.

Like IgG, IgY also has 2 heavy and 2 light chains, shaped in the characteristic Y shape with an antigen valency of 2. IgY and IgG share a similar sedimentation coefficient of about 7S and both are eluted from DEAE cellulose with low ionic strength buffers. Functionally, they play a similar biological role as well. Both IgG and IgY are the major immunoglobulins providing defense against infectious agents and appear in blood at high concentrations following synthesis of a higher molecular weight antibody (IgM).

There are striking differences however: There is little or no immunological cross-reactivity between IgY and mammalian IgG. IgY has a higher molecular weight due to an extra heavy chain constant domain, lacks a well-defined hinge region and has unique oligosaccharide sidechains. It has been proposed that the extra domain (CH_2) may be the evolutionary precursor to the mammalian IgG hinge region. IgY is capable of mediating anaphylactic reactions, a function limited to IgE in mammals. In fact, other similarities between IgY and IgE including similar intrachain disulphide bonding in their extra heavy chain domain, have lead some to suggest that IgY is the ancestral molecule to both IgG and IgE.

Many researchers are now choosing to make their custom polyclonal antibody in chickens. There are many reasons to do so. Some choose to immunize a hen and collect the eggs because it is the least invasive way to produce polyclonal antibodies. The eggs can be stored for up to 3 months in the refrigerator or the yolks separated and frozen in delipidation buffer. For some, the attraction is that chickens often produce better antibodies to conserved mammalian proteins. One hen can produce as much antibody as 10 - 20 rabbits, and it's so much easier to collect eggs than bleed 10 rabbits! Making an IgY antibody in hens isn't that different from producing a rabbit antibody, except that it's easier because bleeding the animal is not necessary. Perhaps the most difficult part of raising antibodies in chickens is to provide a suitable environment for them. Hens prefer to roost on sticks at night, lay their eggs in a nesting box and have regular "dust baths" in sand or wood shavings.

Antigens

An antigen or immunogen is a substance that prompts the generation of antibodies and can cause an immune response. Immunogens are those substances that elicit a response from the immune system, whereas antigens are defined as substances that bind to specific antibodies.

Antigens are usually proteins or polysaccharides. This includes parts (coats, capsules, cell walls, flagella, fimbrae, and toxins) of bacteria, viruses, dust mites etc . Lipids and nucleic acids are antigenic only when combined with proteins and polysaccharides. Non-microbial exogenous (non-self) antigens can include dust mites, pollen, egg white, and proteins from transplanted tissues and organs or on the surface of transfused blood cells.

Both B cells and T cells have surface receptors for antigen. Each cell has thousands of receptors of a single specificity; with a binding site for a particular epitope.

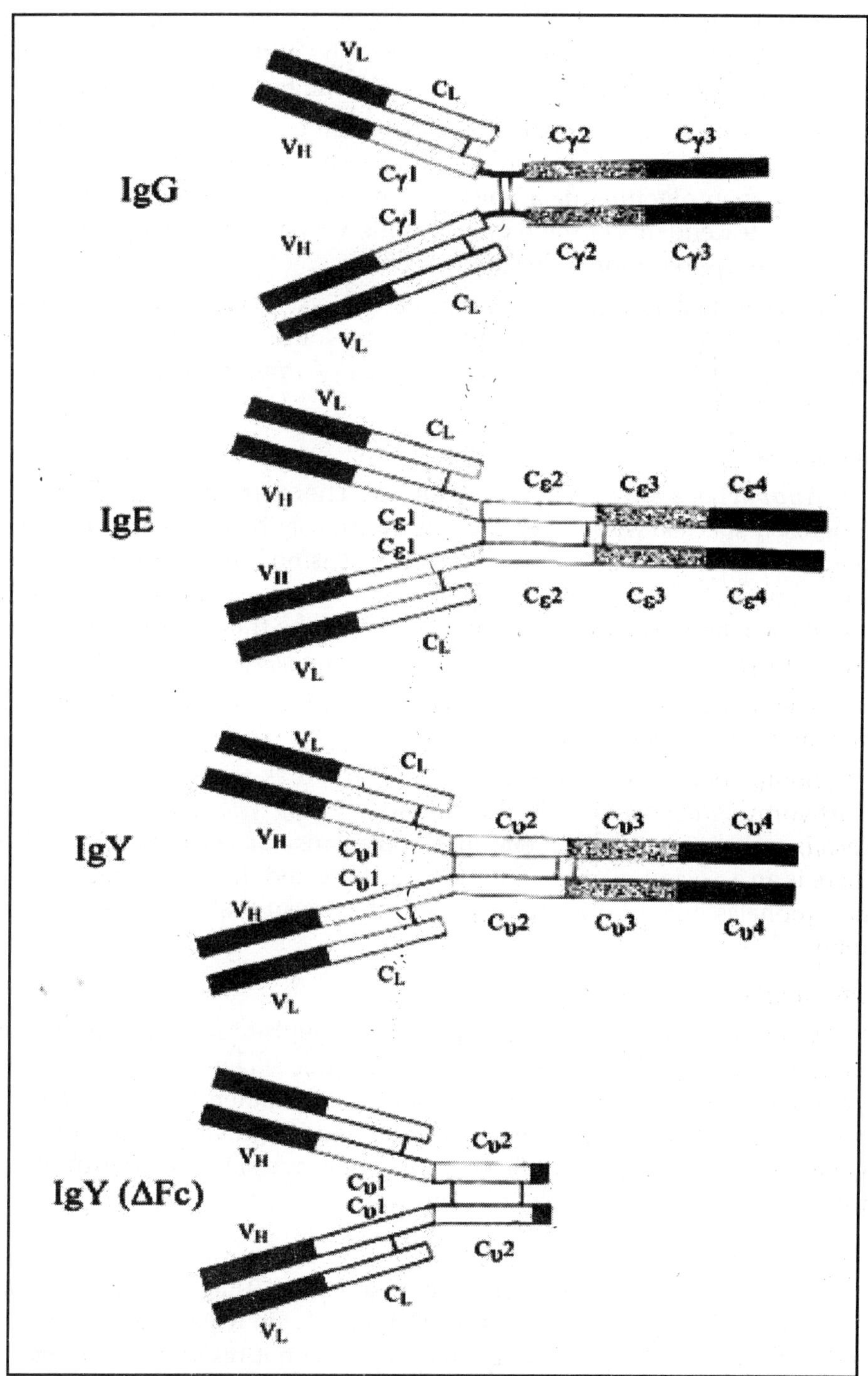
IgG
IgE
IgY
IgY (ΔFc)
V_L
C_L
V_H
$C\gamma1$
$C\gamma2$
$C\gamma3$
$C\varepsilon1$
$C\varepsilon2$
$C\varepsilon3$
$C\varepsilon4$
$C\upsilon1$
$C\upsilon2$
$C\upsilon3$
$C\upsilon4$

Fig. 6.3

- T-cell receptors (TCRs) enable the cell to bind to and, if additional signals are present, to be activated by and respond to an epitope presented by another cell called the antigen-presenting cell or APC.
- B-cell receptors (BCRs) enable the cell to bind to and, if additional signals are present, to be activated by and respond to an epitope on molecules of a soluble antigen. The response ends with descendants of the B cell secreting vast numbers of a soluble form of its receptors. These are antibodies.

Cells present their antigens to the immune system via a histocompatibility molecule. Depending on the antigen presented and the type of the histocompatibility molecule, several types of immune cells can become activated.

Anopheles

Anopheles, is a genus of mosquito. There are approximately 460 recognised species: while over 100 can transmit human malaria, only 30-40 commonly transmit parasites of the genus Plasmodium that cause malaria which affects humans in endemic areas. Anopheles gambiae is one of the best known, because of its predominant role in the transmission of the most dangerous malaria parasite species - *Plasmodium falciparum*.

The name comes from the Greek *an* meaning *not* and *óphelos* meaning *profit* and translates to *useless*.

Some species of *Anopheles* also can serve as the vectors for canine heartworm *Dirofilaria immitis*, the Filariidae *Wuchereria bancrofti* and *Brugia malayi*, and viruses like the one that is the cause of O'nyong'nyong fever. There is an association of brain tumor incidence and malaria, suggesting that the anopheles might transmit a virus or other agent that could cause a brain tumor.

Life Stages

Like all mosquitoes, anophelines go through four stages in their life cycle: egg, larva, pupa, and imago. The first three stages are aquatic and last 5-14 days, depending on the species and the ambient temperature. The adult stage is when the female *Anopheles* mosquito acts as malaria vector. The adult females can live up to a month (or more in captivity) but most probably do not live more than 1-2 weeks in nature.

Eggs

Adult females lay 50-200 eggs per oviposition. The eggs are quite small (~0.5 × 0.2 mm). Eggs are laid singly and directly on water. They are unique in that they have floats on either side. Eggs are not resistant to drying and hatch within 2-3 days, although hatching may take up to 2-3 weeks in colder climates.

Larvae

Mosquito larvae have a well-developed head with mouth brushes used for feeding, a large thorax and a nine segmented abdomen. They don't have legs. In contrast to other mosquitoes, *Anopheles* larvae lack a respiratory siphon and for this reason position themselves so that their body is parallel to the surface of the water.

Larvae breathe through spiracles located on the 8th abdominal segment and therefore must come to the surface frequently. The larvae spend most of their time feeding on algae, bacteria, and other microorganisms in the surface microlayer. They dive below the surface only when disturbed. Larvae swim either by jerky movements of the entire body or through propulsion with the mouth brushes.

Larvae develop through 4 stages, or instars, after which they metamorphose into pupae. At the end of each instar, the larvae molt, shedding their exoskeleton, or skin, to allow for further growth. 1st stage larvae are ~1 mm in length; 4th stage larvae are normally 5-8 mm in length.

The process from egg laying to emergence of the adult is temperature dependent with a minimum time of 7 days.

The larvae occur in a wide range of habitats but most species prefer clean, unpolluted water. Larvae of *Anopheles* mosquitoes have been found in fresh- or salt-water marshes, mangrove swamps, rice fields, grassy ditches, the edges of streams and rivers, and small, temporary rain pools. Many species prefer habitats with vegetation. Others prefer habitats that have none. Some breed in open, sun-lit pools while others are found only in shaded breeding sites in forests. A few species breed in tree holes or the leaf axils of some plants.

Pupae

The pupa is comma-shaped when viewed from the side. The head and thorax are merged into a cephalothorax with the abdomen curving around underneath. As with the larvae, pupae must come to the surface frequently to breathe, which they do through a pair of respiratory trumpets on the cephalothorax. After a few days as a pupa, the dorsal surface of the cephalothorax splits and the adult mosquito emerges.

Adults

The duration from egg to adult varies considerably among species and is strongly influenced by ambient temperature. Mosquitoes can develop from egg to adult in as little as 5 days but usually take 10-14 days in tropical conditions.

Like all mosquitoes, adult *Anopheles* have slender bodies with 3 sections: head, thorax and abdomen.

The head is specialized for acquiring sensory information and for feeding. The head contains the eyes and a pair of long, many-segmented antennae. The antennae are important for detecting host odors as well as odors of breeding sites where females lay eggs. The head also has an elongated, forward-projecting proboscis used for feeding, and two sensory palps.

The thorax is specialized for locomotion. Three pairs of legs and a pair of wings are attached to the thorax.The abdomen is specialized for food digestion and egg development. This segmented body part expands considerably when a female takes a blood meal. The blood is digested over time serving as a source of protein for the production of eggs, which gradually fill the abdomen.

Anopheles mosquitoes can be distinguished from other mosquitoes by the palps, which are as long as the proboscis, and by the presence of discrete blocks of black and white scales on the wings. Adult *Anopheles* can also be identified by their typical resting position: males and females rest with their abdomens sticking up in the air rather than parallel to the surface on which they are resting.

Adult mosquitoes usually mate within a few days after emerging from the pupal stage. In most species, the males form large swarms, usually around dusk, and the females fly into the swarms to mate.

Males live for about a week, feeding on nectar and other sources of sugar. Females will also feed on sugar sources for energy but usually require a blood meal for the development of eggs. After obtaining a full blood meal, the female will rest for a few days while the blood is digested and eggs are developed. This process depends on the temperature but usually takes 2-3 days in tropical conditions. Once the eggs are fully developed, the female lays them and resumes host seeking.

The cycle repeats itself until the female dies. While females can live longer than a month in captivity, most do not live longer than 1-2 weeks in nature. Their lifespan depends on temperature, humidity, and also their ability to successfully obtain a blood meal while avoiding host defenses.

Anopheles dirus

Anopheles dirus is a vector of malaria in Asian forested zones. It is often seen as a species complex including at least seven closely related and efficient forest-based malaria vectors in Asia. Hence, its geographical distribution is overlapping with the areas of high malaria prevalence rates and the occurrence is of drug - resistant *Plasmodium falciparum*. *P. falciparum* is one of the four main protozoan parasites that cause malaria and is one of the leading causes of malaria deaths. This species complex is of high medical importance for malaria control, in view of the biological specificities of the members of this complex. Sympatric sibling species of the complex differ in types of larval habitat, seasonality and behaviour. These differences also exist within the species suggesting the role of environmental factors in determining these. The complex has been reported mainly from Northeast India, Bangladesh, Myanmar and Thailand. GIS-based predictive habitat modelling has revealed that over half of several Northeast Indian states, whole of Thailand and nearly a third of large areas in South Indian states like Kerala and Goa could harbour this complex.

Anopheles dirus	
Scientific Classification	
Kingdom:	Animalia
Phylum:	Arthropoda
Class:	Insecta
Order:	Diptera
Family:	Culicidae
Subfamily:	Anophelinae
Genus:	*Anopheles*
Species:	*A. dirus*

Mosquito Salivary Gland Antigens

The paired salivary glands of mosquitoes are present in the thorax flanking the oesophagus (figurela). Each gland has three lobes, two lateral and one median. In the female mosquito the lateral lobes are formed by proximal, intermediate and distal regions. The median lobe on the other hand, is formed by a short neck region and a distal region. The extreme anterior part of each gland is innervated and the ingluvial ganglia situated at the junction of fore-gut and midgut (Figure 6.4 *b*), supply neurosecretory axons to the gland. Each lobe has a central duct constituted by a layer of epithelial cells that are bound externally by a basal lamina. The ducts from each lobe fuse so as to form a lateral salivary duct which runs forward and fuses with the one from the other gland to form a common salivary duct which opens at the base of the hypopharynx. The extracellular apical cavities of the posterior regions of female salivary glands are highly dilated with salivary secretions. It is interesting to note that the male salivary glands though tri-lobed, are much smaller than the female gland, and the protein profile of the male gland resembles that of the proximal region of lateral lobes 3, 4 of the female salivary glands. Equally interesting is the absence of whole median lobe and the intermediate region of the lateral lobes in non-bloodsucking mosquitoes like *Toxorhynchites brevipalpis* 5 and the absence of polytene chromosomes in the adult mosquitoes.

Salivary Gland Components with Diverse Functions

D7-like fragments of Anopheles Expression of salivary gland-specific genes was first characterized in *A. aegypti*, and more recently in *An. gambiae*. The *A. aegypti D7* gene corresponds to a 37 kDa polypeptide present in the saliva, which is encoded in five exons separated by small introns 33. Isolation and sequencing of 15 unique cDNA fragments from the salivary glands of *An. gambiae* (150-550 bp) following immuno-screening in COS-7 cells have recently been reported. Three of these cDNAs, i.e. D7r1(dB1), D7r2 (iB6) and D7r3(iC5) show a high degree of resemblance to the *D7* and apyrase genes of the salivary glands of *A.aegypti*. These clones hybridize closely to chromosomal positions on the right arm of the third chromosome in the division 30A (D7r2) and 30B (D7r1 and D7r3). The other three of the six *D7*-related cDNAs are new and have not been reported before. These clones are specifically expressed in the female salivary glands only. Although the exact functions of *D7* are unknown, their stage-, sex- and tissue-specificity and location in the secretory cavities suggest their potential role in blood feeding and/or parasite transmission.

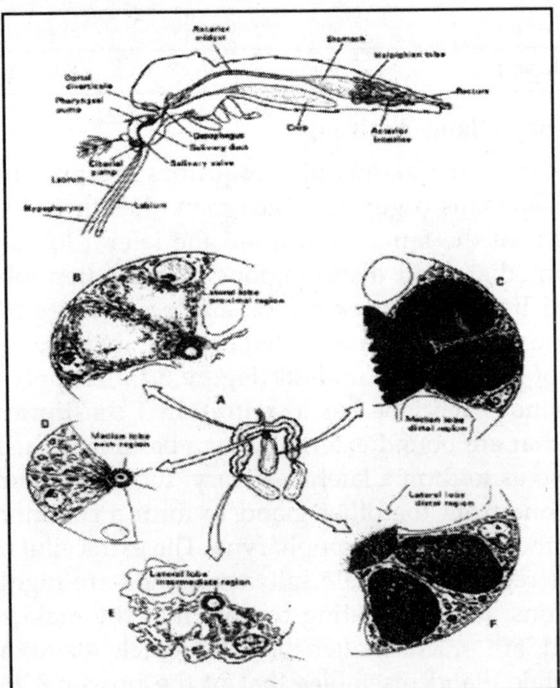

Fig. 6.4

Fig. 6.4: **(*a*) Alimentary Canal of Mosquito Showing Position of the Salivary Glands. (*b*) Salivary Glands of Adult Female *Anopheles stephensi*. (A) Whole Gland and (B–F) Ultrastructure of Different Regions of the Gland in Transverse Section**

Apyrase Gene Product

It is a secretory protein which hydrolyzes ATP and ADP to AMP and Pi, and has been shown to inhibit the ADP induced platelet recruitment and aggregation. A few studies have revealed a relationship between sporozoite infection and the time of probing with a one-third decrease of apyrase activity in *P. gallinaceum*-infected *A.aegypti*. The apyrase activity is more confined to the distal regions of the female salivary glands only. It has also been observed to facilitate mosquito feeding by inhibiting platelet recruitment and aggregation at the site of mosquito bite. The gene has evolved by duplication followed by divergent evolution from membrane-bound 5- nucleotidase due to loss of carboxyl terminus domain involved in membrane-anchoring. Recently, molecular cloning of *An. gambiae* homologue of *Aedes* apyrase has been described.

Defence Molecules

Induction of a 30 kDa protein in the salivary glands of *An. stephensi* in response to infection by *Plasmodium yoelii yoelii* has been suggested to impart tolerance to parasite infections in mosquitoes. On the other hand, *An. gambiae* show an innate immune response after infection by malaria parasites. The molecular markers for such responses include a nitric oxide synthase (*NOS*) gene fragment and *ICHIT* (a gene encoding two putative chitin-binding domains separated by poly threonine-rich mucin region). Interestingly, the salivary gland shows the presence of six immune markers, which raises the possibility that these glands act as immune organs. They respond late in the infection, i.e. induction of *NOS* observed on day-9 post-infection, defensin, *ICHIT* and *NOS* on day-11, and between days 13 and 21 post-infection, respectively40. What is even more fascinating as well intriguing is the observation that the salivary glands did not show any immune induction following the second blood meal. The salivary gland of *Ae. aegypti* has been reported to show bacteriolytic lysozyme activity.

Purification Techniques

Protein purification is a series of processes intended to isolate a single type of protein from a complex mixture. Protein purification is vital for the characterisation of the function, structure and interactions of the protein of interest. The following techniques are used for protein purification.

Ultracentrifugation

Centrifugation is a process that uses centrifugal force to separate mixtures of particles of varying masses or densities suspended in a liquid. When a vessel (typically a tube or bottle) containing a mixture of proteins or other particulate matter, the angular momentum yields an outward force to each particle that is proportional to its mass. The tendency of a given particle to move through the liquid because of this force is off, set by the resistance the liquid exerts on the particle. The net effect of "spinning" the sample in a centrifuge is that massive, small, and dense particles move outward faster than less massive particles or particles with more "drag" in the liquid. When suspensions of particles are "spun" in a centrifuge, a "pellet" may form at the bottom of the vessel that is enriched for the most massive particles with low drag in the liquid. The remaining, non-compacted particles still remaining mostly in the liquid are called the "supernatant" and can be removed from the vessel to separate the supernatant from the pellet.

Sucrose gradient centrifugation, a linear concentration gradient of sugar (typically sucrose, glycerol, or a silica based density gradient media, like Percoll) is generated in a tube such that the highest concentration is on the bottom and lowest on top. A protein sample is then layered on top of the gradient and spun at high speeds in an ultracentrifuge. This causes heavy macromolecules to migrate towards the bottom of the tube faster than lighter material. When the proteins are moving through a sucrose gradient, they encounter liquid of increasing density and viscosity. A properly designed sucrose gradient will counteract the increasing centrifugal force so the particles move in close proportion to the time they have been in the centrifugal field. Samples separated by these gradients are referred to as "rate zonal" centrifugations. After separating the protein/particles, the gradient is then fractionated and collected.

Chromatographic Methods

Usually a protein purification protocol contains one or more chromatographic steps. The basic procedure in chromatography is to flow the solution containing the protein through a column packed with various materials. Different proteins interact differently with the column material, and can thus be separated by the time required to pass the column, or the conditions required to elute the protein from the column. Usually proteins are detected as they are coming off the column by their absorbance at 280 nm. Many different chromatographic methods exist.

Size Exclusion Chromatography (SEC)

It is a chromatographic method in which particles are separated based on their size, or in more technical terms, their hydrodynamic volume. Typically, when an aqueous solution is used to transport the sample through the column, the technique is known as gel filtration chromatography, versus the name gel permeation chromatography which is used when an organic solvent is used as a mobile phase. Different size particles travel different distances in the gel. Consequentially, proteins of a certain range in size will require a variable volume of elutant (solvent) before being collected at the other end of the column of gel. In the context of protein purification, the elutant is usually pooled in different test tubes. All test tubes containing no measurable trace of the protein to purify are discarded. The remaining solution is thus made of the protein to purify and any other similarly-sized proteins.

Ion Exchange Chromatography

It separates compounds according to the nature and degree of their ionic charge. The column to be used is selected according to its type and strength of charge. Anion exchange resins have a positive charge and are used to retain and separate negatively charged compounds, while cation exchange resins have a negative charge and are used to separate positively charged molecules. Before the separation begins a buffer is pumped through the column to equilibrate the opposing charged ions. Upon injection of the sample, solute molecules will exchange with the buffer ions as each competes for the binding sites on the resin. The length of retention for each solute depends upon the strength of its charge. The most weakly charged compounds will elute first, followed by those with successively stronger charges. Because of the nature of the separating mechanism, pH, buffer type, buffer concentration, and temperature all play important roles in controlling the separation.

Affinity Chromatography

It is a chromatographic method of separating biochemical mixtures, based on a highly specific biologic interaction such as that between antigen and antibody, enzyme and substrate, or receptor and ligand. The column is filled with matrix on which ligand specific for protein of interest is covalently bound. When the sample is run through the column the desired protein interact with the ligand and binds to it. The biological interation between ligand and target molecule can be a result of electrostatic or hydrophobic interactions, vanderwaals force or hydrogen bonding. The column is then washed to remove unspecific binding .To elute the target molecule from the affinity medium the interaction can be reversed, either specifically using a competitive ligand,or non-specificall , by changing the ph, ionic strength or polarity.

Affinity chromatoghaphy is unique in purifiacation technology since it is the only technique that enables the purification of biomolecule on the basis of its biological function or individual chemical structure. With high selectivity, hence high resolution and usually high capacity for the proteins of interest ,purification levels in the order of several thousand fold with recovery of active material are achievable. Target protein is collected in purified and concentrated form.

Precipitation Methods

Precipitation is widely used in downstream processing of biological products, such as proteins. This unit operation serves to concentrate and fractionate the target product from various contaminants.

Salting Out

Salting out is the most common method used to precipitate a target protein. Addition of a neutral salt, such as ammonium sulfate, compresses the solvation layer and increases protein-protein interactions. As the salt concentration of a solution is increased, more of the bulk water becomes associated with the ions. As a result, less water is available to partake in the solvation layer around the protein, which exposes hydrophobic patches on the protein surface. Proteins may then exhibit hydrophobic interactions, aggregate and precipitate from solution.

Isoelectric Point Precipitation

The isoelectric point (pI) is the pH of a solution at which the net primary charge of a protein becomes zero. At a solution pH that is above the pI the surface of the protein is predominantly negatively charged and therefore like-charged molecules will exhibit repulsive forces. Likewise, at a solution pH that is below the pI, the surface of the protein is predominantly positively charged and repulsion between proteins occurs. However, at the pI the negative and positive charges cancel, repulsive electrostatic forces are reduced and the dispersive forces predominate. The dispersive forces will cause aggregation and precipitation. The pI of most proteins is in the pH range of 4-6. Mineral acids, such as hydrochloric and sulfuric acid are used as precipitants. The greatest disadvantage to isoelectric point precipitation is the irreversible denaturation caused by the mineral acids. For this reason isoelectric point precipitation is most often used to precipitate contaminant proteins, rather than the target protein. The precipitation of casein during cheesemaking, or during production of sodium caseinate, is an isoelectric precipitation.

Precipitation with Organic Solvents

Addition of miscible solvents such as ethanol or methanol to a solution may cause proteins in the solution to precipitate. The solvation layer around the protein will decrease as the organic solvent progressively displaces water from the protein surface and binds it in hydration layers around the organic solvent molecules. With smaller hydration layers, the proteins can aggregate by attractive electrostatic and dipole forces. Important parameters to consider are temperature, which should be less than 0°C to avoid denaturation, pH and protein concentration in solution. Miscible organic solvents decrease the dielectric constant of water, which in effect allows two proteins to come close together. At the isoelectric point the relationship between the dielectric constant and protein solubility is given by:

$$\log S = k/e^2 + \log S^0$$

S^0 is an extrapolated value of S, e is the dielectric constant of the mixture and k is a constant that relates to the dielectric constant of water. The Cohn process for plasma protein fractionation relies on solvent precipitation with ethanol to isolate individual plasma proteins.

A clinical application for the use of methanol as a protein precipitating agent is in the estimation of bilirubin.

Characterization Techniques

Polyacrylamide Gel Electrophoresis

Gel electrophoresis is a technique used for the separation of deoxyribonucleic acid (DNA), ribonucleic acid (RNA), or protein molecules using an electric current applied to a gel matrix.[1] It is usually performed for analytical purposes, but may be used as a preparative technique prior to use of other methods such as mass spectrometry, RFLP, PCR, cloning, DNA sequencing, or Southern blotting for further characterization.

Proteins, unlike nucleic acids, can have varying charges and complex shapes; therefore they may not migrate into the Polyacrylamide gel at similar rates, or at all, when placing a negative to positive EMF on the sample. Proteins therefore, are usually denatured in the presence of a detergent such as sodium dodecyl sulfate/sodium dodecyl phosphate (SDS/SDP) that coats the proteins with a negative charge. Generally, the amount of SDS bound is relative to the size of the protein (usually 1.4g SDS per gram of protein), so that the resulting denatured proteins have an overall negative charge, and all the proteins have a similar charge to mass ratio. Since denatured proteins act like long rods instead of having a complex tertiary shape, the rate at which the resulting SDS coated proteins migrate in the gel is relative only to its size and not its charge or shape.

Chemical Ingredients and its Roles

- **Tris (tris (hydroxy methyl) aminomethane) ($C_4H_{11}NO_3$; mW: 121.14):** It has been used as a buffer because it is an innocuous substance to most proteins. Its pKa is 8.3 at 20°C, making it a very satisfactory buffer in the pH range from roughly 7 to 9.
- **Glycine (Amino Acetic Acid) ($C_2H_5NO_2$; mW: 75.07):** Glycine has been used as the source of trailing ion or slow ion because its pKa is 9.69 and mobility of glycinate are such that the effective mobility can be set at a value below that of the slowest known proteins of net negative charge in the pH range. The minimum pH of this range is approximately 8.0.
- **Acrylamide (C_3H_5NO; mW: 71.08):** It is a white crystalline powder. While dissolving in water, autopolymerisation of acrylamide takes place. It is a slow spontaneous process by which acrylamide molecules join together by head on tail fashion. But in presence of free radicals generating system, acrylamide monomers are

activated into a free-radical state. These activated monomers polymerise quickly and form long chain polymers. This kind of reaction is known as Vinyl addition polymerisation. A solution of these polymer chains becomes viscous but does not form a gel, because the chains simply slide over one another. Gel formation requires hooking various chains together. Acrylamide is a neurotoxin. It is also essential to store acrylamide in a cool dark and dry place to reduce autopolymerisation and hydrolysis.

- **Bisacrylamide (N,N′-Methylenebisacrylamide) ($C_7H_{10}N_2O_2$; mW: 154.17):** Bisacrylamide is the most frequently used cross linking agent for poly acrylamide gels. Chemically it is thought of having two-acrylamide molecules coupled head to head at their non-reactive ends.
- **Sodium Dodecyl Sulfate (SDS) ($C_{12}H_{25}NaO_4S$; mW: 288.38):** SDS is the most common dissociating agent used to denature native proteins to individual polypeptides. When a protein mixture is heated to 100 □C in presence of SDS, the detergent wraps around the polypeptide backbone. It binds to polypeptides in a constant weight ratio of 1.4 g/g of polypeptide. In this process, the intrinsic charges of polypeptides becomes negligible when compared to the negative charges contributed by SDS. Thus polypeptides after treatment becomes a rod like structure possessing a uniform charge density, that is same net negative charge per unit length. Mobilities of these proteins will be a linear function of the logarithms of their molecular weights.
- **Ammonium persulfate (APS)** ($N_2H_8S_2O_8$; mW: 228.2). APS is an initiator for gel formation.
- **TEMED (N, N, N′, N′-tetramethylethylenediamine)** ($C_6H_{16}N_2$; mW: 116.21). Chemical polymerisation of acrylamide gel is used for SDS-PAGE. It can be initiated by ammonium persulfate and the quaternary amine, N,N,N′,N′-tetramethylethylenediamine (TEMED). The rate of polymerisation and the properties of the resulting gel depends on the concentration of APS and TEMED. Increasing the amount of APS and TEMED results in a decrease in the average polymer chain length, an increase in gel turbidity and a decrease in gel elasticity. Decreasing the amount of initiators shows the reverse effect. The lowest catalysts concentrations that will allow polymerisation in the optimal period of time should be used. APS and TEMED are used, approximately in equimolar concentrations in the range of 1 to 10 mM.

Polyacrylamide gel (PAG) had been known as a potential embedding medium for sectioning tissues as early as 1954. Two independent groups,

Davis and Raymond, employed PAG in electrophoresis in 1959.[4] [5] It possesses several electrophoretically desirable features that make it a versatile medium. PAGE separates protein molecules according to both size and charge. It is a synthetic gel, thermo-stable, transparent, strong, relatively chemically inert, can be prepared with a wide range of average pore sizes [6]. The pore size of a gel is determined by two factors, the total amount of acrylamide present (%T) (T = Total acrylamide-bisacrylamide monomer concentration) and the amount of cross-linker (%C) (C = Crosslinker concentration). Pore size decreases with increasing %T; with cross-linking, 5%C gives the smallest pore size. Any increase or decrease in %C increases the pore size, as pore size with respect to %C is a parabolic function with vertex as 5%C. This appears to be because of nonhomogeneous bundling of strands in the gel.

This gel material can also withstand high voltage gradients, feasible for various staining and destaining procedures, and can be digested to extract separated fractions or dried for autoradiography and permanent recording. DISC electrophoresis utilizes gels of different pore sizes. [7] [8] The name DISC was derived from the discontinuities in the electrophoretic matrix and coincidentally from the discoid shape of the separated zones of ions. There are two layers of gel, namely stacking or spacer gel, and resolving or separating gel.

Stacking Gel

The stacking gel is a large pore PAG (4%T). This gel is prepared with Tris/HCl buffer pH 6.8 of about 2 pH units lower than that of electrophoresis buffer (Tris/Glycine). These conditions provide an environment for Kohlrausch reactions determining molar conductivity, as a result, SDS-coated proteins are concentrated to several fold and a thin starting zone of the order of 19 μm is achieved in a few minutes. This gel is cast over the resolving gel. The height of the stacking gel region is always maintained more than double the height and the volume of the sample to be applied.

Resolving Gel

The resolving gel is a small pore polyacrylamide gel (3 - 30% acrylamide monomer) typically made using a pH 8.8 Tris/HCl buffer. In the resolving gel, macromolecules separate according to their size. Resolving gels have an optimal range of separation that is based on the percent of monomer present in the polymerization reaction; for example an 8%, 10% and 12% resolving gel can effectively used for separating proteins between, 24 - 205 kDa, 14-205 kDa, and 14-66 kDa proteins, respectively (see: SDS gradient gel electrophoresis of proteins).

Visualizing the Gel

Coomassie Brilliant Blue (CBB) (C45H44N3NaO7S2; mW: 825.97). CBB is the most popular protein stain. It is an anionic dye, which binds with proteins non-specifically. The structure of CBB is predominantly non-polar. So is usually used (0.025%) in methanolic solution (40%) and acetic acid (7%). Proteins in the gel are fixed by acetic acid and simultaneously stained. The excess dye incorporated in the gel can be removed by destaining with the same solution but without the dye. The proteins are detected as blue bands on a clear background. As SDS is also anionic, it may interfere with staining process. Therefore, large volume of staining solution is recommended, approximately ten times the volume of the gel.

Analysis of Antigen Antibody Interaction

When the antigen is encounter by antibody the epitope of antigen will react with paratope of antibody this interaction lead to the destruction of antigen or inactive it which is called as antigen antibody interaction.

Antigen-antibody interaction is referred to by many terms these are Antigen – Antibody, Epitope – Paratope, Ligand- Receptor, Antigenic Determinant- Combining Site, Protein- Binding Site.

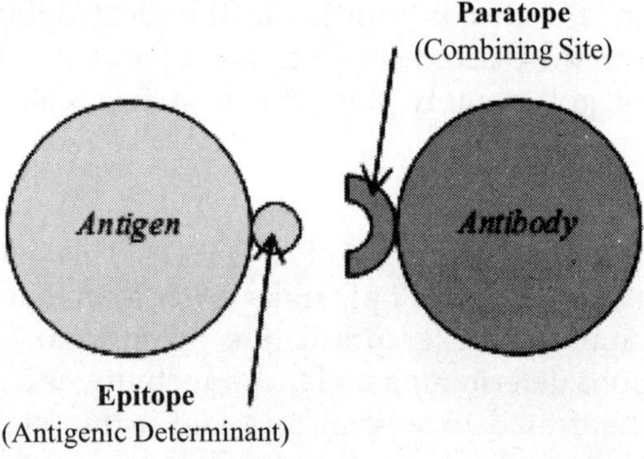

Fig. 6.5

An antibody is a protein molecule that has one or more combining sites called paratopes. An antigen is a general term for a molecule that may trigger antibody generation, with potentially many different features surface. Antigenic determinants are those surfaces features of the antigen that are complementary to an antibodies combining site.

Interactions between antigen and antibody involve non-covalent binding of an antigenic determinant (epitope) to the variable region (complementarity determining region, CDR) of both the heavy and light immunoglobulin chains. These interactions are analogous to those observed in enzyme-substrate interactions and they can be defined similarly. To describe the strength of the antigen-antibody interaction, one can define the affinity constant (K) as shown:

$$\text{Affinity K} = \frac{[\text{Ab} - \text{Ag}]}{[\text{Ab}] \times [\text{Ag}]} = 10^4 \text{ to } 10^{12} \text{ L/mol}$$

If the interaction between antigen and antibody were totally random, one would expect the concentrations of free antigen, free antibody and bound Ag-Ab complex to all be equivalent. In other words,

$$\text{Affinity K} = \frac{1}{1 \times 1} = 10^0 \text{ L/mol}$$

Therefore, the greater the K, the stronger the affinity between antigen and antibody. These interactions are the result of complementarity in shapes, hydrophobic interactions, hydrogen bonds and Van der Waals forces.

There are several immunological tests to identify the Antigen-Antibody Interaction these are:

Ouchterlony Double Diffusion Test

The interaction of Antigen with the Antibody is one of the fundamental reactions, which forms the basis of all immunological techniques. Antibodies are reasonably specific about what antigen they bind or react to, so they can be used to distinguish Antigens (protein). The Ouchterlony procedure is one of the several ways in which titer of an antibody can be measured. In this diffusion, test antigen and antibody diffuse toward each other in a semisolid medium to a point in the medium where optimum concentration of each is reached. A band of precipitation occurs at this point. The method is called "double" referring to the fact that in this procedure, antigen and antibody are allowed to migrate towards each other in a gel and a line of precipitation is formed where the two reactants meet. This precipitation reaction is highly specific. The method is even today widespread and used by people working with diagnosis or protein detection or comparing antigens or antisera.

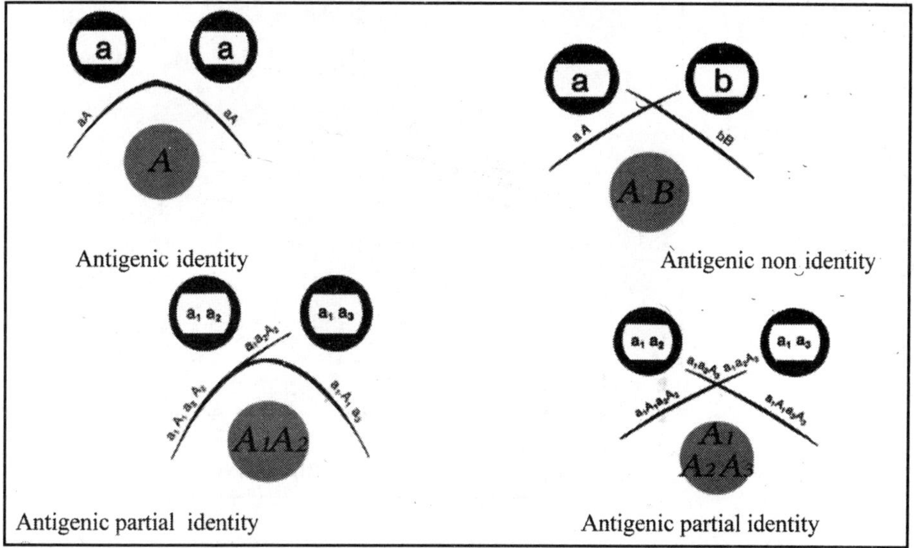

Fig. 6.6

Quantitative Precipitin Technique

It is a simple technique used in the analysis of antibody and antigen interactions and for the estimation of the antibody or antigen content in a sample. The technique is based on the interaction of antibody and antigen to form a large protein complex that in certain solutions (buffer) will result in precipitation. Most real-life antigens, and all immunogens, are bigger than haptens, and in fact have multiple, usually different, antigenic determinants or epitopes. These antigens are therefore multivalent. If we mix such antigens and antibody in solution, not only do the epitopes bind the appropriate antibody's binding sites but the antibody, being at least divalent, has a very good chance of cross-linking two antigens; a lattice will begin to grow (the lattice is commonly called an immune complex). The large immune complexes that are formed at or near equivalence tend to become insoluble and fall out of solution. When the antigen is a molecule, the phenomenon is called precipitation.

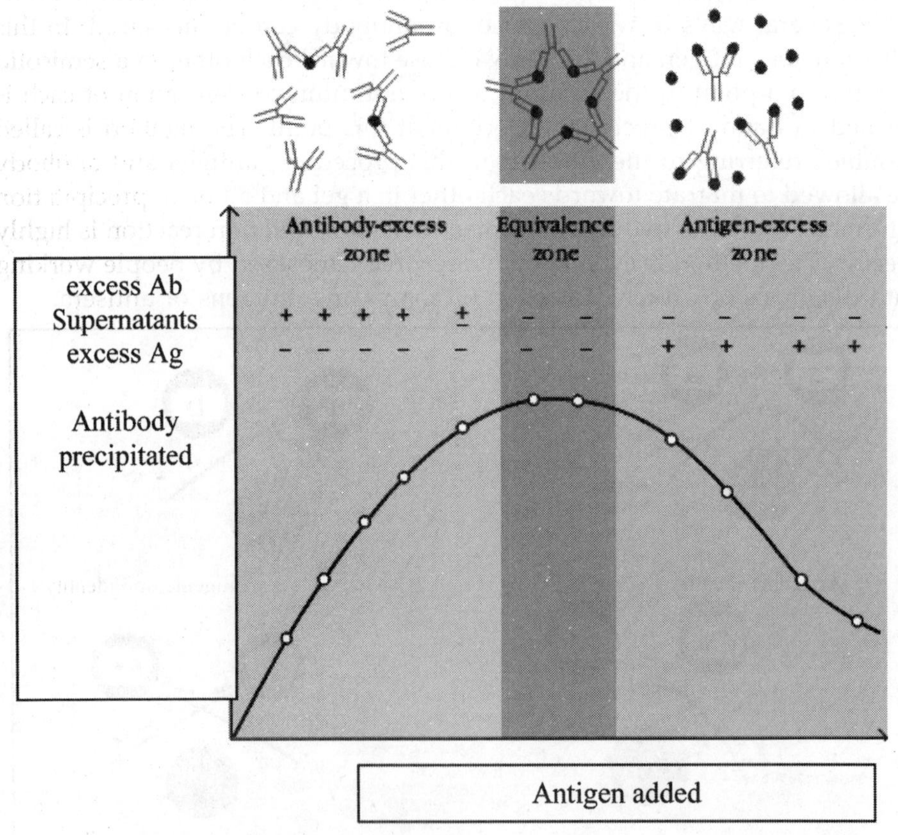

Fig. 6.7

Radial Immunodiffusion

This is a reliable quantitative method and is particularly useful for difficult samples, e.g., that are turbid and for which other methods are inappropriate. This technique detects the quantity of antigen by measuring the radius surrounding samples of the antigen, marking the boundary between it and antibody. As the antigen diffuses into the gel, it reacts with the antibody and when the equivalence point is reached a ring of precipitation is formed. This test is commonly used in the clinical laboratory for the determination of immunoglobulin levels in patient samples.

This Assay is a specialized form of immunodiffusion in which antibody is incorporated into molten agarose, which is poured into a petridish and allowed to solidify. Small wells are cut into the agarose gel and are filled with known concentrations of antigen, which corresponds to the antibody in the agarose. Samples of unknown concentrations are placed in similar wells. The antigens in solution then diffuse outwards from the well in a circular precipitate ring surrounding the well. Generally it takes 24 to 48 hours for optimal diffusion to occur and precipitation to become apparent. The diameter of the precipitin ring is proportional to the concentration of the antigen present in the test sample. By comparing the diameter of the test specimen precipitin ring to known standards, a relatively less sensitive estimation of the concentration of specific antigen can be achieved.

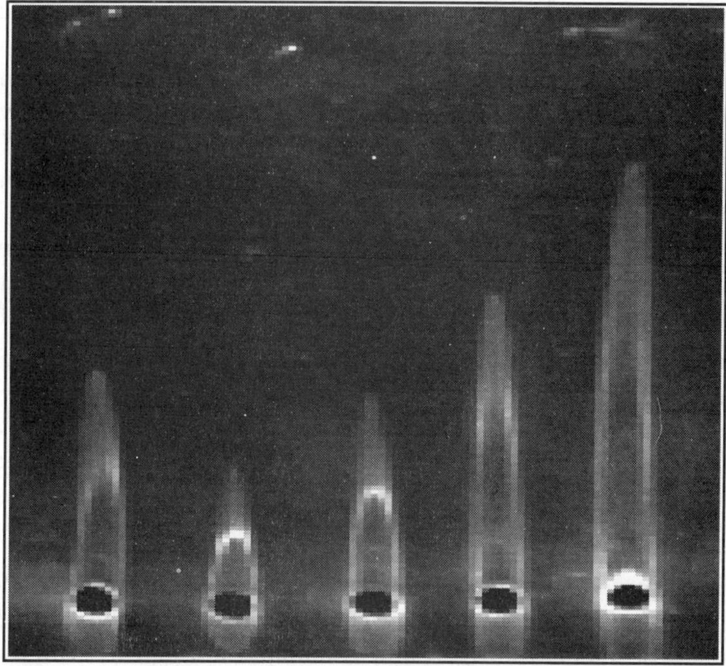

Fig. 6.8

Higher the amount of antigen loaded in the well, farther the antigen will travel through the gel. Hence, with increasing antigen concentration, a series of rockets of increasing heights are seen that is proportional to amount of antigen in the well. Therefore, a direct measurement of the height of rocket will reflect upon the antigen concentration.

A standard graph of antigen concentration versus peak height is then constructed and from the peak height of the unknown sample, concentration of antigen is determined.

Immunoelectrophoresis

Immunoelectrophoresis is a powerful technique to characterize antibodies. The technique is based on the principles of electrophoresis of antigens and immunodiffusion of the electrophoresed antigens with a polyspecific antiserum to form precipitin bands. During electrophoresis, molecules placed in an electric field acquire a charge and move towards appropriate electrode.

Thus, when antigens are subjected to electrophoresis in an agarose gel, they get separated according to their acquired charge, size and shape, by migrating to different positions. The antigen mixture is first electrophoresed to separate its components by charge. Troughs are then cut into the agar gel parallel to the direction of the electric field, and antiserum is added to the troughs. Antibody and antigen then diffuse toward each other and produce lines of precipitation where they meet in appropriate proportions Antigens thus resolved by electrophoresis are subjected to immunodiffusion with antiserum added in a trough cut in the agarose gel. Due to diffusion, density gradient of antigen and antibody are formed and at the zone of equivalence, antigen antibody complex precipitates to form an opaque arc shaped line in the gel. The precipitin line indicates the presence of antibody, specific to the antigen. If the antibody is homogeneous only one precipitin line is visible. Presence of more than one precipitin line establishes the heterogeneity of antibody, while the absence of precipitin line indicates that the antiserum does not have antibody to any of the antigens separated by electrophoresis.

Because immunoelectrophoresis is a strictly qualitative technique that only detects relatively high antibody concentrations (greater than several hundred g/ml), it utility is limited to the detection of quantitative abnormalities only when the departure from normal is striking, as in immunodeficiency states and immunoproliferative disorders.

Radioimmunoassay

Radioimmunoassay (RIA) is one of the most sensitive techniques for detecting antigen or antibody. The principle of RIA involves competitive binding of radio labeled antigen and unlabeled antigen to a high-affinity antibody. The labeled antigen is mixed with antibody at a concentration that saturates the antigen-binding sites of the antibody. Then test samples of unlabeled antigen of unknown concentration are added in progressively larger amounts. The antibody does not distinguish labeled from unlabeled antigen, so the two kinds of antigen compete for available binding sites on the antibody. As the concentration of unlabeled antigen increases, more labeled antigen will be displaced from the binding sites. The decrease in the amount of radio labeled antigen bound to specific antibody in the presence of the test sample is measured in order to determine the amount of antigen present in the test sample.

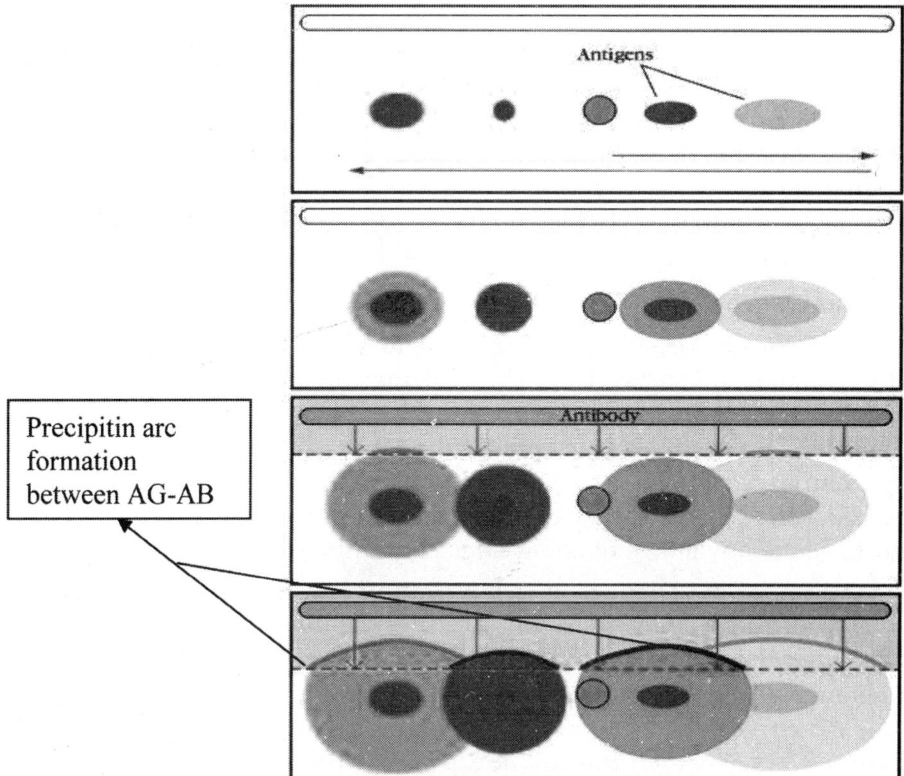

Fig. 6.9

The ratio of antibody (Ab) to antigen (Ag) is chosen to ensure that the number of epitopes presented by the labeled antigen always exceeds the total number of antibody binding sites. Consequently, unlabeled antigen added to the sample mixture will compete with radio labeled antigen for the limited supply of antibody. Even a small amount of unlabeled antigen added to the assay mixture of labeled antigen and antibody will cause a decrease in the amount of radioactive antigen bound, and this decrease will be proportional to the amount of unlabeled antigen added. To determine the amount of labeled antigen bound, the Ag-Ab complex is precipitated to separate it from free antigen (antigen not bound to Ab), and the radioactivity in the precipitate is measured. A standard curve can be generated using unlabeled antigen samples of known concentration (in place of the test sample), and from this plot the amount of antigen in the test mixture may be precisely determined.

Several methods have been developed for separating the bound antigen from the free antigen in RIA. ne method involves precipitating the Ag-Ab complex with a secondary anti-isotype antiserum. For example, if the Ag-Ab complex contains rabbit IgG antibody, then goat anti-rabbit IgG will bind to the rabbit IgG and precipitate the complex. Another method makes use of the fact that protein A of Staphylococcus aureus has high affinity for IgG. If the Ag-Ab complex contains an IgG antibody, the complex can be precipitated by mixing with formalin-killed S. aureus. After removal of the complex by either of these methods, the amount of free labeled antigen remaining in the supernatant can be measured in a radiation counter; subtracting this value from the total amount of labeled antigen added yields the amount of labeled antigen bound.

Enzyme-Linked Immunosorbent Assay (ELISA)

ELISA (or EIA), is similar in principle to RIA but depends on an enzyme rather than a radioactive label. An enzyme conjugated with an antibody reacts with a colorless substrate to generate a colored reaction product. Such a substrate is called a chromogenic substrate. A number of enzymes have been employed for ELISA, including alkaline phosphatase, horseradish peroxidase and â-galactosidase. These assays approach the sensitivity of RIAs and have the advantage of being safer and less costly.

A number of variations of ELISA (Indirect, Sandwich and Competitive) have been developed, allowing qualitative detection or quantitative measurement of either antigen or antibody. Each type of ELISA can be used qualitatively to detect the presence of antibody or antigen. Alternatively, a standard curve based on known concentrations of antibody or antigen is prepared, from which the unknown concentration of a sample can be determined.

Types of ELISA

Indirect ELISA

Antibody can be detected or quantitatively determined with an indirect ELISA. Serum or some other sample containing primary antibody (Ab1) is added to an antigen-coated microtiter well and allowed to react with the antigen attached to the well. After any free Ab1 is washed away, the presence of antibody bound to the antigen is detected by adding an enzyme conjugated secondary anti-isotype antibody (Ab2), which binds to the primary antibody.

Any free Ab2 then is washed away, and a substrate for the enzyme is added. The amount of colored reaction product that forms is measured ELISA plate reader.

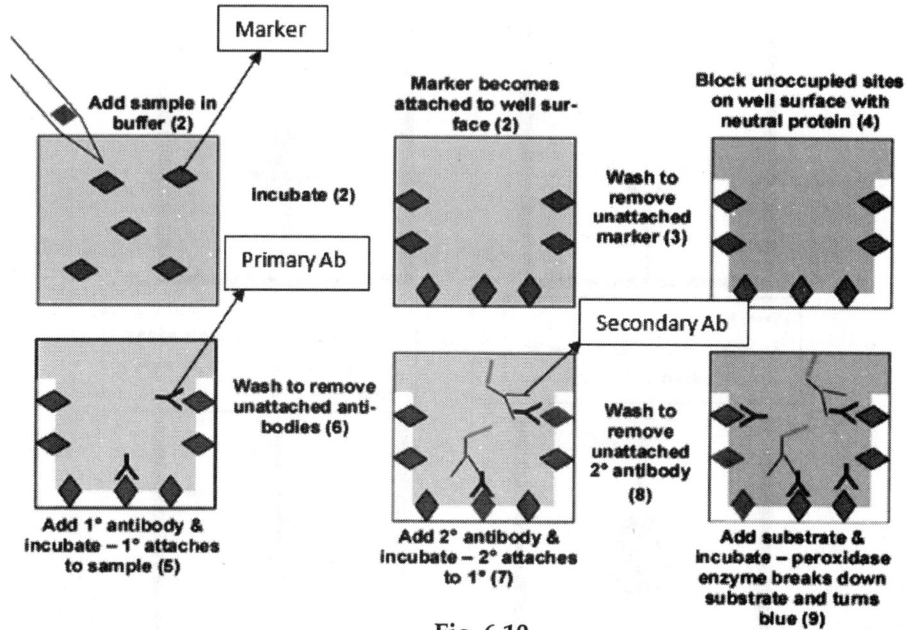

Fig. 6.10

Sandwich ELISA

Antigen can be detected or measured by a sandwich ELISA. In this technique, the antibody is immobilized on a microtiter well. A sample containing antigen is added and allowed to react with the immobilized antibody. After the well is washed, a second enzyme-linked antibody specific for a different epitope on the antigen is added and allowed to react with the bound antigen. After any free second antibody is removed by washing, substrate is added, and the colored reaction product is measured.

Competitive ELISA

Another variation for measuring amounts of antigen is competitive ELISA. In this technique, antibody is first incubated in solution with a sample containing antigen. The antigen-antibody mixture is then added to an antigen coated microtiter well. The more antigens present in the sample, the less free antibody will be available to bind to the antigen-coated well. Addition of an enzyme-conjugated secondary antibody (Ab2) specific for the isotype of the primary antibody can be used to determine the amount of primary antibody bound to the well as in an indirect ELISA.

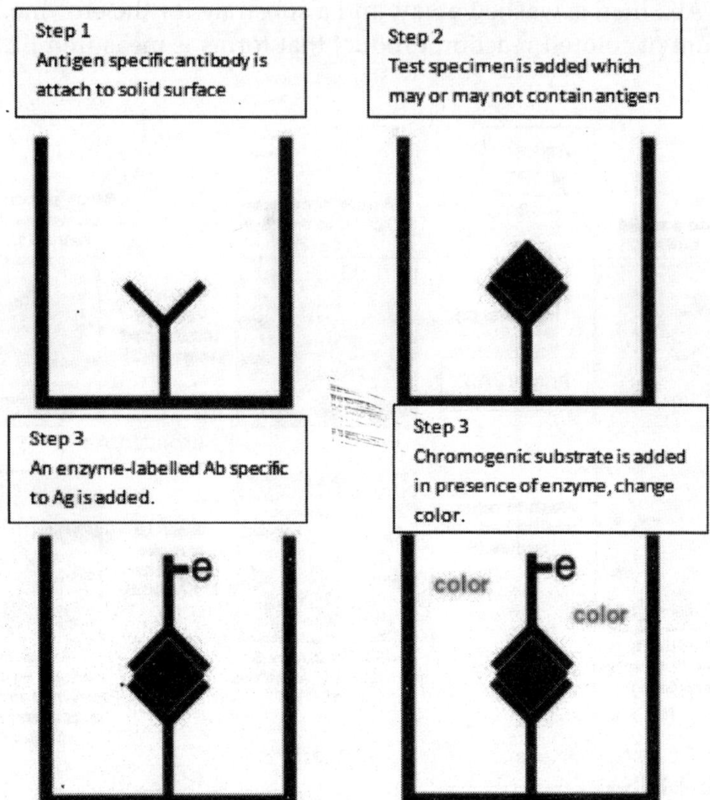

Fig. 6.11

Sensitivity of Various Immunoassays

Assay Method	Sensitivity μg/ml Antibody
Precipitation reaction in fluids	20-200
Precipitation reactions in gels	
Ouchterlony double immunodiffusion	20-200
Immunoelectrophoresis	20-200
Rocket electrophoresis	2
Radioimmunoassay	0.0006-0.006
Enzyme-linked immunosorbent assay (ELISA)	0.0001-0.01
Immunofluorescence	1.0
Flow cytometry	0.06-0.006

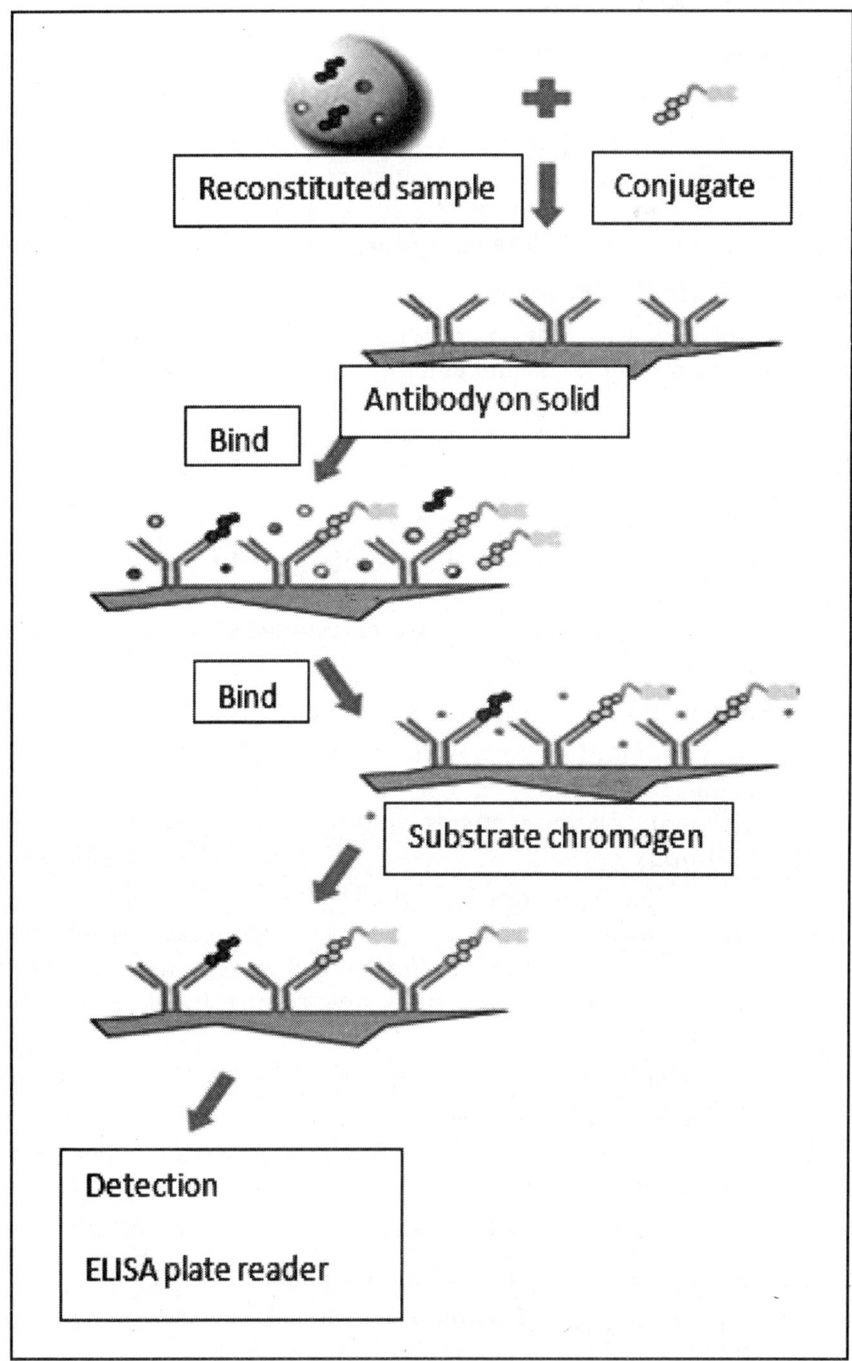
Reconstituted sample
Conjugate
Antibody on solid
Bind
Bind
Substrate chromogen
Detection
ELISA plate reader

Fig. 6.12

MATERIALS AND METHODS

1. Isolation of Immunoglobulin Y

Water Dilution Method

10 ml of yolk was diluted 1:9 with distilled water acidified with 0.1M HCl to reach pH 5.0 and incubated for atleast 6 hours at 4°C. After incubation samples were centrifuged at 10000g for 20 min, the supernatants were separated from the pellets, filtered on filter papers.

Sodium Alginate Precipitation

10 ml of yolk was diluted 1:4 with TBS buffer, 6 ml of 10% sodium alginate and 15 ml of 1M calcium chloride were added and the mixture was incubated for 20 min at room temperature. After incubation samples were centrifuged at 10000g for 20 min, the supernatants were separated from the pellets, filtered on filter papers.

Chloroform Method

10 ml of yolk was diluted with chloroform at 1:1 ratio and incubated for 20 min at room temperature. After incubation samples were centrifuged at 10000g for 20 min, the supernatants were separated from the pellets, filtered on filter papers.

2. Partial purification by ammonium sulphate precipitation:

1. Add 5.0 ml of respective 10, 20, 40, 60 and 100% of ammonium sulfate solutions individually to 5.0 ml of the sample obtained form different isolation methods drop by drop, vortex to mix between additions.

   Note: If the salt is added too quickly, then high local concentrations will develop and proteins will be precipitated that would remain soluble at the target ammonium sulfate concentration. Such proteins may not readily re-dissolve, and reduce the effectiveness of fractionation.

2. The mixture is allowed to stand on ice for 30 min to allow protein precipitation taking place.
3. Centrifuge at 12,000 rpm for 5 min. Remove the supernatant by pipette as much as possible.
4. Add 1 ml of 1% NaCl to resuspend the pellet (crude albumin).

3. Purification by PEG method (Immunoglobulin Y)

1. Mix 5 ml of egg yolk solution and 10ml of phosphate buffer solution (PBS). Take 50µl of this solution and mark it as sample 1.
2. Add 500mg of PEG (Poly-ethylene Glycol) and mix it. Invert about 5-10 minutes.

3. Centrifuge at 6000rpm for 10 minutes.
4. Pour the supernatant into syringe filter and collect about 50µl of this solution and mark it as sample 2.
5. Add 850mg PEG to the collected fraction and centrifuge at 10000rpm for 10 minutes.
6. Collect the supernatant and take 50 µl of this solution and mark it as sample 3.
7. Add 5ml of PBS to the pellet and collect 50 µl of this solution and mark it as sample 4.
8. Add 600mg PEG , mix and centrifuge at 10000rpm for 10 minutes.
9. To the pellet, add 1ml PBS and mark the sample as no. 5
10. Perform SDS-PAGE using the five samples. The last sample obtained contains about 80-90% pure Ig Y.

4. SDS-PAGE

1. Assemble the plates for casting gel as shown below:

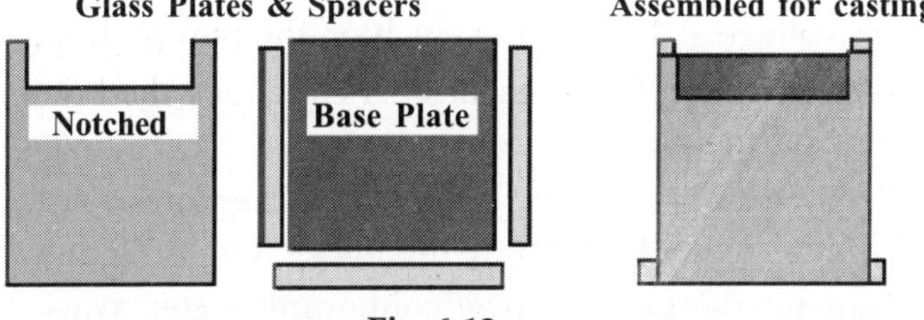

Fig. 6.13

2. Clamp the assembly of plates. Ensure the assembly is leak proof by filling water between the plates. Silicon grease can be applied to spacers or 1% agarose can be used for sealing to make it leak proof.
3. Add 50 µl of ammonium persulphate to 5 ml of separating gel mix and mix thoroughly.Pour the gel solution between the plates till the level is about 2 cm below the top edge of notched plate.
4. Add 200 to 250 µl of water to make the surface even.
5. After the gel is set (approximately 20-30 minutes), wash the top of the separating gel with distilled water and drain off the water completely.
6. Add 20 µl of APS solution to 2 ml of stacking gel mix, mix thoroughly and pour directly onto the polymerized separating gel.
7. Insert the comb into the gel solution carefully without trapping any air bubbles, approximately 1 cm above the separating gel. The stacking gel will set in about 10 minutes.

8. Pipette out 25 µl of protein samples (A, B and C) and 10 µl of protein marker into individual vials. Label them appropriately. To each of these vials add 15 µl of sample loading buffer.
9. Place the vials in a boiling water bath for 5 minutes.
10. After the stacking gel has set, carefully remove the comb and the bottom spacer. Wash the wells immediately with distilled water to remove non-polymerized acrylamide.
11. Fill the bottom reservoir with 1X reservoir buffer.
12. Carefully fix the plate to the PAGE apparatus without trapping any air bubbles between the buffer and the bottom of the gel, with the notched plate facing the top reservoir.
13. Fill the top reservoir with 1X reservoir buffer.
14. Load samples into the wells, rinse the micropipette tip in the bottom reservoir buffer between each load. Note down the order in which the samples have been loaded.
15. Connect the cords to the power supply, red: anode, black: cathode.
16. Set voltage at 100 V and switch on the power supply.
17. When the dye front reaches 0.5 cm above the bottom of the gel, turn off the power.
18. Remove the gel plates and gently pry the plates apart. Use a spatula or similar tool to separate the plates (not at the notch).
19. Transfer the gel to a tray containing water, wash the gel for 5 minutes. Discard the water.
20. Add 20 ml of Ezee blue and stain the gel for 30-60 minutes. Continue staining the gel overnight if the bands appear light.
21. Destain the gel with water, if the background is not clear. (This is an optional step).

    Note: For uniform staining and washing, place the tray on a rocker or shake intermittently every 10 to 15 minutes.
22. Place the gel between two sheets of plastic wrap and place it on a piece of white paper.
23. Use a ruler to measure the distance migrated by each band of the protein marker from the start of separating gel.
24. Similarly, measure the migration distance of protein sample C and the tracking dye from the start of separating gel.
25. Calculate the relative mobilities of the proteins (total serum and IgG)

5. Radial Immuno Diffusion Protocol:

Prepare a 1% solution of agarose using 1X immunobuffer (PBS).

1. Cool the agarose solution to around 50 c.
2. Mix 500 ul of antiserum to 5ml of agarose. By using glass pipette, add molten Agarose onto a glass microscopic side kept on a leveled surface/The agarose would be about3-4mm thick. Avoid spillage, even a little spillage cause the whole Agarose get drawn from the slide due to capillary action.
3. Allow solidify. Place template under the gel plate and punch corresponding to the marking on the template, after the Agarose has hardened sufficiently.
4. Agarose plugs can be removed from the wells using a sharp needle. Optimal results are obtained if reagents are added to the wells just after the plugs are removed from the gel.
5. Add 10ul test antigen in the centre well and 10ul of standard antigens to the surrounding wells as shown above.
6. Each well should be filled with 10ul of antigen. This amount will fill the well without overflowing into the adjacent well.
7. After the wells are filled keep the slide in the moist chamber.
8. keep the glass plate in moist chamber for 16-18 hours.

6. Quantitative Precipitation Assay Protocol:

1. Add antigen, 1X assay buffer and test antibody as given in the table.

Tube No.	Antigen [1mg/ml]	Conc. of Antigen (in µg)	1X Assay Buffer(µl)	Test antiserum (µl)
1.	0 µl		250	100
2.	25µl	25	225	100
3.	50µl	50	200	100
4.	75µl	75	175	100
5.	100µl	100	150	100
6.	150µl	125	100	100

2. Mix well and incubate at 37 degrees centigrade for 40 minutes. Mix gently after every 10 minutes.
3. Incubate for another 20 minutes at 2-8° c.
4. Centrifuge for 10-15 minutes at 10000 to 12000 rpm.

Aspirate the supernatant carefully. Minute pellet will stick on vial.

5. Resuspend the pellet in 1 ml of 1X assay buffer.

6. Centrifuge for 10-15 minutes at 10000-12000 rpm.
7. Dissolve the precipitate in 1 ml of 1X NaOH.
8. Read the absorbance at 280 nm (A280).

   Calculation:

   Protein content in precipitate= A280 * m/1.4 mg

   Where 'm' is amount of NaOH added.

7. Ig G purification by Ion exchange chromatography:

Sample Preparartion

Thaw serum sample on ice and tranfer 500ul into test tube or suitable tube. Add 0.5ml of serum dilution buffer slowly and gently mix. Check Ph using PH paper. It must be PH 7. If not, adjust serum Ph by adding serum dilution buffer.

Column Equilibration:

- Fix column into stand and fix well.
- Open top column cap gently and place an empty beaker under column.
- Remove column outlet and add equlibration buffer and allow buffer draining out slowly. Equlibrate column with minimum 50 ml equilibration buffer.
- Once equlibration is complete, close outlet when buffer touches the matrix bed.

Loading Serum sample:

- Loading Serum sample which is already mixed with serum dilution buffer(1ml) by pipetting slowly into column.
- With the help of glass Pipette or 1ml micropipette, slowly mix serum sample with matrix bed. While mixing, make sure that glass wool placed under matrix is not disturbed.
- After a brief mix, incubate column on room temperaturefor 15 minutes. Again mix gently, incubates for another 10 minutes.
- Label % eppendrof tubes as fraction 1 to 5.
- Open outlet carefully, start collecting 0.25ml fraction untill flow stops.(Collect 4 to 5, 1ml)
- Start pouring recharge buffer to column slowly and allow it to drain.
- Regenerate column with minimum of 25ml of recharge buffer.
- Store column with 5 ml of recharge buffer at 4c.

RESULTS AND DISCUSSIONS

1. Collection of Eggs and Separation of egg yolk:

4 different types of eggs(Normal, Brown color, Double yolk, Shell less) were collected from a poultry farm in Vijayawada.

Fig. 6.14

2. Isolation and Partial Purification of Ig Y

Ig y is preliminarily isolated from the egg yolk using 3 different methods (Water dilution, Chloroform, Sodium alginate). These samples were then subjected to Ammonium sulfate precipitation.

3. Characterization of the partially purified samples:

In order to determine the best method of isolation the partially purified samples were characterized using SDS-PAGE.

From the results of PAGE the following methods seems to be good for the isolation of IgY from Egg Yolk.

Normal – Water Dilution Method

Brown – Chloroform Method

Double Yolk – Water Dilution Method

Shell less – Sodium Algenate Method

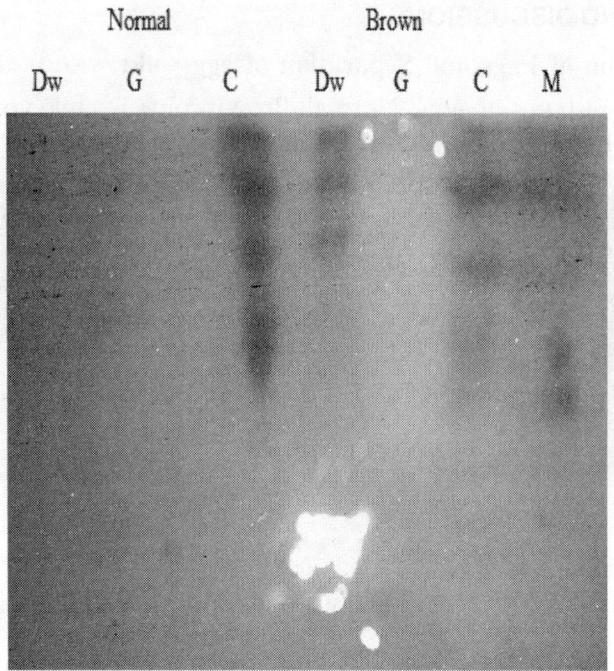

Fig. 6.15

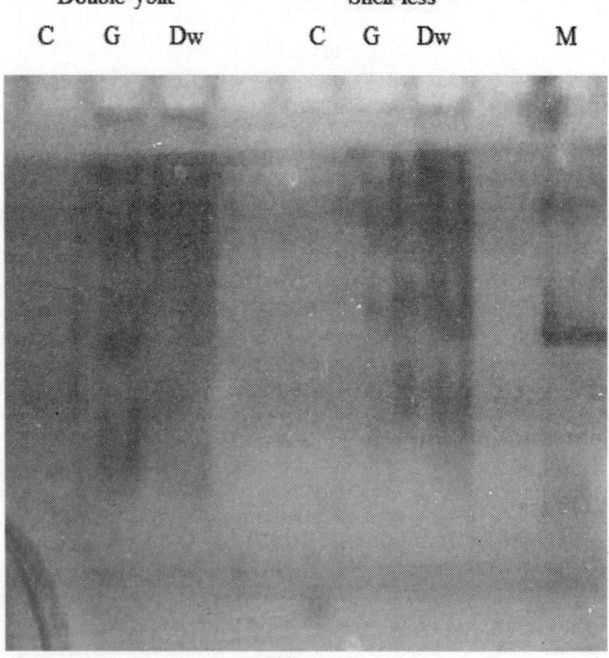

Fig. 6.16

These samples were then used for further purificaion.

4. Complete Purification of Ig Y using Column Chromatography

Samples were then completely purified using Gel Filtration Chromatography is collected in eppendrof tubes and used for subsequent tests.

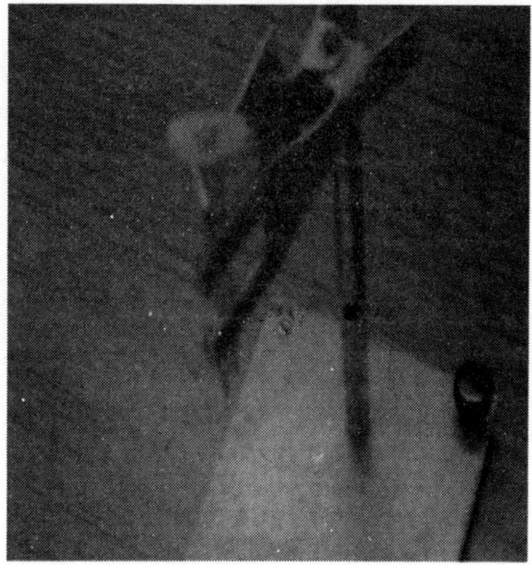

Fig. 6.17

5. Characterization of Ig Y by SDS-PAGE

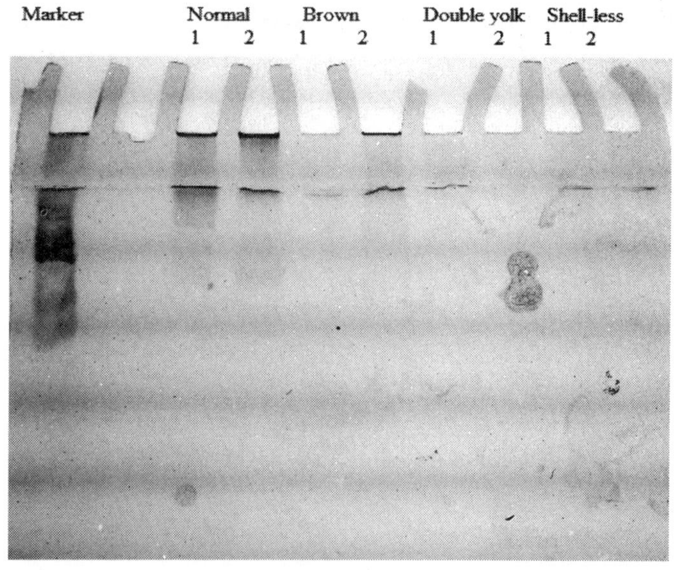

Fig. 6.18

6. Purification of Ig G by column chromatography

7. Characterization of Ig G by SDS-PAGE

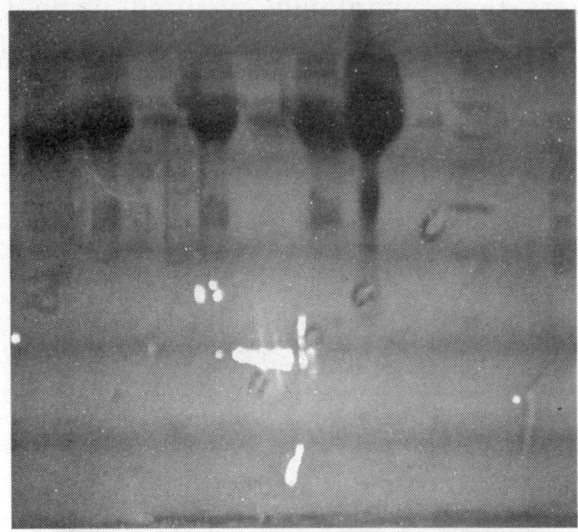

Fig. 6.19

8. Antigen Collection:

Anopheles Dirus Salivary gland Antigens were procured from Vimta Labs, Hyderabad

9. Tests for Antigen Antibody Interactions:

1. ***Radial Immunodiffusion:***

The diameter of rings formed by Ag-Ab interaction are as follows:

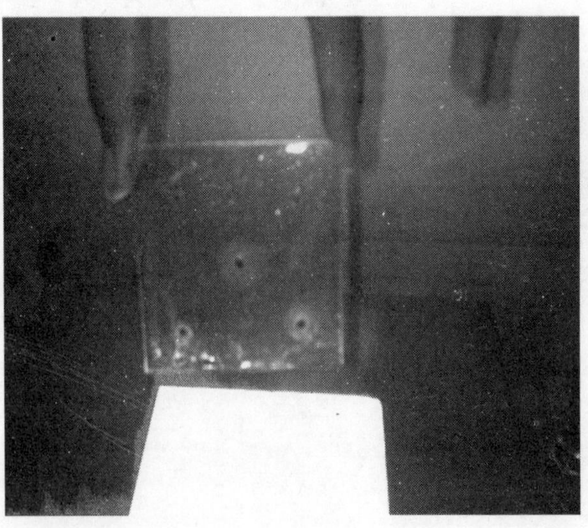

Fig. 6.20

	Normal Egg	Brown Egg	Double Yolk	Shell Less Egg	Blood Serum
Concentration (µg/ml)	Diameter of ring (mm)	Diameter of ring (mm)	Diameter of ring (mm)	Diameter of ring (mm)	Diameter of ring (mm)
10	5	3	4	4	2
20	8	6	7	6	3
30	11	7	10	7	4
40	13	11	12	8	6
50	17	14	15	10	8

2. ***Quantitative precipitin Assay:***

From the optical density obtain from different concentration of antigen towards antibody the following graphs were obtained.

	Normal Egg		Brown Egg		Double Yolk Egg		Shell Less Egg		Blood Serum	
Antigen (µg)	O.D (A_{280})	Protein (µg)	O.D (A_{280})	Protein (µg)	O.D (A_{280})	Protein (µg)	O.D (A_{280})	Protein (µg)	O.D (A_{280})	Protein (µg)
25	0.06	42.8	0.09	64.28	0.022	15.7	0.04	28.5	0.018	12.8
50	0.13	92.8	0.180	128.57	0.151	107.8	0.16	114.2	0.120	85.7
75	0.28	200	0.25	178.57	0.114	81.4	0.19	135	0.107	76.4
100	0.14	100	0.10	71.42	0.066	47.1	0.08	57.1	0.046	32.8
150	0.05	28.5	0.08	57.14	0.105	75	0.102	72.8	0.101	72.1

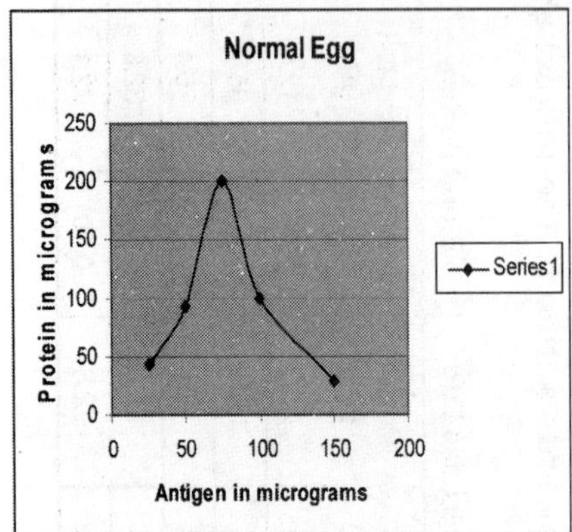

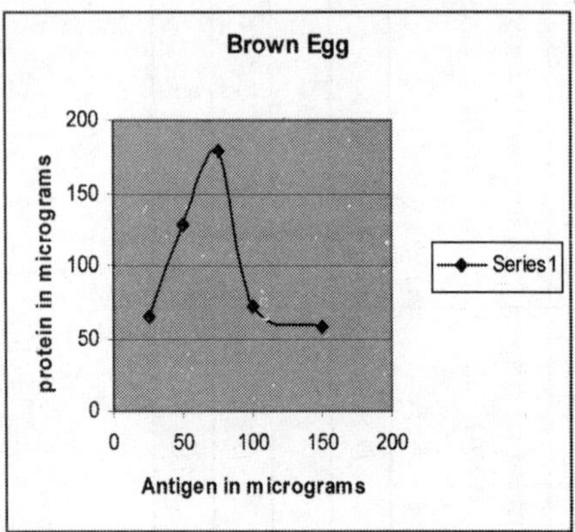

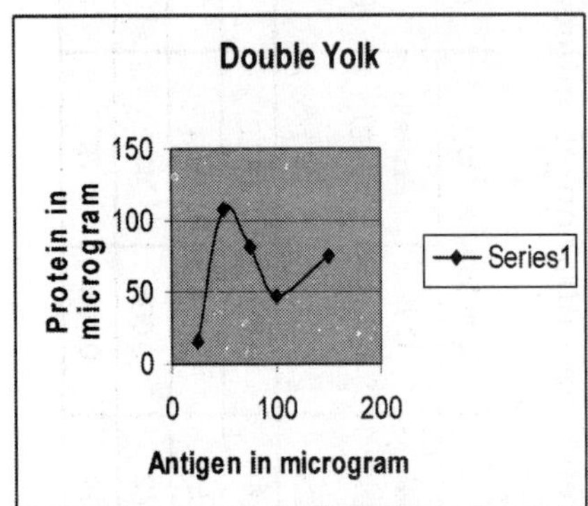

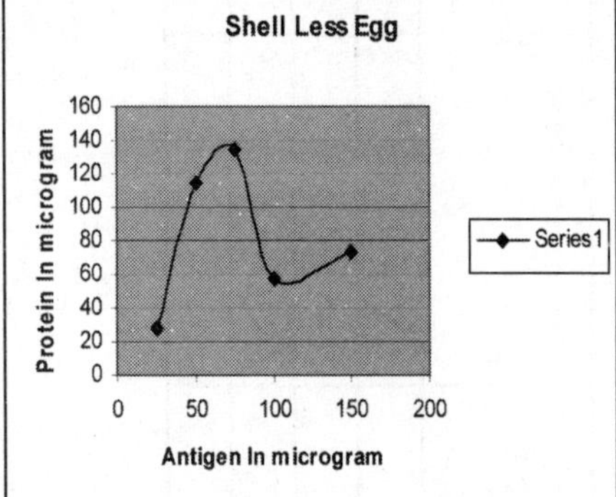

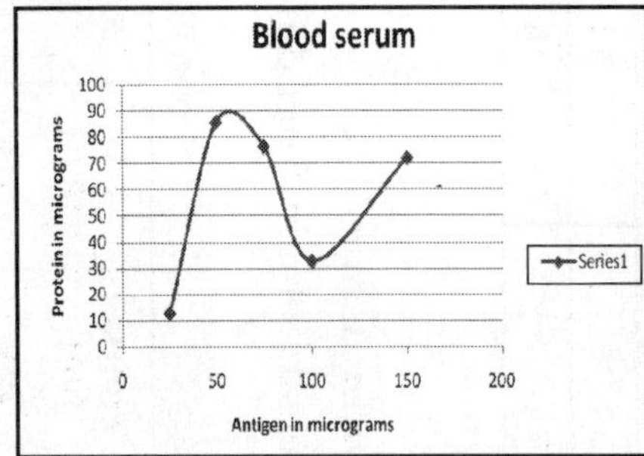

Fig. 6.21

Amount of Antibody in Antiserum was calculated by:

(Pm-Ag)/V mg/ml

Where

Pm - Amount of maximum precipitate in µg.

Ag - Amount of antigen in µg added in the tube.

V - Volume of antiserum taken in µl.

Therefore,

1. For Normal Egg: Amount of Ab in antiserum was (200-75)/100 = 1.25 mg/ml.
2. For Brown Egg: Amount of Ab in antiserum was (178.57-100)/100 = 0.786 mg/ml.
3. For Double Yolk Egg: Amount of Ab in antiserum was (107.8-50)/ 100 = 0.578 mg/ml.
4. For Shell Less Egg: Amount of Ab in antiserum was (135-75)/100 = 0.6 mg/ml.
5. For Blood serum: Amount of Ab in antiserum was (76.4-75)/ 100=0.014 mg/ml.

REFERENCES

1. Akita, E.M. and Nakai, S. (1993). Comparison of Four Purification Methods for the Production of Immunoglobulins from Eggs Laid by Hens Immunized with an Enterotoxigenic E. coli Strain. J. Immunol. Methods 160:207.
2. A. Polson, M.B. von Wechmar, M.H.V van Regenmortel (1980) Isolation of viral IgY Antibodies from Yolks of Immunized Hens, Immunol. Commun. 9, 475-493.
3. Arca, B.; Lombardo, F.; De Lara Capurro M. et al. - Trapping cDNAs Encoding Secreted Proteins from the Salivary Glands of the Malaria Vector Anopheles Gambiae. Proc. nat. Acad. Sci. (Wash.), 96: 1516-1521, 1999.
4. Baimai, V.; Green, C.A.; Andre, R.G.; Harrison, B.A. & Peyton, E.L. -Cytogenetic Studies of Some Species Complexes of Anopheles in Thailand and Southeast Asia. Southeast Asian J. trop. Med. publ. Hlth., 15: 536-546, 1984.
5. Barrow, P.M.; Mcciver, S.B. & Wright, K.A. - Salivary Glands of Female Culex Pipiens: Morphological Changes Associated with Maturation and Blood Feeding. Canad. J. Zool., 107: 1153-1160, 1975.
6. Calvo, E.; Andersen, J.; Francischetti, I.M. et al. – The Transcriptome of Adult Female Anopheles Darlingi Salivary Glands. Insect Molec. Biol., 13: 73-88, 2004.
7. D.G. Hardie, P.S. Guy, P. Cohen, in J. Lowenstein, Ed. (1981) Methods in Enzymology, Vol. 71, Academic Press, San Diego, CA,pp. 26-33.
8. E.M. Akita, S. Nakai (1993) Comparison of Four Purification Methods for the Production of Immunoglobulins from Eggs Laid by Hens Immunized with Enterogenic E. coli Strain, J. Immunol. Methods 160, 207-214.
9. F. Calabi and M.S. Neuberger; Molecular Genetics of Inimunoglobulin; Elsevier Science Publishers; ISBN 0-444-XO915-5; Medical Research Council Laboratory of Molecular Biology, Hills Road, Combridge CB2 2QH, UK.
10. G.W. Warr, K.E. Magor, D.A. Higgins (1995) IgY: Clues to the Origin of Modern Antibodies, Immunol. Today 16, 392-398.
11. H. Towbin, T. Staehelin, J. Gordon (1979) Electrophoretic Transfer of Proteins from Polyacrylamide Gels to Nitrocellulose Sheets: Procedure and Some Applications, Proc. Natl. Acad. Sci. U.S.A. 76, 4350-4354.

12. Jangen, H.G. & Wright, K.A. - The Salivary Glands of Aedes aegypti (L.): An Electron Microscope Study. Canad. J. Zool., 49: 1343-1345, 1971.
13. Jensenius, J.C., et al. (1981). Eggs: Conveniently Packaged Antibodies. Methods for Purification of Yolk IgG. J. Immunol. Methods 46: 63.
14. Jensenius, J.C. and Koch, C. (1997) Antibodies Packaged in Eggs, in Immunochemistry: A Practical Approach, Vol. 1 (Johnstone, A.P. and Turner, M.W., eds.), IRL Press, Oxford,UK, pp. 89-107.
15. K.C. Ingham, in M.P. Deutscher, Ed. (1990) Methods in Enzymology, Vol. 182, Academic Press, San Diego, CA, pp. 301-306.
16. Larsson, A. and Sjoquist, J. (1990). Chicken IgY: Utilizing the Evolutionary Difference. Comp. Immun. Microbiol. Infect. 13: 199.
17. Larsson, A., et al. (1993). Chicken Antibodies: Taking Advantage of Evolution – A Review. Poultry Sci. 72:1807.
18. M. Allansmith, B. McClellan and M. Butterworth; The Influence of Heredity and Environment on Immunolobulin Levels; The Journal of Immunology Vol. 102, No. 6, June 1909.
19. Polson, A., et al. (1985). Improvements in the Isolation of IgY from the Yolks of Eggs Laid by Immunized Hens. Immunol. Invest. 14: 323.
20. Polson, G.M. Potgieter, J.F. Largier, G.E.F. Mears, F.J. Joubert (1964). The Fractionation of Protein Mixtures by Linear Polymers of High Molecular Weight, Biochim. Biophys. Acta 82, 463-475.
21. Polson, T. Coetzer, J. Kruger, E. von Maltzahn, K.J. vander Merwe (1985) Improvements in the Isolation of IgY from the Yolks of Eggs Laid by Immunized Hens, Immunol. Investig. 14, 323-327.
22. Raymond M.seun & Shalima Gorden; Critical Review of IgG Immunoglobulins; US Biotech Laboratories 13500 linden Avn. N. Seattle,WA9 8133; 2003.
23. R.F. Boyer (1993) Modern Experimental Biochemistry, 2nd ed., Benjamin/Cummings, San Francisco, CA, pp. 249-250.
24. Richard A. Goldsby, Thomas J. Kindt and Barbara A. Osborne; *Kuby Immunology 4e*; ISBN-13: 9781429202114.
25. Roald Nezlin; The Immunoglobulins: Structure and Function; ISBN 0-12-517970-7; Academic Press Limited; 24-28 Oval Road, London NW 1 7DX, UK.
26. Roitt,I., J.Brostoff, and D.Male; "Immunology", Mosby., London, England, (1996) Fourth Edition.
27. R. Schade, I. Nehn, M. Erhard, A. Hlinak, C. Staak, Eds. (2001) Chicken Egg Yolk Antibodies, Production and Application. Springer-Verlag, Berlin, pp. 65-107.
28. T.H.T. Coetzer (1993) Type IV Collagenase and Cathepsins L and H: Proteinases Involved in Tumour Invasion. Ph.D. Thesis, University of Natal, Pietermaritzburg, South Africa.
29. U.K. Laemmli (1970) Cleavage of Structural Proteins during the Assembly of the Head of Bacteriophage T4, Nature 227, 680-685.
30. Vlug,A. and P. van Remortel: "The Structure and Function of Human IgG Subclasses". Eur.Clin.Lab. 8, 26 (1989).

Fate and Effects of Microorganisms in the Control of Common Diseases of Tomato

Caroline F Ajilogba and **Olubukola O Babalola**

Department of Biological Sciences, Faculty of Agriculture, Science and Technology, North-West University Mafikeng Campus, Private Bag X2046 Mmabatho 2735, South Africa.

ABSTRACT

Tomato (*Lycopersicon esculentum* mill) is a very important vegetable and fruit crop. It is nutritious and contains vitamin A, B and the antioxidant lycopene that is useful in the prevention and treatment of common cancers. Tomatoes are easily susceptible to fungal, bacterial, viral, and nematodal diseases and infections. Such diseases include wilts, root rots, canker, spots and specks, tomato spotted wilt virus, tomato bushy stunt virus and root knot. These diseases lead to stunted growth in tomato seedlings, wilting and death of the tomato plants. This in turn leads to little or no yield from the tomato to the farmer. The effects microorganisms on tomatoes can both be beneficial and adverse. The beneficial effects include promoting plant growth and biocontrol while the adverse effects include non-target microorganisms being displaced from their habitats, the microorganisms being pathogenic to non-target organisms, the microorganisms being toxic to non-target organisms and humans/other animals beings allergic to the microorganisms. The fate of these microorganisms can be determined by monitoring them and generating data about their microbial ecology over time to ascertain how they will fare if they are formulated as this helps to determine their future. This review seeks to outline the importance of tomato plant, the various diseases affecting it, and the fate and the effect of using microorganisms to stop these infections.

Keywords: Biological control, diseases, effects, fates, microorganisms, tomato.

INTRODUCTION

Knowledge on the fate and effect of microorganisms as alternative to other ways of controlling plant diseases and pest is essential to the future of biocontrol. Regulatory bodies require concrete information on the possible effects of releasing some microorganisms into the environment. That information can only be generated from research and studies on the fate and effects of microorganisms (Kiewnick 2007). Some species of microorganisms such as *Saccharomyces cerevisae, Bacillus licheniformis* and *Aspergillus niger* have long been recognized as 'Generally recognised as safe' (GRAS) by regulatory bodies such as the European Food Safety Authority (EFSA) and the Food and Drug Administration (FDA), and are being utilized in environmental applications. The safety assessment of these microorganisms is made easy because of previous evaluation; so more attention is concentrated on those microorganisms that could pose greatest risks (Leuschner et al. 2010).

The fate of microorganisms involves four particular areas of microbial ecology which are: community effects, population dynamics, microbial dissemination, and persistence in the environment (Holmberg 2011). These effects go a long way to affect the strategies that will be used in their formulation into biocontrol products. In a situation where little is known about their interaction with other target and nontarget organisms in the environment, the process towards registration as anti-microbial product is slowed down.

When a microorganism is introduced into a new environment, it is faced with different challenges as well as opportunities. These challenges include its ability to persist, which also varies between strains of the same species; also there is the issue of competition with the resident population in the new community, and the issue of it being predated upon by other pathogens or bacteriophages (Babalola and Glick 2012b; Xiang et al. 2010). To overcome these challenges, microorganisms may be introduced into sterile soil prior to introduction to the field as it helps them to adapt and deal with the issue of stress in the new environment (Van Dyke and Prosser 2000).

Monitoring the interaction with and response to both biotic and abiotic influences help to determine the fate of microorganism. This involves following the microorganism overtime and generating data on the microbial population concerning its size, its distribution and survival times (Whipps 2001). A microorganism that will be used as a biocontrol strain will be successful if it will be able to find its own protective niche within the new environment, colonise it and spread from there to the other parts of the environment (Johansen et al. 2005). Microorganisms have been used in the control of diseases in most solanaceous crops and that includes tomato.

Tomato comes second to potato worldwide, as a vegetable crop. It is known as a healthy food because of its nutritive value which include low sodium, saturated fat and cholesterol value, rich vitamin E (Alpha tocopherol), thiamine, niacin, vitamin B6, folate, magnesium, phosphorus, copper, dietary fiber, vitamin A, vitamin C, vitamin K, potassium and manganese values. The world yearly production was estimated as 145 751 507 Mt in 2010 (FAO 2012). It is an important cash crop for smallholders and medium-scale commercial farmers (Naika et al 2005). Tomato is rich in minerals, vitamins, essential amino acids, sugars and dietary fibres. They contain much vitamin B and C, iron and phosphorus. Yellow tomato contains vitamin A which is important for good eyesight. Red tomato contains lycopene, which is responsible for the red coloration and also an anti-oxidant that may contribute to protection against carcinogenic substances. Lycopene has the ability to neutralize the free radicals that can cause damage to cells (Boyer 2011). As a matter of fact, it is thought to be twice as effective as many other kinds of antioxidants, and it has been shown to play a role in the prevention of such common cancers as prostate cancer, lung cancer and breast cancer. In addition, lycopene is thought to help inhibit the aging process, allowing tomato eaters to remain active longer.

Tomato is an important cash crop for smallholders and medium-scale commercial farmers in Africa (Babalola and Glick 2012a) but it is prone to infections and diseases by soil-borne pathogens. There are several microorganisms used in the control of tomato disease. Some of these microorganisms are *Bacillus, Trichoderma,* and *Pseudomonas* species.

Origin, Taxonomy and Morphology of Tomato

Tomato was native to the South American Andes before Spanish explorers introduced it to the whole world. Scientifically, tomato is known as *Solanum lycopersicon* with synonym as *Lycopersicon esculentum* while botanically, it belongs to the nightshade family or solanaceae which also includes chili peppers, potato and eggplant. The taxonomy of tomato is outlined below:

Kingdom Plantae – Plants, Subkingdom Tracheobionta – Vascular plants, Superdivision Spermatophyta – Seed plants, Division Magnoliophyta – Flowering plants, Class Magnoliopsida – Dicotyledons, Subclass – Asteridae, Order – Solanales, Family Solanaceae – Potato family, Genus Solanum L. – nightshade, Species *Solanum lycopersicum* L. – garden tomato, Other names of *Solanum lycopersicon* includes, *Lycopersicon esculentum* Mill, *Lycopersicon esculentum* var. *esculentum, Lycopersicon lycopersicum, Lycopersicum esculentum, Solanum esculentum, Solanum esculentum* Dunal, *Solanum lycopersicon,* Common names for tomato are: jitomate (Mexico), pomodoro (Italy), tomate (Spain, France), tomatl (Nahuatl), tomat (Indonesia), faan ke'e (China), nyanya (Swahili) and tomati (West Africa).

In South Africa, like it is worldwide, tomato is the second most important vegetable crop after potato. It is planted in over 6000 hectares of land in areas like, Mpumalanga, Lowveld and Middleveld, Western Cape, Limpopo, Southern part of the Eastern Cape and the Pongola region of Kwazulu-Natal (DAFF 2012).

Distribution

Tomato was introduced into Spain by the Spanish explorers and from there it was taken to Europe and Africa. Initially it was thought to be poisonous but was later accepted to be non-poisonous in the 18th century. Tomato is grown in every country in the continent (Philouze and Hedde 1993). Most of the wild species are found in the Andean mountains of South America while the domesticated one are widely distributed throughout the world (Chetelat et al. 2009). Asia and African account for more than 65% of tomato grown in the world. These countries include China, India, Turkey and Nigeria (Srinivasan 2010). It is now one of the most widely eaten vegetables worldwide (DAFF 2012, Hanson et al. 2004). In South Africa, of the total vegetables eaten, tomato constitutes about 24% (DAFF 2012). Tomato is cultivated on all continents except Antarctica, from sea level to an elevation of 3000 metres above sea level, and in temperate climates they are grown as annuals. Tomato can also be grown as perennials. Sometimes tomato can become weeds when they escape outside the garden and grow where they are not planted.

Planting and Harvesting Requirement

Tomato can easily be killed by frost and is seen as warm season crop. The plant needs daily optimum temperature of between 20°C and 24°C (Whiting et al. 2012). Temperatures below 12°C lead to poor growth, yield and poor quality of the fruit. During windy dry season, the plant losses many of its flowers while during wet season, it is prone to foliar disease infection. They can grow in quite dry areas, but grow bigger and produce more fruit when they are well-watered (DAFF 2012). It grows well in a rich well aerated loam soil with nutrients and pH of 6-7. It requires a good amount of nitrogen for growth and better flower and fruit set, phosphorus for vigorous growth and development of root and potassium for the acids and solids of the fruit, firmness and improved taste. It also requires other micronutrients like iron, manganese, calcium, magnesium, boron and molybdenum for its growth and development.

Tomato is a perishable and must be handled with care when they are harvested as they can be harvested manually by picking them in most cases. They can be harvested when they are properly ripe, not fully ripe or not ripe at all. In handling them, care should be taken to avoid injury that could lead to them being infected with microbes which eventually leads to spoilage and low taste quality.

Importance of Tomato in Health

Tomato is so important for its phytochemical properties and it has more health benefitting properties compared to other vegetables. It is one of the vegetables with low calorie, 18 calories per 100 g compared to 902 calories per 100 g in animal fat and 218 calories per 100g in kidney beans. It has no cholesterol and is recommended in cholesterol reduction diet. It is a rich source of many important nutrients, and is quite important to a healthy diet. It is rich in minerals, vitamins, essential amino acids, sugars and dietary fibres. It contains much vitamin B and C, iron and phosphorus. Yellow tomato contains vitamin A which is important for good eyesight. Red tomato contains lycopene which is responsible for the red coloration and also an anti-oxidant that may contribute to protection against carcinogenic substances (Miller et al. 2002). It has the ability to neutralize the free radicals that can cause damage to cells (Boyer 2011). As a matter of fact, lycopene is thought to be twice as effective as many other kinds of antioxidants, and it has been shown to play a role in the prevention of such common cancers as prostate cancer, lung cancer and breast cancer. In addition, lycopene is thought to help to inhibit the aging process, allowing tomato eaters to remain active longer (Bramley 2000; Heber and Lu 2002).

Flavonoids contained in tomato include zeaxanthin, which helps to prevent ultra-violet rays from filtering into elderly people's eyes thereby preventing age related macular disease. It also contains other flavonoid antioxidants such as á and ß-carotenes, xanthins and lutein which enhance good vision and healthy bones and help in preventing oral cavity cancer. It contains reasonable amount of vitamin B complex like folates, thiamine, niacin, riboflavin and other essential minerals like iron, calcium, manganese. 21% of the recommended daily levels per 100 g of vitamin C requirement are found in tomato and it helps to detoxify the blood by removing free radicals (Rupprada 2013).

Diseases of Tomato

Several soil-borne fungal pathogens attack tomato plants and cause serious diseases such as root rot, crown rot and wilt (Montealegre et al. 2005)

Fungi

Septoria leaf spot, this is caused by the fungus *Septoria lycopersici* and is a foliar disease of tomato. Infection starts with the lower leaves after fruiting is set, so in most cases fruits are not affected but sometimes, the stems might be affected (Damicone and Bradenberger 2010). Infected leaves have grey sporulating centres in the midst of a dark spot or dark border (DAFF 2012). Crop rotation, weeding and destruction of infected parts are important for the control of this infection. Also using drip method instead of sprinkling method of irrigation reduces leaf wetness and susceptibility to the infection.

Early blight, this is caused by the fungus *Alternaria solani*. It is also known as *Alternaria* leaf spot or target spot. Early defoliation starts from the lower part of the plant thereby exposing fruits to sunscald (Damicone and Bradenberger 2010). Infected seeds and plant remains, rain and wind help to spread the infection. Round concentric black lesions appear on leaf. Small lumps appear on stems and leaves and tend to make flowers and small fruits to fall off as a result of the yellowing and wilting that takes place. Damaged plants or plants with wound are more susceptible to the infection (Naika et al. 2005). Crop rotation, good hygiene and sanitation can help to reduce disease severity (DAFF 2012).

Anthracnose, this is caused by the fungus *Colletotrichum coccodes*, is one of the most common fruit-attacking disease of tomato. Sclerotia are formed in the centres of the spots. It causes infection when rain or sprinkled water splashes on the fruit. The sclerotia can remain in the soil for up to 3 years causing infection. Symptom includes grey brown spot on the fruit. The disease is easily spread through infected fruit and in humid weather. Proper hygiene helps to control the spread. Using drip irrigation instead of overhead irrigation and plucking fruits immediately they are dry can also help to control the disease (Damicone and Bradenberger 2010).

Fusarium wilt, caused by *Fusarium oxysporum* and *F. solani* attacks the vascular tissues of the plant causing yellowing and wilting that progresses from the bottom to the top and on one side of the plant. When the stem or root is cut open, brown stain can be observed (Babalola 2010). Use of resistant cultivars, removing and burning infected plant parts and practicing crop rotation can reduce spread of the disease (Naika et al. 2005; DAFF 2012).

Verticillium albo-atrum and *V. dahliae*, the fungi that cause *Verticillium* wilt, can attack more than 200 plant species, especially solanaceous plants including potato, eggplant, pepper, strawberry, radish and watermelon. Its symptoms are close to that of *Fusarium* wilt but the appearance is slow and mainly occurs in areas with very cool climate. Crop rotation with crops other than solanaceous plants, proper hygiene and resistant cultivars will help reduce disease incidence (Naika et al. 2005).

Late blight, this is caused by the fungus *Phytophthora infestans* in cold or rainy weather and can destroy tomato plants. Grey or whitish fungal growth is seen on the underside of leaf, the leaf wilts and brown spot is seen on the fruits regular weeding, mulching to prevent water getting in contact with the plants and removing and burning of infected plants can reduce infection (Naika et al. 2005; Damicone and Bradenberger 2010; Miller et al. 2002). The effects of biocontrol agents on some of these fungal disease pathogens are listed in Table 7.1.

Table 7.1: Effect of Biocontrol Agents on Some Fungal Pathogens of Tomato Plants

Pathogen Suppressed	Plant Disease	Biocontrol Agent	Mechanism	Effect	Reference
P. infestans	Tomato Late blight	*Bacillus. pumilus* SE34	ISR	Improved plant growth	Yan et al. 2003
F. solani	Root rot disease	*Bacillus. subtilis, Trichoderma viride*	Mycoparasitism, competition and antibiosis	Biocontrol activity against the diseases and high yield of tomato.	Zaghloul 2007
Botrytis cinerea	Grey mold of tomato	*Microdochium dimerum*		*M. dimerum* was very effective inprotecting pruning wounds of tomato plants against *B. cinerea* and reduced disease severity significantly.	Bardin et al. 2008
F. oxysporum f.sp *radicis-lycopersici* (FORL)	Crown and root rot disease of tomato	*B. subtilis* EU07	Production of antibiotics, fengycin, bacillomycin and iturin	Growth of FORL was efficiently inhibited	Baysal et al. 2008
A. solani	Early blight disease of tomato	*Bacillus coagulans, B. pumilus, Serratia plymuthica, S. mercescens, Paenibacillus macerans*	Antifungal metabolites and competition	Reduced disease severity significantly on the field compared to control	Yazici et al. 2011
Non-pathogenic strain of *F. oxysporum* Fo47	Tomato wilt	Pathogenic strain of *F. oxysporum* f.sp *lycopercisi* Fol8	Induced systemic resistance	Improved growth and reduced infection	Aimé et al. 2008
Rhizoctonia solani	Damping-off of tomato	*B. subtilis* RB14-C	Antibiosis	Promoted plant growth and reduced disease severity	Szczech and Shoda 2006
Pythium ultimium, Macrophomina phaseolina, Pyricularia oryzae	Damping-off disease	*Pseudomonas fluorescens*	Antifungal metabolites-antibiosis	Inhibited growth of pathogens	Goud and Muralikrishnana 2009)
Pythium aphanidermatum	Damping-off disease of tomato	*Bacillus* spp.	Antifungal metabolites	Inhibited mycelia growth and improved plant growth	Intana et al. 2008

Bacteria

Bacterial spot, this is caused by the bacterium *Xanthomonas campestris* pv. *vesicatoria*, and infects both tomato and pepper. This bacterial disease is severe where there is heavy downpour and easily transmitted by the rain drops, insects, infected seeds and plant parts. Symptoms include small brown spots on infected leaves and fruits. To prevent this, hot treatment can be used on seeds (Miller et al. 2002), weeding and crop rotation is also helpful (Naika et al. 2005).

Bacterial specks, similar to bacterial spot are, caused by the bacterium *Pseudomonas syringae*. This bacterial pathogen of tomato does not only affect pepper or other solanaceous crops but may survive on non-host plants. Necrotic spots are noticed on leaves with smaller spots on fruits and may also come with heavy rain drops (Miller et al. 2002). Hot treatment on seeds and weeding will help reduce disease severity

Bacterial canker, caused by the bacterium *Clavibacter michiganensis* subsp. *michiganensis*, is a very serious bacterial disease. It leads to leaf spot or discolouration as a result of a burning effect on the leaves. Leaves turn yellow and wilt and spotting can also be seen on the fruits. Crop rotation with a non-host plant, soil and seed sterilization, proper hygiene and sanitation can help reduce disease severity (Naika et al. 2005; Miller et al 2002).

Bacterial wilt is caused by *Ralstonia solanacearum*. It is similar to *Fusarium* wilt but the leaves have no yellowing before wilting. When a portion of the stem is cut and put inside water there is this secretion of milky or whitish ooze. This helps to distinguish it from *Fusarium* wilt. The symptoms also include brown discoloration of the stem. It can be controlled by burning and destroying affected plant. Effects of biocontrol agents on some of these bacterial disease pathogens are listed in Table 7.2.

Virus

Tomato spotted wilt virus (TSWV) is transmitted by several species of the thrip. Common manifestations of TSWV are ring spots (yellow or brown rings) or other line patterns, black streaks on petioles or stems, necrotic leaf spots, or tip dieback. Prevention is the best way of controlling TSWV. Adequate control can also be achieved by using a combination of cultural, physical and chemical control. Remove infected plant materials and weeds that can harbour the vector (Hanssen et al. 2010).

Tomato yellow leaf curl virus is transmitted by the biotype B (or silverleaf) whitefly (*Bemisia argentifolii*) and the sweet potato whitefly (*Bemisia tabaci*). It is not transmitted by means of farm equipment or touching and cannot be spread by seeds. Symptoms include wrinkled leaves, curled up leaf margin and yellow veins in leaves. Infected plants should be removed, bagged and discarded. Pesticides are applied in a way that prevents build-up of pesticides-resistant flies, resistant cultivars are available and use of cultural control is also encouraged (Melzer et al. 2009; Hanssen 2010). The effects of biocontrol agents on some of these viral disease pathogens are listed in Table 7.3.

Nematodes

Root knot nematode caused is by *Meloidogyne* spp. Symptoms includes stunting, general unthriftiness, premature wilting, leaf chlorosis, gall formation etc. Control or management of nematodes include use of resistant cultivars, cultural practices and preplant nematicide treatments (Mohammed et al. 2008). Biocontrol agents have inhibitory effects on some of these nematode disease pathogens by colonizing the roots and suppressing their growth and number of galls (Table 7.4).

Effects of Microorganisms on Tomato Pathogens

Some of the effects of rhizobacteria on different tomato pathogens are reflected in research that has been published by other authors as stated below:

The reduction in disease incidence which was the greatest in tomato seedlings infested with bacterial spot diseases resulted from foliar application with *P. fluorescens* (Abo-Elyousr and El-Hendawy 2008). Also, when tomato seeds were treated with *P. fluorescens* and *P. chlororaphis*, the root gall of *M. incognita* race 1 in tomato cv rutgers were significantly reduced (Jonathan et al. 2000).

B. subtilis RB14-C has been shown to be effective in colonizing tomato plant roots and producing the antibiotic iturin A which is effective against *R. solani* and thus reduced the infection of damping-off in the plant (Szczech and Shoda 2006). In the fight against fungi, fungi have been effective. In order to stop the development of *B. cinerea* on wounds of tomato, the fungus *M. dimerum* has proved to be highly effective (Bardin et al. 2008).

Out of twenty-three bacterial isolates tested for their inhibitory effects against *A. solani*, five reduced the severity of early blight disease of tomato significantly and can be considered as biocontrol agents of *A. solani* in tomato (Yazici et al. 2011).

P. fluorescens inhibited the growth of *Pythium ultimum* causal agent of damping off by 80%; *M. phaseolina*, causal agent of root rot by 70% and *P. oryzae* causal agent of rice blast disease by 50%. It produced antifungal metabolites (crude antibiotics) (Goud and Muralikrishnan 2009).

According to (Baysal et al. 2008), a new strain of *B. subtilis* EU07 inhibited the growth of *F. oxysporum* f sp. *radicis-lycopersici* (FORL) the causal agent of crown and root rot of tomato. The growth of the seedlings in pot experiments showed highest average value for plant length in treatments by EU07.

Table 7.2: Effects of Biocontrol Agents on Some Bacterial Disease-causing Pathogens of Tomato Plants

Pathogen Suppressed	Plant Disease	Biocontrol Agent	Mechanism	Effect	Reference
R. solacearum	Tomato bacterial wilt	*Bacillus* spp	ISR	Improved plant growth	Jetiyanon 2002
X. campestris pv. *vesicatoria* strain 2	Bacterial spot of tomato	*Rahnella aquatilis*	Antibiosis	Reduction in the deleterious effect on tomato seedlings	El-Hendawy et al. 2005
Xanthomonas axonopochy	Bacterial spot disease of tomato	*P. fluorescens*	Antibiosis	Promoted plant growth and reduced disease severity	Abo-Elyousr et al 2008
C. michiganensis subsp. *michiganensis*	Bacterial canker of tomato	*P. fluorescens*	Competition	Improved plant growth by colonizing seedling' roots	Boudyach et al 2001

Table 7.3: Effect of Biocontrol Agents on Viral Pathogens of Tomato Plants

Pathogen Suppressed	Plant Disease	Biocontrol Agent	Mechanism	Effect	Reference
Cucumber mosaic virus (CMV)	Tomato leaf spot	*B. pumilus SE34; B. subtilisIN937b; acillus amyloliquefaciensIN937b*	ISR	Improved plant growth	Zehnder et al 2002
Tomato spotted wilt virus (TSWV)	Tomato spotted wilt	*P. fluorescens*	ISR	Significantly reduced incidence of disease	Kandan et al. 2002
Tomato yellow leaf curl virus and B. tabaci	Tomato yellow leaf curl	*Eretmocerus californicus; Encarsia formosa*	Parasitism	Reduction in the number of *B. tabaci* leading to reduction availability of the virus and so improved tomato production	Attard 2002

Table 7.4: Effects of Biocontrol Agents on Nematodes (or Meloidogyne Species) that Infest Tomato

Pathogen Suppressed	Plant Disease	Biocontrol Agent	Mechanism	Effect	Reference
Meloidogyne javanica	Root nematode	*P. fluorescens* CHAO	ISR-2, 4DAPG	Improved plant growth and reduction in galls	Siddiqui and Shaukat 2003
Meloidogyne. incognita	Root nematode	*P. fluorescens*	Colonization of roots and direct antagonism	Improved plant growth and reducing galling and nematode multiplication	Siddiqui 2004
M. incognita	Root knot nematodes of tomatoes	*Bacillus thurigiensis*	Competition	Bt7N controlled root knot by reducing the number of eggs of root nematodes by 76-84%	Mohammed et al. 2008
M. incognita	Root gall	*P. fluorescens* *Pseudomonas chlororaphis*	Antagonism	Improved plant growth and reduction in galling	Jonathan 2000

Effects of Microorganisms on Plant

Some microorganisms are very useful for plant growth directly and indirectly. Those microorganisms that live in the rhizosphere and enhance the growth of plant and also control diseases are known as Plant Growth-Promoting Rhizobacteria, (Ajilogba and Babalola 2013). Beneficial effects of microorganisms can be grouped as Plant growth promoting effect and biological control effect. (Whipps 2001; Vassilev et al. 2006).

Mechanisms of Plant Growth Promoting Effect of Biocontrol Agents

Plant growth promoting effect of biocontrol agents is a primary effect because of its direct effect in promoting plant growth. This effect can be seen in early seedling emergence, helping to colonize roots to ward off pathogens colonising them, promoting production of plant hormones such as gibberellins, auxins and cytokinins, enhancing plant mineral uptake and water utilization. This it does through the following mechanisms:

Phosphate solubilization: This involves the ability of some bacteria to make available to plants soluble phosphorus that has been liberated from insoluble Ca (PO4) in the soil. Some microorganisms that liberate and solubilize phosphate include *Agrobacteria, Aspergillus, Bacillus, Enterobacter, Pseudomonas* and *Trichoderma*. Studies have shown that when these microbes are applied around the roots of plants in soils, they promote the growth of such plants and protect the plants from pathogens and their effects (Ouahmane et al. 2007; Rudresh et al. 2005).

Hydrogen cyanide production (*HCN*): Some microorganisms produce Hydrogen cyanide (HCN) which effectively blocks the cytochrome oxidase pathway and is highly toxic to all aerobic microorganisms at picomolar concentrations (Pal and Gardener 2006). Some of the Rhizobacteria involved in the production of HCN are *Bacillus* (50%) and *Pseudomonas* (88.89%) and they produce it in the plant root noodles and rhizospheric soils (Ahmad et al. 2008; Charest et al. 2005a).

Nitrogen fixation: Nitrogen-fixing organisms are generally active in the rhizosphere. They make atmospheric nitrogen available to plants and are also referred to as plant growth-promoters. Some of these nitrogen-fixing microorganisms are *Rhizobium* spp, *Azospirillum* spp, *Azotobacter* spp, *Azolla* spp and *Cyanobacteria* spp (Shridhar 2012). Others that are non-symbiotic nitrogen–fixers are *Bacillus* spp, *Pseudomonas* spp, *Enterobacter* spp and *Clostridium* spp.

Siderophore production: All living things require iron for growth and when it is insufficient, the issue of competition comes up. Under this condition of insufficient rhizospheric iron, rhizobacteria produce siderophore which is a low-molecular-weight compound to competitively acquire ferric ion (Whipps 2001). Microorganisms produce and secrete siderophores to sequester iron (Pérez-Miranda et al. 2007). Siderophore solubilises iron in the environment and make it available to the plant. It is a high-affinity chelating agent for ferric iron (Crumbliss and Boukhalfa 2002) and it helps in inhibiting the growth of phytopathogens (Qing-Ping and Jian-Guo 2011). *B. subtilis* CAS 15 produced siderophore in pepper plant where it reduced the incidence of Fusarium wilt and promoted growth (Yu et al. 2011). Ability to sequester iron differs from one bacterial siderophore to another but since pathogenic fungi siderophore have a relatively lower affinity for iron they are deprived of this essential element. Sometimes some Rhizobacteria go further to sequester iron from heterologous siderophore of cohabiting microorganisms (Whipps 2001).

Production of Indole acetic acid (IAA): IAA is one of the most physiologically active auxins which is a plant hormone that regulates the amount, type, and direction of plant growth. *Rhizobium* spp is an example of microorganisms that release IAA which helped to promote growth and pathogenesis in plants (Mandal et al. 2007). While working with chickpea, all isolates of *Bacillus* spp, *Pseudomonas* spp and *Azotobacter* spp produced IAA while only 85.7% of *Rhizobium* was able to produce it and promoted growth (Joseph et al. 2007).

Production of 1-aminocyclopropane-1-carboxylic acid (ACC)-deaminase

Ethylene is one of plant hormones that are gaseous and it helps to regulate a number of developmental processes in plants. ACC is an immediate precursor of ethylene and it can be exuded from plant roots. Ethylene helps to break seed dormancy in many plants but after the seed has germinated, any further increase in the level of ethylene inhibits root elongation (Contesto et al. 2008). Increased growth and yield of plants have been reported with plants that were inoculated with rhizobacteria containing ACC-deaminase (Shaharoona et al. 2007; Zahir et al. 2009).

Antagonistic and Biological Control Effects of some Biocontrol Agents on Different Plants

Biological control is the use of microorganisms to suppress or control diseases and infections in plants. These microorganisms might be residents in the soil or introduced into the soil. Some of the Rhizobacteria shown to have biocontrol abilities include; *Pseudomonas* spp., *Bacillus* spp., *Acinetobacter* spp., *Enterobacter* spp., *Micrococcus* spp., (Kumar et al. 2012).

Workers at Montana State university found two strains of *B. pumilus* (strains 203-6 and 203-7) and one of *B. mycoides* (strain Bac J) that reduced the severity of Cercospora leaf spot of sugar beet, caused by *Cercospora beticola* sacc (Kloepper et al. 2004). The plant root-colonizing *B. amyloliquefaciens* strain F2B42 is a naturally occurring isolate and has the ability to stimulate plant growth and suppress plant pathogens (Idris et al. 2007a). Research has it that on several hosts, specific strains of the species *B. amyloliquefaciens, Bacillus cereus, Bacillus mycoides, Bacillus pasteurii, B. pumilus, Bacillus sphaericus* and *B. subtilis,* has shown significant reductions in disease incidences and severity (Kloepper et al. 2004).

Bacillus-based biological control agents (BCAs) have great potential in integrated pest management (IPM) systems (plant diseases inclusive). The biocontrol potential of *Bacillus* spp. as important agents to combat root and soil borne pathogen has been reported in many crops including chickpea. Antagonistic and antifungal activities against Fusarium wilt caused by *F. oxysporum* have been shown especially by several *Bacillus* spp isolated from the rhizosphere of chickpea (Idris et al. 2007a). In terms of plant disease control, biocontrol effects have been observed in sporulating gram positive bacteria like spp (Kloepper et al. 2004).

Bacillus spp was shown to have biocontrol potential against phytopathogenic fungi. For example *B. subtilis* was evaluated for biocontrol activities against *Botrytis cinerea*, a phytopathogenic fungus causing grey mold rot of tomatoes after harvest. The bacterium effectively suppressed the disease at 4°C and 23°C (Siripornvisal 2010). Antagonistic activity by *B. amyloliquefaciens* LBM 5006 was observed against phytopathogenic fungi, including *Aspergillus* spp, *Bipolaris sorokiniana* and *Fusarium* spp and pathogenic bacteria (Benitez et al. 2010).

Biological control effects in most cases have secondary effect on the plant in that it helps to suppress the growth of plant pathogens and invariably promotes growth. Some of the mechanisms used to suppress or inhibit the growth of plant pathogens and diseases are:

Detoxification and degradation of virulence factors: Detoxification and degradation of virulence factors is one of the mechanism of biological control for example, albicidin is a toxin produced by *Xanthomonas albilineans* and which can be detoxified by certain biocontrol agents. This involves a protein that is produced and can irreversibly detoxify albicidin as a result of the occurrence of an esterase in *Pantoea dispersa*. This protein can also bind the toxin in both *Klebsiella oxytoca* and *Alcaligenes denitrificans* in an irreversible manner. Also, strains of *Burkholderia cepacia* and *Ralstonia solanacearum* have been observed to hydrolyse a phytotoxin known as fusaric acid, produced by various *Fusarium* species (Compant et al. 2005).

Parasitism and Lytic enzyme production: Parasitism depends on the production of extracellular lytic enzymes and can be observed when pathogenic fungi degrade cell walls. This can be seen in some microorganisms like *Bacillus* degrading chitin because of its ability to produce enzymes that can break it down. Chitin is a major component of the cell wall of fungi and so *Bacillus* can serve as a biocontrol agent against plant fungal by degrading its chitinase cell wall (Kouki et al. 2012).

Antibiosis: Many biological control agents such as *Trichoderma* spp. and *Bacillus* spp. could be effectively used in suppressing diseases caused by *Fusarium* spp, *Drechslera halodes* and *Rhizoctonia solani* as reported by many workers (Abdel-Monaim 2010; Hashem and Hamada 2002). A lot of *Bacillus* strains have been considered to be better biocontrol agents compared to fungal and gram negative bacterial biocontrol agents because of their ability to produce spores which invariably enhance their ability to withstand harsh environmental conditions. Also they can produce several broad spectrum antibiotics which can suppress the growth of a wide range of bacterial pathogens (Cui et al. 2012). In addition to their antibiotic properties, *Bacillus* spp enhance their antagonistic effects against fungal pathogens by competition for basic nutrients and space (Khokhar et al. 2012). Also, some bacterial antagonists produce antifungal antibiotics (Sadfi et al. 2002).

Induced systemic resistance (*ISR*): When some plants are infected by a disease, they respond with a signal that is salicylic-dependent. This normally led them to express a resistance that is broad-spectrum and long-lasting which is also efficient against bacteria, fungi and viruses. This is because the endogenous levels of salicylic acid (SA) normally increase in the phloem locally and systemically after infection before the occurrence of ISR but in some cases, SA is produced in non-infected parts and this also leads to systemic expression of ISR (Heil and Bostock 2002). In a natural situation where the pathogen for a particular infection is more than one, the level of the basal resistance from the host is increased as a result of induced resistance (Van Loon and Glick 2004). In greenhouse or field trials, elicitation of ISR by some strains of *Bacillus* spp has been demonstrated on *Arabidopsis* spp, bell pepper, cucumber, loblolly pine, muskmelon, sugar beet, watermelon, tobacco, tomato and two tropical crops (green kuang futsoi and long cayenne pepper) (Kloepper et al. 2004).

Adverse Effects of Microorganisms Used as Biocontrol Agents on Nontarget Organisms

Some of the adverse effects identified with the use of microorganisms for the biological control of plant diseases and seen as safety issues (hazards) include:

Allergenicity to humans and other animals: Allergenicity is a concern because of direct exposure of workers to the microorganisms but it is not a public health problem because most workers in agricultural settings are exposed to all kinds of allergenic particles. So in using biocontrol agents, allergy is not a new problem but it should be looked into during product formulation and development as safety issues (Hunsberger 2000).

Displacement of non-target microorganisms: Competitive displacement is defined as the removal of a formerly established species from a habitat as a result of direct or indirect competitive interactions with another species. This can be through competition for carbon or energy; it can also be competition through the activity of PGPR that produce siderophore and make iron unavailable to root pathogens (Reitz and Trumble 2002).

Pathogenicity to non-target organisms: This is one of the effects of using biocontrol which most people are concerned about. This could mean that the microbial biocontrol agent can also cause disease or is pathogenic to other beneficial organisms. It could also be that apart from helping the plant or pest to be able to induce disease resistant, it could cause disease in other plants or living organisms in that community. This is the most important issue where pathogenicity is concerned. For example, as far as pathogenicity to non-target organism is concerned no harmful effects have been reported on non-target organisms including mammals in using registered strains of *Bacillus* species for biocontrol (Lacey et al. 2001).

Toxigenicity to non-target organisms: Some microorganisms produce antibiotics to help inhibit the growth of pathogens. These antibiotics can become toxic to non-target microorganisms. Even though this potential is there, so far there are no documented examples yet; perhaps because most of these antibiotics are produced in minute quantities and are basically used against the target organisms. For example, the research conducted using wheat take-all (*Gaeumannomyces graminis* (Sacc.) Arx & Olivier var. tritici Walker) showed that *P. fluorescens* strain Q8r1-96 2-79 produced 2,4-diacetylphloroglucinol (2, 4-DAPG) of 1850 µg/mL (Okubara and Bonsall 2008) and which showed no effect on the establishment of mycorrhizal fungi in the rhizosphere (Khan 2006).

Finally, apart from allergenicity, these other attributes such as displacement of non-target microorganisms, pathogenicity to non-target organisms and toxigenicity to non-target organisms are the same attributes that contribute to the efficacy and usefulness of microbial biocontrol agents.

Fate of Microbial Biocontrol Agents

Looking at the various effects of using biocontrol for diseases in tomato plants, the non-use of microbial agents for disease control could be due to the following reasons:

Lack of fundamental information on the various microorganisms to be used as biocontrol is an issue that should be addressed. More research and knowledge into the ecology of these various microorganisms would improve on the technical difficulties experienced so far in the use of microorganisms for biocontrol.

Another important problem hindering the usage of biocontrol to control plant disease is the fact that some of the microbial formulations may not be viable in long term plant disease controls (Handelsman 2002).

Finally, the cost of product development and meeting with the regulatory agencies is high compared to the limitation of the market and its usability by farmers (Handelsman 2002).

Future Prospects

Tomato is very important to nutrition and health. The different diseases that affect them always affect their yield, taste and nutrient content. The use of microorganisms to increase plant growth and invariably yield is very crucial in reducing environmental pollution. The effects of these microorganisms can be seen in both plant growth and disease control. So far, there are no known examples of documented adverse effects to animals or people that might eat microbially treated plant parts. More research into the management of these diseases using biocontrol may be carried out. Farmers need to be oriented, taught and educated on the different ways to protect their tomato plants and fruits from being infected and destroyed by these infections. Preplanting methods that will discourage these diseases will be included in the training and also, planting, harvesting, preservation, transporting and marketing procedures that will also discourage and ameliorate the situation should also be included in such trainings. Integrating the use of microorganisms into management of tomato diseases is a step further into food security as a part of the Millennium Development Goals.

REFERENCES

Abdel-Monaim, M.F. (2010): Integrated Management of Damping-off, Root and/or Stem Rot Diseases of Chickpea with Sowing Date, Host Resistance and Bioagents. Egyptian Journal Phytopathology, 38: 45-61.

Abo-Elyousr, A., Kamal, A. M. and El-Hendawy, H.H. (2008): Integration of *Pseudomonas fluorescens* and Acibenzolar-S-methyl to Control Bacterial Spot Disease of Tomato. Crop Protection, 27: 1118-1124.

Ahmad, F.A., Ahmad, I. and Khan, M. S. (2008): Screening of Free-living Rhizospheric Bacteria for Their Multiple Plant Growth Promoting Activities. Microbiological Research, 163: 173-181.

Aimé, S., Cordier, C., Alabouvette, C. and Olivain, C. (2008): Comparative Analysis of PR Gene Expression in Tomato Inoculated with Virulent *Fusarium oxysporum* f. sp. *lycopersici* and the Biocontrol Strain *F. oxysporum* Fo47, Physiological and Molecular Plant Pathology, 73: 9-15.

Ajilogba, C.F. and Babalola, O.O. (2013): Integrated Management Strategies for Tomato Fusarium Wilt, Biocontrol Science, 18(3): 117-127.

Attard, D. (2002): Methods of Controlling Tomato Yellow Leaf Curl Virus (TYLCV) and its Vector *Bemisia tabaci* in Maltese Island, Bulletin OEPP/EPPO, pp: 39-40.

Babalola, O.O. (2010): Pectinolytic and Cellulolytic Enzymes Enhance *Fusarium compactum* Virulence on Tubercles Infection of Egyptian Broomrape, International Journal of Microbiology Article ID 273264, 7 pages doi: 10.1155/2010/273264.

Babalola, O.O. and Glick, B.R. (2012a): The Use of Microbial Inoculants in African Agriculture: Current Practice and Future Prospects, Journal of Food Agriculture and Environment, 10: 540-549.

Babalola, O.O. and Glick, B.R. (2012b): Indigenous African Agriculture and Plant Associated Microbes: Current Practice and Future Transgenic Prospects, Science Research Essays, 7: 2431-2439.

Bardin, M., Fargues, J. and Nicot, P.C. (2008): Compatibility Between Bio pesticides used to Control Grey Mould, Powdery Mildew and Whitefly on Tomato, Biological Control, 46: 476-483.

Baysal, Ö., Çali°kan, M. and Ye°ilova, Ö. (2008): An Inhibitory Effect of a New *Bacillus subtilis* strain (EU07) Against *Fusarium oxysporum* f. sp. *radicis-lycopersici*. Physiological and Molecular Plant Pathology, 73: 25-32.

Benitez, L.B., Velho, R.V., Lisboa, M.P., da Costa Medina, L.F. and Brandelli, A. (2010): Isolation and Characterization of Antifungal Peptides Produced by *Bacillus amyloliquefaciens* LBM5006, Journal of Microbiology, 48: 791-797.

Boudyach, E.H., Fatmi, M., Akhayat, O., Benizri, E., Aoumar, A. and Ben, A. (2001): Selection of Antagonistic Bacteria of *Clavibacter michiganensis* subsp. *michiganensis* and Evaluation of Their Efficiency Against Bacterial Canker of Tomato, Biocontrol Science and Technology, 11: 141-149.

Bramley, P.M. (2000): Is Lycopene Beneficial to Human Health? Photo-chemistry, 54: 233-236.

Boyer, L. (2011): Best antioxidants. http://www.livestrong.com/article/394965-best-antioxidants/. Assessed 04 July 2012

Charest, M.H., Beauchamp, C.J. and Antoun, H. (2005): Effects of the Humic Substances of De-inking Paper Sludge on the Antagonism Between Two Compost Bacteria and *Pythium ultimum,* FEMS Microbiology Ecology, 52: 219-227.

Chetelat, R.T., Pertuze,´ R.A., Fau´ndez, Graham. E.B. and Jones, C.M. (2009): Distribution, Ecology and Reproductive Biology of Wild Tomatoes and Related Nightshades from the Atacama Desert Region of Northern Chile, Euphytica, 167: 77-93.

Compant, S., Duffy, B., Nowak, J., Clément, C. and Ait Barka, E. (2005): Use of Plant Growth-promoting Bacteria for Biocontrol of Plant Diseases: Principles, Mechanisms of Action, and Future Prospects, Applied and Environmental Microbiology, 71: 4951-4959.

Contesto, C., Desbrosses, G., Lefoulon, C., Bena, G., Borel, F., Galland, M., Gamet, L., Varoquaux, F. and Touraine, B. (2008): Effects of Rhizobacterial ACC Deaminase Activity on *Arabidopsis* Indicate that Ethylene Mediates Local Root Responses to Plant Growth-promoting Rhizobacteria, Plant Science, 175: 178-189.

Crumbliss, H. and Boukhalfa, A. L. (2002): Chemical Aspects of Siderophore Mediated Iron Transport, Biometals, 15: 325-339.

Cui, T., Chai, H. and Jiang, L. (2012): Isolation and Partial Characterization of an Antifungal Protein Produced by *Bacillus licheniformis* BS-3, Molecules, 17: 7336-7347.

DAFF (2012) Production Guidelines for Tomato, Directorate of Agricultural Services, Pretoria, pp. 1-22.

Damicone, J. and Bradenberger, L. (2010): Common Diseases of Tomatoes Part I. Diseases Caused by Fungi Oklahoma State University—Division of Agricultural Sciences and Natural Resources—Cooperative Extension Service.

Dukare, A.S., Prasana, R., Dubey, S.C., Nain, L., Chaudhary, V., Singh, R. and Saxena, A.K. (2011): Evaluating Novel Microbe Amended Composts as Biocontrol Agents in Tomato, Crop Protection, 30: 436-442.

El-Hendawy, H. H., Osman, M.E. and Sorour, N.M. (2005): Biological Control of Bacterial Spot of Tomato Caused by *Xanthomonas campestris* pv. *vesicatoria* by *Rahnella aquatilis*, Microbiological Research, 160: 343-352.

FAO (2012): Agriculture Data, Food and Agriculture Organisation of the United Nations. Available at http://faostat.fao.org

Goud, M.P. and Muralikrishnana, V. (2009): Biological Control of Three Phytopathogenic Fungi by *Pseudomonas fluorescens* Isolated from Rhizosphere, Internet Journal of Microbiology, 7 doi: 10.5580/c13

Handelsman, J. (2002): Future Trends in Biocontrol. In: Gnanamanickam, SS (ed) Biological Control of Crop Diseases, Marcel Dekker, Inc, New York, pp. 443-448.

Hanson, P.M., Yang, R., Wu, J., Chen, J., Ledesma, D., Tsou, S.C.S. and Lee, T.C. (2004): Variation for Antioxidant Activity and Antioxidants in Tomato, Journal of American Society of Horticultural Science, 129: 704-711.

Hanssen, I.M., Lapidot, M. and Thomma, B.P.H.J. (2010): Emerging Viral Diseases of Tomato Crops, American Phytopathology Society, 23: 539-548.

Hashem, M., Abo-Elyousr, A. and Kamal, A. (2002): Evaluation of Two Biologically Active Compounds for Control of Wheat Root Rot and its Causal Pathogens. Microbiology 30: 233-239.

Heber, D. and Lu, Q-Y. (2002): Overview of Mechanism of Action of Lycopene. Experimental Biology and Medicine, 227: 920-923.

Heil, M. and Bostock, R.M. (2002): Induced Systemic Resistance (ISR) Against Pathogens in the Context of Induced Plant Defences, Annals of Botany, 89: 503-512.

Holmberg, A.J. (2011): Tracking the Fate of Biocontrol Microorganisms in the Environment Using Intrinsic SCAR Markers. Dissertation, Swedish University of Agricultural Sciences.

Hunsberger, A. (2000): Bt (*Bacillus thuringiensis*), A Microbial Insecticide, ENY-275, University of Florida publication Florida pp. 6.

Idris, H.A., Labuschagne, N. and Korsten, L. (2007): Screening Rhizobacteria for Biological Control of Fusarium Root and Crown rot of sorghum in Ethiopia, Biological Control, 40: 97-106.

Intana, W., Yenjit, P., Suwanno, T., Sattasakulchai, S., Suwanoon, M. and Chamswarng, C. (2008): Efficacy of Antifungal Metabolites of *Bacillus* spp. for Controlling Tomato Damping-off Caused by *Pythium aphanidermatum*, Walailak Journal of Science and Technology, 5: 29-38.

Jetiyanon, K. and Kloepper, J.W. (2002): Mixture of Plant Growth-promoting Rhizobacteria for Induction of Systemic Resistance Against Multiple Plant Diseases. Biological Control, 24: 285-291.

Johansen, A., Knudsen, I.M.B., Binnerup, S.J., Winding, A., Johansen, J.E., Jensen, L.E., Andersen, K.S., Svenning, M.M. and Bonde, T.A. (2005): Non-target Effects of the Microbial Control Agents *Pseudomonas fluorescens* DR54 and *Clonostachys rosea* IK726 in Soils Cropped with Barley Followed by Sugar Beet: A Greenhouse Assessment, Soil Biology and Biochemistry, 37: 2225-2239.

Jonathan, E.I., Basker, K.R., Abdel-Alim, F.F., Vrain, T.C. and Dickson, D.W. (2000): Biological Control of *Meloidogyne incognita* on Tomato and Banana with Rhizobacteria, *Actinomycetes* and *Pasteuria penetrans*, Nematropica, 30: 231-240.

Joseph, B., Patra, R.R. and Lawrence, R. (2007): Characterization of Plant Growth Promoting Rhizobacteria Associated with Chickpea (*Cicer arietinum* L), International Journal of Plant Production, 1: 141-152.

Kandan, A., Commare, R., Nandakumar, R., Ramiaii, M., Raguchander, T. and Samiyappan, R. (2002): Induction of Phenylpropanoid Metabolism by *Pseudomonas fluorescens* Against Tomato Spotted wilt Virus in Tomato, Folia Microbiology, 47: 121-129.

Khan, A.G. (2006): Mycorrhizoremediation—An Enhanced Form of Phytoremediation, Journal of Zhejiang University of Science B.,7: 503-514.

Khokhar, M.K., Gupta, R. and Sharma, R. (2012): Biological Control of Plant Pathogens Using Biotechnological Aspects: A Review, Science Reports, 1: 277.

Kiewnick, S. (2007): Practicalities of Developing and Registering Microbial Biological Control Agents, CAB Reviews: Perspectives in Agriculture, Veterinary Science, Nutrition and Natural Resources, 2: 1-11.

Kloepper, J.W., Ryu, C.M. and Zhang, S. (2004): Induced Systemic Resistance and Promotion of Plant Growth by *Bacillus sp*., Phytopathology, 94: 1259-1266.

Kouki, S., Saidi, N., Ben Rajeb, A., Brahmi, M., Bellila, A., Fumio, M., Hefiène, A., Jedidi, N., Downer, J. and Ouzari, H. (2012): Control of *Fusarium* Wilt of Tomato Caused by *Fusarium oxysporum* F. Sp. *radicis-lycopersici* Using Mixture of Vegetable and *Posidonia Oceanica* Compost, Applied Environmental Soil Science, doi:10.1155/2012/239639.

Kumar, A., Kumar, A., Shikha, D., Sandip, P., Chandani, P. and Sushila, N. (2012): Isolation, Screening and Characterization of Bacteria from Rhizospheric Soils for Different Plant Growth Promotion (PGP) Activities: an in vitro Study, Recent Research in Science and Technology, 4: 1-5.

Lacey, L.A., Frutos, R., Kaya, H.K. and Vail, P. (2001): Insect Pathogens as Biological Control Agents: Do They have a Future? Biological Control, 21: 230-248.

Leuschner, R.G.K., Robinson, T.P., Hugas, M., Cocconelli, P.S., Richard-Forget, F., Klein, G., Licht, T.R., Nguyen-The, C., Querol, A., Richardson, M., Suarez, J.E., Vlak, J.M. and von Wright, A. (2010): Qualified Presumption of Safety (QPS): A Generic Risk Assessment Approach for Biological Agents Notified to the European Food Safety Authority (EFSA), Trends in Food Science and Technology, 21: 425-435.

Mandal, S.M., Mondal, K.C., Dey, S. and Pati, B. R. (2007): Optimization of Cultural and Nutritional Conditions for Indol-3-Acetic acid (IAA) Production by a *Rhizobium* sp. Isolated from Rot Nodules of *Vigna mungo* (L) Hepper, Research Journal of Microbiology, 2: 239-246.

Melzer, M.J., Ogata, D.Y., Fukuda, S.K., Shimabuku, R., Borth, W.B., Sether, D. M. and Hu, J.S. (2009): Tomato Yellow Leaf Curl. Plant Disease. The College of Tropical Agriculture and Human Resources (CTAHR), Manoa.

Miller, E.C., Hardley, C.W., Schwartz, S.J., Erdman, J.W., Boileau, T.M.W. and Clinton, S.K. (2002): Lycopene, Tomato Products and Prostate Cancer Prevention. Have we Established Casualty? Pure and Applied Chemistry, 74: 1435-1441.

Mohammed, S.H., El Sarey, M.A., Enan, M.R., Ibrahim, N.E., Ghareeb, A. and Moustafa, S.A. (2008): Biocontrol Efficiency of *Bacillus thuringiensis* Toxins Against Root-knot Nematode, *Meloidogyne incognita*, Cell Molecular Biology, 7: 57-66.

Montealegre, J.R., Herrera, R., Velasquez, J.C., Silva, P., Besoain, X. and Perez, L. M. (2005): Biocontrol of Root and Crown Rot in Tomatoes Under Greenhouse Conditions Using *Trichoderma harzianum* and *Paenibacillus lentimorbus*. Additional Effect of Solarization, Electron Journal of Biotechnology, 6: 115-127.

Naika, S., Van Lidt de Jeude, J., Goffau, M., Hilmi, M. and Van Dam, B. (2005): Cultivation of Tomato: Production, Processing and Marketing. In: Van Dam B (ed). Agromisa and CTA, Wageningen, The Netherlands.

Okubara, P.A. and Bonsall, R.F. (2008): Accumulation of *Pseudomonas*-derived 2, 4- diacetylphloroglucinol on Wheat Seedling Roots is Influenced by Host Cultivar, Biological Control 46: 322-331.

Ouahmane, L., Thioulouse, J., Hafidi, M., Prin, Y., Ducousso, M., Galiana, A., Plenchette, C., Kisa, M. and Duponnois, R. (2007): Soil Functional Diversity and P Solubilization from Rock Phosphate After Inoculation with Native or Allochtonous Arbuscular Mycorrhizal Fungi, Forest Ecology and Management, 241: 200-208.

Pal, K.K. and Gardener, B.M. (2006): Biological Control of Plant Pathogens, The Plant Health Instructor, 10: 1094.

Panthee, D. R. and Chen, F. (2010): Genomics of Fungal Disease Resistance in Tomato, Current Genomics, 11: 30-39.

Pérez-Miranda, S., Cabirol, N., George-Téllez, R., Zamudio-Rivera, L.S. and Fernández, F.J. (2007): O-CAS, a Fast and Universal Method for Siderophore Detection, Journal of Microbiological Methods, 70: 127-131.

Philouze, J and Hedde, L. (1993): Tomato Available at http://www.oecd.org/env/ehs/biotrack/1946244.pdf, (Assessed on 13 September 2013)

Qing-Ping, H. and Jian-Guo, X. (2011): A Simple Double-layered Chrome Azurol S agar (SD-CASA) Plate Assay to Optimize the Production of Siderophores by a Potential Biocontrol Agent Bacillus, African Journal of Microbiological Research, 5: 4321-4327.

Reitz, S.R. and Trumble, J.T. (2002): Competitive Displacement Among Insects and Arachnids, Annual Review of Entomology, 47: 435-465.

Rudresh, D.L., Shivaprakash, M.K. and Prasad, R.D. (2005): Tricalcium Phosphate Solubilizing Abilities of *Trichoderma* spp. in Relation to P uptake and Growth and Yield Parameters of Chickpea (*Cicer arietinum* L.), Canadian Journal of Microbiology, 51: 217-222.

Rudrappa, U. (2013): Tomato Nutrition Facts and Health Benefits, www.nutrition-and-you.com/tomato.htmlý

Sadfi, N., Cherif, M., Hajlaoui, M.R., Boudabbous, A. and Bélanger, R. (2002): Isolation and Partial Purification of Antifungal Metabolites Produced by *Bacillus cereus*, Annals of Microbiology, 52: 323-337.

Shaharoona, B., Jamro, G.M., Zahir, Z.A., Arshad, M. and Memon, K.S. (2007): Effectiveness of Various *Pseudomonas* spp. and *Burkholderia caryophylli* Containing ACC-deaminase for Improving Growth and Yield of Wheat (*Triticum aestivum* L.), Journal of Microbiology and Biotechnology, 17: 1300-1307.

Shridhar, B.S. (2012): Review: Nitrogen Fixing Microorganisms. International Journal of Microbiology Research, 3: 46-52.

Siddiqui, I.A. and Shaukat, S.S. (2003): Effects of *Pseudomonas aeruginosa* on the Diversity of Culturable Microfungi and Nematodes Associated with Tomato: Impact on Root-knot Disease and Plant Growth, Soil Biology and Biochemistry, 35: 1359-1368.

Siddiqui, Z. (2004): Effects of Plant Growth Promoting Bacteria and Composed Organic Fertilizers on the Reproduction of *Meloidogyne incognita* and Tomato Growth, Bioresource Technology, 95: 223-227.

Siripornvisal, S. (2010): Biocontrol Efficacy of *Bacillus subtilis* BCB3-19 Against Tomato Gray Mold. KMITL Science and Technology Journal, 10: 37-44.

Szczech, M. and Shoda, M. (2006): The Effect of Mode of Application of *Bacillus subtilis* RB14-C on its Efficacy as a Biocontrol Agent Against *Rhizoctonia solani*, Journal of Phytopathology, 154: 370-377.

Van Dyke, M.I. and Prosser, J.I. (2000): Enhanced Survival of *Pseudomonas fluorescens* in Soil Following Establishment of Inoculum in a Sterile Soil Carrier. Soil Biology and Biochemistry, 32: 1377-1382.

Van Loon, L.C. and Glick, B.R. (2004): Increased Plant Fitness by Rhizobacteria. In: Sandermann H (ed) Molecular Ecotoxicology of Plants. Springer, Berlin, pp. 177-205.

Vassilev, N., Vassileva, M. and Nikolaeva, I. (2006): Simultaneous P-solubilizing and Biocontrol Activity of Micro-organisms: Potentials and Future Trends. Applied Microbiology and Biotechnology, 71: 137-144.

Whipps, J. M. (2001): Microbial Interactions and Biocontrol in the Rhizosphere. Journal of Experimental Botany 52: 487-511.

Whiting, D., O'Meara, C. and Wilson, C. (2012): Growing Tomatoes In: Colorado Master Gardener Garden Notes, pp. 1-8.

Xiang, S.R., Cook, M., Saucier, S., Gillespie, P., Socha, R., Scroggins, R. and Beaudette, L.A. (2010): Development of Amplified Fragment Length Polymorphism-derived Functional Strain-specific Markers to Assess the Persistence of 10 Bacterial Strains in Soil Microcosms, Applied Environmental Microbiology, 76: 7126-7135.

Yan, Z., Reddy, M.S., Ryu, C., McInroy, J.A., Wilson, M. and Kloepper, J.W. (2002): Induced Systemic Protection Against Tomato Late Blight Elicited by Plant Growth-Promoting Rhizobacteria, Phytopathology, 92: 1329-1333.

Yazici, S., Yanar, Y. and Karaman, I. (2011): Evaluation of Bacteria for Biological Control of Early Blight Disease of Tomato, African Journal of Biotechnology, 10: 1573-1577.

Yu, X., Ai, C., Xin, L. and Zhou, G. (2011): The Siderophore-producing Bacterium, *Bacillus subtilis* CAS15, has a Biocontrol Effect on *Fusarium* Wilt and Promotes the Growth of Pepper, European Journal of Soil Biology 47: 138-145.

Zahir, A.Z., Ghani, U., Naveed, M., Nadeem, S.M. and Asghar, H.N. (2009): Comparative Effectiveness of *Pseudomonas* and *Serratia* sp. Containing ACC-deaminase for Improving Growth and Yield of Wheat (*Triticum aestivum* L.) Under Salt-stressed Conditions, Archea Microbiolology, 191: 415-424.

Functional Interactions of Diazotrophs and Antagonistic Rhizobacteria in Sustainable Development of Agricultural Products

Upendra Kumar[1]*; S.K.Gupta[2]
Tushar Kanti Dangar[1]; Kannepalli Annapurna[3]

1. Microbiology Laboratory, Crop Production Division, Central Rice Research Institute, Cuttack –753 006, Odisha, (India)
2. Directorate of Cold Water Fisheries Research, (DCFR) Chhirapani Fish Farm, District – Champawat, Uttrakhand – 262 523, (India).
3. Division of Microbiology, Indian Agricultural Research Institute, New Delhi – 110 012 (India).

ABSTRACT

Rhizosphere and soil bacteria are important drivers in nearly all biochemical cycles in terrestrial ecosystems and participate in maintaining health and productivity of soil in agriculturally managed systems. Fundamental research on plant growth promoting rhizobacteria (PGPR) in India has a long history. In the 1980's the main interest was in leguminous symbiotic diazotrophs and rice-blue green algae (BGA) interaction. Presently, scientific interests are focused on mechanisms of actions, active compounds and genetic regulation in the major PGPR groups like *Azospirillum, Bacillus* and *Pseudomonas* in monocots including rice. There has been much research interest in PGPR as biofertilizer and biocontrol that is why an increasing number of PGPR are being commercialized for various crops. In this chapter, we have discussed various endo- and rhizobacteria which act as PGPR, their mechanisms and the desirable properties exhibited by them to increase production and productivity of rice crop.

Keywords: Biocontrol, Biofertilizer, Diazotrophs, PGPR, Rice.

INTRODUCTION

Rice has a paramount importance in human diet and considered to be staple food for half the human population. Rice is grown in both wetland and upland cultures, with about 85% of the planet's total area of rice being in flooded wetlands. In upland culture where soils are drained by gravity, the rice roots are more aerobic and N_2 might be assimilated as NO_3^- after fertilizer addition or mineralization of organic N. In addition, aerobic diazotrophs may fix atmospheric N_2. In wetland culture of flooded paddies, N is mainly available to rice plants from soil water as NH_4^+, requiring less energy to assimilate into amino acids than NO_3^- (Kennedy,1992).

Rhizobacterial strains increase plant growth after inoculation of seeds and therefore, called "Plant growth promoting rhizobacteria" (Kloepper et al, 1980). The mechanisms of growth promotion by these PGPR are complex and appear to comprise both changes in the microbial balance in the rhizosphere and alterations in host plant physiology (Glick et al, 1999). Plant growth promoting rhizobacteria survive and colonize the rhizosphere of all field crops. They promote plant growth by secreting auxins, gibberellins and cytokinin. PGPR has a significant impact on plant growth and development in both, direct or indirect ways. Indirect promotion of plant growth occurs when bacteria prevent some of the deleterious effects of a phytopathogenic organism by one or more mechanisms. On the other hand, the direct promotion of plant growth by PGPR generally entails providing the plant with compounds that are synthesized by the bacterium or facilitating the uptake of nutrients from the environment (Glick, 1995; Glick et al, 1999). Table 8.1 depicts the different functional traits of a typical PGPR.

Table 8.1: Growth Promoting Substances Released by PGPR

PGPR	Plant Growth Promoting Traits	References
1	2	3
Rhiozobium leguminosarum, Mesorhizobium sp., *Rhizobium* sp.	IAA, HCN, ammonia and siderophore	Ahemad and Khan (2009, 2010 a, b)
Azospirillum amazonence	IAA and nitrogenase activity	Elisete et al (2008)
Mesorhizobium sp.	IAA, HCN, ammonia and siderophore	Wani et al (2008)
Proteus vulgeris	Siderophore	Rani et al (2009)
Mesorhizobium ciceri	IAA and siderophore	Wani et al (2007c)
Pseudomonas, Bacillus	IAA, phosphate solubilization and siderophore	Wani et al (2007c)
Klebsiella oxytoca	IAA, phosphate solubilization and nitrogenase activity	Jha and Kumar (2007)
Bacillus spp., *Pseudomonas* spp.	IAA and ammonia production	Joseph et al (2007)
Azotobacter spp., *Bradyrhizobium* spp.	IAA, Siderophore and ammonia production	Wani et al (2007 a, c)
Rhizobium sp.	IAA, HCN, ammonia and siderophore	Wani et al (2007b)
Pseudomonas fluorescens	Induced systemic resistance and antifungal activity	Saravanakumar et al (2007)
Bacillus subtilis	Antifungal activity	Cazorla et al (2007)

(Contd...)

1	2	3
Gluconacetobacter diazotrophicus	Zinc solubilization	Sarvanan et al. (2007)
Bravibacillus spp.	Zinc resistance and IAA	Vivas et al. (2006)
Pseudomonas putida	ACC deaminase, Pb and Cd resistance and siderophore	Govindasamy et al (2008a, b), Tripathi et al (2005)
Pseudomonas fluorescens., *Azospirillum bracilense*	IAA, siderophore and antifungal activity	Day et al (2004), Upendra Kumar et al (2010)
Azospirillum amazonence	IAA, phosphate solubilization, nitrogenase activity, antifungal activity	Thakuria et al. (2004)
Pseudomonas fluorescens *Kluyvera ascorbata*	IAA, phosphate solubilization ACC deaminase, IAA, siderophore, metal resistance	Jeon et al (2003) Burd et al (2000)
Paenibacillus polymyxa strain HKA15	Antifungal activity	Senthil et al. (2007), Mageshwaran et al (2012)

Plant growth benefits due to the addition of PGPR include increase in germination rates, root growth, yield including grain, leaf area, chlorophyll content, magnesium, nitrogen and protein content, hydraulic activity, tolerance to drought and salt stress, shoot and root weights and delayed leaf senescence. Mashooda Begum et al 2003 studied the effectiveness of plant growth promoting rhizobacterial isolates against some seed borne fungal diseases. Among them, *B. pumilus* (SE-34), *B. pasteurii* (T4) and *B. subtilis* (IN 937-6., GB-03) strains stood first in the improvement of crop, both in greenhouse and field condition. Potential strains increased the biomass of plants, total number of leaves, fruits, length, girth and biomass of the fruit. The colonization of these bacterial strains reduced the incidence of seed mycoflora which indirectly enhanced the seed germination and vigour index of the seedlings. Studies of Mahmoud et al 2011 revealed that pseudomonads have plant growth promoting properties. They showed high ability of IAA production, phosphate solubilization and siderophore production, while genotyping analysis showed that pseudomonads isolated from the rhizosphere of rice are genetically diverse. Most endophytes with plant growth-enhancing properties are producers of phytohormones: indolacetic acid, gibberellins and cytokinins (Verma et al, 2001), iron-sequestering siderophores (Yanni et al, 2001), phosphate-solubilising enzymes (Verma et al, 2001) and production of 1-aminocyclopropane- 1-carboxylate (ACC) deaminase (Khalid et al, 2005). Release of auxins and ACC deaminase *in vitro* by the rhizobacteria was linearly correlated with the host plant growth promotion (Khalid et al, 2005). Subsequently, indole-3-acetic acid and ACC deaminase production is being deployed as tool for identification and screening of endophytes (Khalid et al, 2005; Shaharoona et al, 2006).

FUNCTIONAL INTERACTIONS OF PGPR IN RICE

Indole-3-Acetic Acid (IAA) Production

IAA is a phytohormone which is known to be involved in root initiation, cell division and cell enlargement. This hormone is very commonly produced by PGPR (Barazani and Friedman, 1999). Vessey 2003 has reviewed the production of this hormone and implicated it in the growth promotion by PGPR. However, the effect of IAA on plants depends on the plant sensitivity to IAA and the amount of IAA produced from plant associated bacteria and induction of other phytohormones. Patten and Glick 1996 demonstrated that IAA production from *P. putida* played a major role in the development of host plant root system. Picard et al 2005 showed that out of 2430 *Pseudomonas* isolates, originating from maize hybrid, 412 isolates were auxin producers, 27 were *phl*D$^+$. Bric et al 1990 developed a new assay that differentiates between IAA producing and non-producing bacteria on a colony plate lift and used this assay for quantifying epiphytes and endophytes populations of IAA producing isolates of *Pseudomonas syringae* subsp. *savastanoi* and for detecting IAA producing colonies of other pseudomonads and *Erwinia herbicola*. The assay provided a rapid and convenient method to screen large number of bacteria.

Phosphate Solubilization

According to Gaur 1990 who had carried out extensive work on phosphate solubilisation, used of co-inoculants of *Pseudomonas, Azotobacter* and *Bacillus* with Mussoorie Rock Phosphate (MRP) could make phosphorus availability equivalent to 50 kg of P_2O_5 applied in the form of Single Super Phosphate (SSP). The efficient phosphate solubilizers are *Pseudomonas* species *viz., aeruginosa, cepacia, fluorescence and putida*. Srivastava et al 2007 showed that out of 30 cultures of bacteria and fungi, 26 isolates solubilized varying amount of phosphorus, some of the isolates showed positive antifungal activities as well and were identified as *Pseudomonas* spp., *Pseudomonas striata* (IARI culture) continue to perform best in phosphate solubilization even under field conditions.

Siderophore Production

Siderophores are low molecular weight, extracellular compounds with a high affinity for ferric iron, that are secreted by microorganisms to take up iron from the environment and their mode of action in suppression of disease were thought to be solely based on competition for iron with the pathogen. Fluorescent pseudomonads are characterized by the production of yellow-green pigments termed pyoverdines which fluoresce under UV light and function as siderophores. The role of siderophores produced by fluorescent pseudomonads in plant growth promotion was first reported by Kloepper et al 1980. The siderophores of rhizobacteria were later reported to be implicated in the suppression of plant pathogens, competition for iron between pathogens and siderophores of rhizobacteria has been implicated in the biocontrol of wilt diseases caused by *Fusarium oxysporum*, damping off cotton caused by *Pythium ultimum* and pythium root rot of wheat. Pyoverdines chelate iron in the rhizosphere and deprive pathogens of iron which is required for their growth and pathogenesis (Leong, 1986).

Rhizobacteria produce various types of siderophores (pseudobactin and ferrooxamine B) that chelate the scarcely available iron and thereby prevent pathogens from acquiring iron. Though siderophores are part of primary metabolism (iron is an essential element), on occasions they also behave as antibiotics which are commonly considered to be secondary metabolites (Haas and Defago, 2005). Suryakala et al 2004 have reported that siderophores exerted maximum impact on *F. oxysporum* than on *Alternaria* sp. and *Colletotrichum capsici*. Leong 1986 reported that the fluorescent pseudomonads had the property to form ferric siderophores complex which prevent the availability of iron to the microorganisms. Ultimately this led to iron starvation and arrested survival of the microorganisms including nematodes. *Pseudomonas aeruginosa* strain IE-6 and its streptomycin resistant strain IE-6+ markedly suppressed nematode population densities in root and subsequent rootknot development. The iron concentration in soil was lowered by the addition of an iron chelator (Siddiqui and Shaukat, 2003).

Hydrogen Cyanide (HCN) Production

The cyanide ion is exhaled as HCN and metabolized to a lesser degree in to other compounds. HCN first inhibits the electron transport and the energy supply to the cell is disrupted leading to death of the organisms. It inhibits proper functioning of enzymes and natural receptors and it is also known to inhibit the action of cytochrome oxidase. HCN is produced by many rhizobacteria and is postulated to lay a role in biological control of pathogens (Defago et al, 1990). Suppression of take-all of wheat (Defago et al, 1990) by *P. fluorescens* strain CHAO was attributed to the production of HCN. Ramatte et al 2003 reported that hydrogen cyanide is a broad spectrum antimicrobial compound involved in biological control of root disease by many plant associated rhizobacteria. Further, Laville et al 1998 noted that the enzyme HCN synthase is encoded by three biosynthetic genes (*hcnA*, *hcnB* and *hcnC*).

BIOCONTROL AGENTS OF RICE PATHOGENS

Rice Diseases

Research on biological control of rice pathogens started in the 1980s. Research is still concentrated on the identification, evaluation and formulation of potential biocontrol agents for deployment. A number of fungi, bacteria, virus, nematode and mycoplasma-like organisms cause disease of rice plants.

Among these the fungal diseases viz. blast (*Pyricularia grisea*), brown spot (*Bipolaris oryzae*), stem rot (*Sclerotium oryzae*), sheath blight (*Rhizoctonia solani*), sheath rot (*Sarocladium oryzae*), bacterial disease such as bacterial blight (*Xanthomonas oryzae pv. oryzae*) and viral disease such as tungro (rice tungro virus) are most important (Table 8.2). These diseases are considered as a serious constraint for rice production.

Table 8.2: Major Rice Diseases and Their Biocontrol Agents

Disease	Causal Organism	Biocontrol Agent
Blast	*Pyricularia grisea* (Cooke) Sacc.	*Pseudomonas fluorescens*
Brown spot	*Bipolaris oryzae* (Breda de Haan) Shoemaker	*Pseudomonas sp.* *P. aeruginosa, B. subtilis*
Bacterial blight	*Xanthomonas oryzae pv. Oryzae* (Ishiyama)	*Bacillus* sp.
Sheath blight	*Rhizoctonia solani* Kuhn	*P. fluorescens* *B. subtilis* *B. laterosporus* *Serratia marcescens* *P. aeruginosa*
Sheath rot	*Sarocladium oryzae* (Sawada) W. Gams & D. Hawksworth	*P. fluorescens* *B. subtilis* *P. aeruginosa*
Stem rot	*Sclerotium oryzae* Cattaneo	*P. fluorescens* *P. aeruginosa* *B. subtilis* *B. pumilus*
Tungro	Rice tungro virus Vector - *Nephotettix* spp.	*P. fluorescens* (for vector)

Source: Vasudevan et al (2002)

Rice disease management strategies mainly aim at prevention of outbreak or epidemics through the use of host plant resistance and chemical pesticides. The persistent, injudicious use of chemicals has toxic effects on non-target organisms and can cause undesirable changes in the environment. Most of these chemicals are too expensive for the resource poor farmers of Asia, where 90% of the world's rice is grown. Large-scale and long-term use of resistant cultivars is likely to result in significant shifts in the virulence characteristics of pathogens, culminating in resistance breakdown. However, research during the previous two decades indicated another potential option for rice disease management, that is, biological control of rice diseases. Biocontrol assumes special significance being an eco-friendly and cost effective strategy which can be used in integration with other strategies for a greater level of protection with sustained rice yields.

Biological Control Agents for Rice Pathogens

A diverse group of biocontrol agents, such as, bacteria, fungi, viruses exist in nature. Among them bacterial antagonist are considered ideal candidates because of their rapid growth, ease of handling and aggressive colonizing character. Bacterial antagonists, *Pseudomonas*, and *Bacillus* in particular, are good candidates for biological control. Bacilli are gram-positive endospore-producing bacteria that are tolerant to heat and desiccation; a very good feature required for field application. The pseudomonads are gram-negative rods and have simple nutritional requirements; they are excellent colonizers and widely prevalent in rice rhizosphere. The fluorescent and non-fluorescent strains of a number of antagonistic bacteria associated with upland and lowland rice rhizosphere soils have been found effective *in vitro*, greenhouse and the field against *R. solani* (sheath blight). As many as 23 bacterial antagonists belonging to the genera *Bacillus, Pseudomonas, Serratia* and *Erwinia* have been found to inhibit mycelial growth of *R. solani*, while a few of them also inhibit growth of other fungal pathogens like *S. oryzae* (stem and sheath rot), *B. oryzae* (brown spot), *P. grisea* (blast) and *Fusarium fuijkuroi* (bakanae). Laboratary studies also revealed that a large nuber of bacterial strains possess the ability to protect rice plants from diseases. About 40 bacterial isolates antagonistic to the rice sheath blight pathogen have been identified. Important fungal antagonists include *Trichoderma* spp., *Penicillium, Myrothecium verrucaria, Chaetomium globosum* and *Laerisaria arvalis*. The important biocontrol agents of major rice diseases are listed in Table 8.2.

Potential of Biocontrol Agents in Rice Disease Management

The success of potential biocontrol agents in disease suppression depends on a suitable form for application to the plant system. Biocontrol agents can be applied either by direct inoculation (dipping seeds in culture, aerial spraying or spreading in sowing furrows by a drip system) or by the use of various solid-phase inoculants. The effects of some of the biocontrol agents on the pathogens and/or rice plant are summarized by Vasudevan et al 2002:

1. The bacterium *P. fluorescens* applied (prior to pathogen inoculation) against several rice pathogens to the seed and rice plants can reduce disease severity by 20-42% in a greenhouse and the field. Such bacterization of rice plants can enhance plant height, number of tillers and grain yield by 3 to 160%.
2. Seed treatment by antagonistic bacteria can reduce bakanae disease (*F. fujikuroi*) by 72-96%.
3. Different species of *Bacillus* applied to rice plants as a seed treatment before sowing, root dip prior to transplanting and two foliar sprays prior to inoculation can suppress bacterial blight pathogen by up to 59%, resulting in a two-fold increase in plant height and grain yield.
4. Recent laboratory study demonstrated that *P. fluorescens* have insecticidal effect on the rice tungro virus disease vector *Nephotettix virescens*. Bacterial strains of Pf 7-14 and PpV14i can cause about 90% mortality if they feed on treated rice leaves for 7 days.

BIOLOGICAL NITROGEN FIXATION IN RICE

Diazotrophic PGPR Association with Rice Crop

Malik et al 1997 established the association of nitrogen fixing, plant growth promoting rhizobacteria with Kallar grass and rice. The expression of nitrogenase of *Azoarcus* cells inside roots of rice seedlings. A variety of nitrogen-fixing rhizobacteria found to colonize the root interior of axenically and field grown rice, maize and other grass plants were studied by You and Zhou 1989.

Endophytic diazotrophs proposed to be responsible for the supply of biologically fixed nitrogen to their host plant was revealed by Boddy et al 1995. Chaintreuial et al 2000 investigated the presence of endophytic rhizobia within the roots of the wetland wild rice *O. breviligulata*, which is the ancestor of the African cultivated rice *O. glaberrima* and found that most endophytic and aquatic isolates were photosynthetic and belonged to the same phylogenetic *Bradyrhizobium/Blastobacter* sub-group as the typical photosynthetic *Bradyrhizobium* strains previously isolated from *Aeschynomene* photosynthetic strain. They also detected the *Bradyrhizobium and Rhizob*ium strains colonizing rice roots (*O. sativa*) by 16S-23S rDNA intergenic spacer-targeted PCR.

Isolation and identification of natural endophytic rhizobia from rice (*O. sativa*) through PCR-RFLP and their sequence was studied by Ramesh et al 2006 and described large diversities of apparently diazotrophic (~10%) and non-diazotrophic endophytic bacteria which were isolated from rice tissue. Some of them were re-colonizing their host, when re-inoculated onto sterile rice seedlings. Some of diazotroph bacterial endophytes associated with cereal plants are represented in Table 8.3.

Past isolations of nitrogen fixing bacteria from rice roots have already revealed a broad diversity of diazotrophs inhabiting the rice rhizosphere by Yanni et al 2001. Ueda et al 1995 reported the recent studies based on molecular phylogeny of the DNA sequences generated by PCR amplification of nitrogen fixing genes found in the rice rhizosphere and also suggested the existence of broad range of different rhizosphere diazotrophs.

Francine et al 2007 investigated certain rhizobial strain R4 intimately associated with rice seedling by using the green fluorescent protein (GFP) as a visual marker. Freng et al 2005 revealed the ascending migration of endophytic *Rhizobia* from roots to leaves inside rice plants and examined the infection, dissemination, and colonization of healthy rice plant tissues by four species of *gfp*-tagged rhizobia and their influence on the growth physiology of rice. Some scientists also reported the presence of non-nodulating pink-pigmented facultative *Methylobacterium* sp. with a functional *nif* H gene.

Table 8.3: Diazotrophic Bacterial Endophytes Associated with Rice Crop

Endophyte/ Diazotroph Inoculants	Colonization	Condition of Cultivation and % increase	References
Azoarcus	Roots of grasses	Gnotobiotic, 16% (total dry weight)	Reinhold- Hurekand Hurek (1997)
Burkholderia	Roots	Greenhouse, 68% (Shoot biomass)	Baldani et al (2000)
Photosynthetic *Bradyrhizobium*	Rhizosphere	Gnotobiotic, 20% (Total plant biomass)	Chaintruel et al (2000)
Gluconacetobacter diazotrophicus	Stem, Roots	Gnotobiotic, 30% (total dry weight)	Muthukumarasamy et al (2005, 2007)
Herbaspirillum seropedicae	Roots	Gnotobiotic, 38-54% (root biomass), 22-50% (shoot biomass), 37.6% (plant dry weight), 52-112%, 71% (fresh and dryweight)	Elbeltagy et al (2001) Gyaneshwar et al (2002) James et al (2002) Baldani et al (2000)
Serratia Marcescens	Roots, Stem	Gnotobiotic, 23% (total dry weight)	Gyaneshwar et al (2002)
Consortia	*Roots*	Greenhouse, increase 17% and 8% (Uptake of P and N)	Upendra Kumar et al (2012)

Saveetha et al 2009 observed that KH-1, a *P. fluorescens* strain exhibit plant growth promotional activity in rice under both *in vitro* and *in vivo* conditions. But the mechanism underlying such promotional activity of *P. fluorescens* were not understood clearly thus efforts were made to elucidate the molecular responses of rice plants to *P. fluorescens* treatment through protein profiling. Two-dimensional polyacrylamide gel electrophoresis strategy was adopted to identify the PGPR responsive proteins and the differentially expressed proteins were analyzed by mass spectrometry. Rice seeds treated with different bacterial suspensions showed improvement in plant growth parameters over untreated seeds. Among six strains of fluorescent pseudomonads, *P. fluorescens* strain KH-1 significantly increased the vigor index of rice seedlings. The increase in mean root length (25.30 cm) and shoot length (11.88 cm) was significantly higher in seedlings treated with *P. fluorescens* KH-1 compared to untreated control. The maximum vigor index of 3718 was observed in rice seedlings treated with KH-1 suspension and less vigor index of 1654 was recorded from untreated control. In addition, greater wet (1025.2 mg) and dry (806.4 mg) weight was recorded in *P. fluorescens* KH-1 treated seedlings where as in untreated control only 490.6 and 249.4 mg of dry and wet weight was recorded.

Pedraza et al 2009 assessed the *Azospirillum* inoculation and N-fertilization effect on grain yield and on the phyllosphere endophytic diversity of nitrogen-fixing bacteria in a rice rainfed crop. They used cultivation-based techniques and cultivation-independent methods involving PCR-16S rRNA and denaturing gradient gel electrophoresis (DGGE). In general, they observed that grain yield was improved when inoculated with *Azospirillum* (depending on the genotype) and/or fertilized with urea. A similar behavior was observed in total N-content in grain and the MPN determination, as the highest values occurred when seeds were inoculated with *A. brasilense* REC3 than with *A. brasilense* 13-2C. A positive nitrogenase activity and PCR-*nifH* amplification suggests that the bacteria associated to inner tissues of rice phyllosphere could have contributed to the different N-contents detected. The DGGE profiles revealed great stability in the dominating bands, which presumably represent numerically dominant species. Application of *A. brasilense* strains as inoculants did not influence the dominant members of the endophytic microbial communities in the phyllosphere, but improved N-content and production of rainfed rice crop.

Recently, it was observed that non-leguminous plant, rice forms an extended niche for various species of nitrogen fixing (NF) bacteria (Table 8.4). These bacteria thrive within the plant, successfully colonizing roots, stems and leaves. During the association, the invading bacteria benefit the acquired host with a marked increase in plant growth, vigor and yield.

Table 8.4: Colonization of Various PGPR with Rice Crop

Sl. No.	PGPR	Colonization	Condition of Cultivation and % Increase	References
1.	*Pantoea agglomerans*	Root and shoot tissue	Gnotobiotic, 63.5 (Total biomass)	Verma et al (2001), Feng et al (2006)
2.	Combination of *G. diazotrophicus* LMG7603, *H. seropedicae* LMG6513, *A. lipoferum* 4B LMG4348, and *B. vietnamiensis*LMG10929	–	Pot trial and field, 9.5, 23.6 (Yield)	Govindarajan et al (2007)
3.	*B. vietnamiensis MGK3*	Roots, shoots	Pot trial and field, 5.6-12.16 (Yield)	Govindarajan et al (2008)
4.	*Rhizobium leguminosarum bv. Trifolii*	Roots	Greenhouse and field,15-22, 8-22 (grain yield)	Yanni et al. (1997, 2001), Biswas et al (2000a, b)
5.	*B. vietnamiensis*	Rhizosphere	Nursery pot trial and field, 23 and 59 (shoot/root weight) 19 (yield), 13-22 (yield)	Trân Van et al (2000)

With increasing population, the demand of non-leguminous plant products is growing. In this regard, the richness of NF flora within non-leguminous plants and extent of their interaction with the host definitely shows a ray of hope in developing an eco-friendly alternative to the nitrogenous fertilizers. Bhattacharjee et al 2008 reviewed the association of NF bacteria with various non-leguminous plants emphasizing on their potential to promote host plant growth and yield. In addition, plant growth-promoting traits observed in these NF bacteria and their mode of interaction with the host plant have been described briefly.

Some workers observed that the overall growth promotion and nitrogen assimilation in a plant inoculated with bacteria is not solely due to BNF by the endophyte (Chi et al, 2005). During extensive greenhouse and field experiments using unsterilized soils, Riggs et al 2001 observed that when maize seeds are inoculated with *H. seropedicae* under greenhouse conditions, the yield increased by 49-82% with applied fertilizer N, whereas without fertilization, the increase was only 16%. This indicated the participation of factors other than BNF, which improved the maize plant's proficiency to use the available fertilizer N. Similarly, Sevilla et al 2001 also suggested the participation of other growth-promoting factors in addition to N fixation as both wild and *nifH* mutants of *A. diazotrophicus* promoted growth of sugarcane in the presence of nitrogen. Further, in the association of *R. trifolii* or *Bradyrhizobia* and rice, there was no evidence of *in planta* nitrogen fixation by the bacteria (Perrine-Walker et al, 2007).

Conclusions and Future Prospects

The present chapter concentrated on the overall functional prospects of plant growth promoting rhizobacterial association with rice crop. The potential contribution of PGPR to the sustainable cultivation of rice crop to exert their most significant effect on crop growth is by enhanced nutrient uptake and biopesticides. PGPR represent a less significant threat to the environment than the use of inorganic N or pesticide application, in the longer term, the consequence of inoculation of soils with PGPR on microbial soil diversity is unknown. Inoculants technology has developed significantly in recent years, in terms of scale and quality, particularly for legumes but not for cereal crops. Genetically engineered strains are possible but remain an expensive and potentially more controversial approach to the technology. The effective utilization of PGPR in the future will demand that there is a much more rational approach to the choice and delivery of the particular bacterium into the rice field.

REFERENCES

Ahemad, M. and Khan, M.S. (2009): Effect of Insecticide-tolerant and Plant Growth Promoting *Mesorhizobium* on the Performance of Chickpea Grown in Insecticide Stressed Alluvial Soil. *Journal of Crop Science and Biotechnology*, 12: 213-222.

Ahemad, M. and Khan, M.S. (2010a): Comparative Toxicity of Selected Insecticide to Pea Plants and Growth Promotion in Response to Insecticide Tolerant and Plant Growth Promoting *Rhizobium leguminorarum. Crop Protection,* 29: 325-329.

Ahemad, M. and Khan, M.S. (2010b): Growth Promotion and Protection of Lentil (*Lens esculenta*) Against Herbicide Tolerant *Rhizobium sp. Annals of Microbiology,* 60: 735-745.

Baldani, V.L.D. Baldani, J.I. and Döbereiner, J. (2000): Inoculation of Rice Plants with the Endophytic Diazotrophs *Herbaspirillum seropedicae* and *Burkholderia spp. Biology and Fertility of Soils,* 30: 485-491.

Biswas, JC. Ladha, J.K. and Dazzo, F.B. (2000a): Rhizobia Inoculation Improves Nutrient Uptake and Growth of Lowland Rice. *Soil Science Society of American Journal,* 64: 1644-1650.

Biswas, J.C. Ladha, J.K. Dazzo, F.B. Yanni, Y.G. and Rolfe, B.G. (2000b): Rhizobial Inoculation Influences Seedling Vigor and Yield of Rice. *Journal of Agronomy,* 92: 880-886.

Bhattacharjee, R.B. Singh, A. and Mukhopadhyay, S.N. (2008): Use of Nitrogen-fixing Bacteria as Biofertilizer for Non-legumes: Prospects and Challenges. *Applied Microbiology and Biotechnology,* 80: 199-209.

Boddey, R.M. Oliveira, O.C.D. Urquiaga, S. Reis, V.M. Olivares, F.L.D. Baldani, V.L.D. and Döbereiner, J. (1995): Biological Nitrogen Fixation Associated with Sugarcane and Rice: Contributions and Prospects for Improvement. *Plant and Soil,* 174: 195-209.

Bric, J.M. Bostock, R.M. and Silverstone, S.E. (1991): Rapid *in situ* Assay for Indoleacetic Acid Production by Bacteria Immobilized on a Nitrocellulose Membrane. *Applied and Environmental Microbiology,* 57: 535-538.

Burd, G.I. Dixon, D.G. and Glick, B.R. (2000): Plant Growth-promoting Bacteria that Decrease Heavy Metal Toxicity in Plants. *Canadian Journal of Microbiology,* 46: 237-245.

Cazrola, F.M. Romero, D. Perej Garasia, A. Lugtenberg, B.J.J. de Vicente, A. and Bloemberg, G. (2007): Isolation and Characterization of Antagonistic *Bacillus subtilis* Strains from Avocado Rhizoplane Displaying Biocontrol Activity. *Applied and Environmental Microbiology,* 103: 1950-1959.

Chaintreuil, C. Giraud, E. Prin, Y. Lorquin, J. Ba, A. Gillis, M. de Lajudie, P. and Dreyfus, B. (2000): Photosynthetic Bradyrhizobia are Natural Endophytes of the African Wild Rice *Oryza breviligulata. Applied and Environmental Microbiology,* 66: 5437-5447.

Chi, F. Shen, S.H. Cheng, H.P. Jing, J.X. Yanni, Y.G. and Dazzo, F.B. (2005): Ascending Migration of Endophytic Rhizobia, from Roots to Leaves, Inside Rice Plants and Assessment of Benefits to Rice Growth Physiology. *Applied and Environmental Microbiology,* 71: 7271-7278.

Defago, G. and Haas, D. (1990): Pseudomonads as Antagonists of Soil Borne Plant Pathogens: Mode of Action and Genetic Analysis. *Soil Biochemistry,* (Eds) Bolley, J.M, and Stortzky, G. New York, Baul, 6: 249-291.

Dey, R. Pal, K.K. Bhatt, D.M. and Chauhan, S.M. (2004): Growth Promotion and Yield Enhancement of Peanut (*Arachis hypogaea* L.) by Application of Plant Growth-promoting Rhizobacteria. *Microbiology Research,* 159: 371-394.

Elbeltagy, A,K. Sato, N.T. Suzuki, H. Ye, B. Hamada, T. Isawa, T. Mitsui, H. and Minamisawa, K. (2001): Endophytic Colonization and in Planta Nitrogen Fixation by a *Herbaspirillum sp.* Isolated from Wild Rice Species. *Applied and Environmental Microbiology,* 67: 5285-5293.

Elisete, P.R. Luciana, S.R. Andre, L.M.D.O. Lucia, D.B.V. Regina, D.S.T.K. Segundo, U. and Varonica, M.R. (2008): *Azospirillum amazonense* inoculation: Effect of Growth, Yield and Nitrogen Fixation of Rice (*Oryza sativa*). *Plant and Soil*, 302: 249-261.

Freg, C. Shi-Hua, S. Hai-Ping, C. Yu-Xing, J. Yanni, Y.G. and Dazzo, F.B. (2005): Ascending Migration of Endophytic Rhizobia, from Roots to Leaves Inside Rice Plants and Assessment of Benefits to Rice Growth Physiology. *Applied and Environmental Microbiology*, 71: 7271-7278.

Gaur, A.C. (1990): Phosphate Solubilizing Microorganisms as Biofertilizers. *Omega Science Publishers, New Delhi*, pp. 176-182.

Glick, B.R. (1995): The Enhancement of Plant Growth by Free-living Bacteria. *Canadian Journal of Microbiology*, 41: 109-117.

Glick, B.R. Patten CL, Holguin G, Penrose DM (1999): Biochemical and Genetic Mechanisms Used by Plant Growth Promoting Pacteria. *Imperial College Press, London, Frankenberger WT*, pp. 125-141.

Govindarajan, M. Kwon, S.W. Weon, H.Y. (2007): Isolation, Molecular Characterization and Growth-promoting Activities of Endophytic Sugarcane Diazotroph *Klebsiella* sp. *World Journal of Microbiology and biotechnology*, 23: 997-1006.

Govindarajan, M. Balandreau, J. Muthukumarasamy, R. Kwon, S.W. Weon, H.Y. and Lakshminarasimhan, C. (2008): Effects of the Inoculation of *Burkholderia vietnamiensis* and Related Endophytic Diazotrophic Bacteria on Grain Yield of Rice. *Microbial Ecology*, 55: 21-37.

Govindasamy, V. Senthil Kumar, M. Upendra Kumar, Annapurna, K. (2008a): PGPR: Biotechnology for Management of Abiotic and Biotic Stresses in Crop Plants. In: Potential Microorganisms for Sustainable Agriculture. Maheshwari, D.K. and Dubey, R.C. (Eds). *I K International Publication, India*. pp. 26-48.

Govindasamy, V. Senthilkumar, M. Gaikwad, K. Annapurna, K. (2008b): Isolation and Characterization of ACC Deaminase Gene from Two Plant Growth Promoting Rhizobacteria. *Current Microbiology*, 57: 312-317.

Gyaneshwar, P. James, E.K. Reddy, P.M. and Ladha, J.K. (2002): *Herbaspirillum* Colonization Increases Growth and Nitrogen Accumulation in Aluminium-tolerant Rice Varieties. *New Phytology*, 154: 131-145.

Haas, D. and Defago, G. (2005): Biological Control of Soil Borne Pathogens by Fluorescent Pseudomonads. *Nature Reviews of Microbiology*, 1: 1-13.

James, E.K. Gyaneshwar, P. Mathan, N. Barraquio, W.L. Reddy, P.M. Iannetta, P.P.M. Olivares, F.L. and Ladha, J.K. (2002): Infection and Colonization of Rice Seedlings by the Plant Growth-promoting Bacterium *Herbaspirillum seropedicae* Z67. *Molecular Plant–Microbe Interactaction*, 15: 894-906.

Jeon, J.S. Lee, S.S. Kim, H.Y. Ahn, T. S. Song, H.G. (2003): Plant Growth Promotion in Soil by Some Inoculated Microorganisms. *Journal of Microbiology*, 41: 271-276.

Jha, P.N. and Kumar, A. (2007): Endophytic Colonization of *Typha australis* by a Plant Growth-promoting Bacterium *Klebsiella oxytoca* Strain GR-3. *Journal of Applied Microbiology*, 104: 1311-1320.

Joseph B, Ranjan Patra R, Lawrence R (2007): Characterization of Plant Growth Promoting Rhizobacteriaassociated with Chickpea (*Cicer arietinum* L.) Int. J. Plant Prod. 2: 141-152.

Kennedy, I.R. and Tchan, Y. (1992): Biological Nitrogen Fixation in Non-leguminous Field Crops: Recent Advances. *Plant and Soil,* 141: 93-118.

Khalid, A. Arshad, M. and Zahir, Z. (2005): Screening Plant Growth Promoting Rhizobacteria for Improving Growth and Yield of Wheat. *Journal of Applied Microbiology,* 96: 473-480.

Kloepper, J.W. Leong, J. Teintze, M. and Schroth, M.N. (1980): *Pseudomonas* Siderophores: A Mechanism Explaining Disease Suppressive Soils. *Current Microbiology,* 4: 317-320.

Laville, J. Blumer, C. Von Schroetter, C. Gaia, V. Défago, G Keel, C. and Haas, D. (1998): Characterization of the *hcn* ABC Gene Cluster Encoding Hydrogen Cyanide Synthase and Anaerobic Regulation by ANR in the Strictly Aerobic Biocontrol Agent *Pseudomonas fluorescence* CHAO. *Journal of Bacteriology, 180: 3187-3196.*

Leong, J. (1986): Siderophores: Their Biochemistry and Possible Role in the Biocontrol of Plant Pathogens. *Annual Reviews of Phytopathology,* 24: 187-209.

Mageshwaran, V. Mondal, K.M. Upendra Kumar and Annapurna, K. (2012): Role of Antibiosis on Suppression of Bacterial Common Blight Disease in French Bean by *Paenibacillus polymyxa* Strain HKA-15. *African Journal of Biotechnology,* 11(60): 12389-12395.

Mahmoud, R.R. Yuri, P. Kazem, K. Hadi, A.R. (2011): Molecular Genosystematic and Physiological Characteristics of Fluorescent Pseudomonads Isolated from the Rice Rhizosphere of Iranian Paddy Fields. *African Journal of Agricultural Research,* 6: 145-151.

Malik, K.A. Bilal, R. Mezhnez, S. Rasul, G. Mirza, M.S. and Ali, S. (1997): Association of Nitrogen Fixing, Plant-growth-promoting Rhizobacteria (PGPR) with Kallar Grass and Rice. *Plant and Soil,* 194: 37-44.

Mashooda Begum, Ravisankar Rai, V. and Lokesh, S. (2003): Effect of Plant Growth Promoting Rhizobacteria on Seed Borne Fungal Pathogens in Okra. *Indian Phytopathology,* 56: 156-158.

Muthukumarasamy, R. Cleenwerck, I. Revathi, G. Vadivelu, M. Janssens, D. Hoste, B. Ui Gum, K. Park, K. Son, C.Y. Sa, T. and Caballero-Mellado, J. (2005): Natural Association of *Gluconacetobacter diazotrophicus* and Diazotrophic *Acetobacter peroxydans* with Wetland rice. *Systematic and Applied Microbiology,* 28: 277-286.

Muthukumarasamy, R. Kang, U.G. Park, K.D. Jeon, W.T. Park, C.Y. Cho, Y.S. Kwon, S.W. Song, J. Roh, D.H. and Revathi, G. (2007): Enumeration, Isolation and Identification of Diazotrophs from Korean Wetland Rice Varieties Grown with Long-term Application of N and Compost and Their Short-term Inoculation Effect on Rice Plants. *Journal of Applied Microbiology,* 102: 981-991.

Patten, C.L. and Glick, C.R. (1996): Bacterial Biosynthesis of Indole 3-acetic Acid. *Canadian Journal of Microbiology,* 42: 207-220.

Pedraza, R.O. Carlos, H. B. Silvia, C. Paulo, M.F. Boa, S. and Katia. R.S.T. (2009): *Azospirillum* Inoculation and Nitrogen Fertilization Effect on Grain Yield and on the Diversity of Endophytic Bacteria in the Phyllosphere of Rice Rainfed Crop. *European Journal of Soil Biology,* 45: 36-43.

Perrine-Walker FM, Prayitno J, Rolfe BG, Weinman JJ and Hocart CH (2007): Infection Process and the Interaction of Rice Roots with Rhizobia. *Journal of Experimental Botany,* 58: 3343-50.

Picard, C. and Bosco, M. (2005): Maize Heterosis Affects the Structure and Dynamics of Indigenous Rhizospheric Auxins–Producing *Pseudomonas* Populations. *FEMS Microbiology Ecology,* 53: 349-357.

Ramatte, A. Frapolli, M. Defago, G. and Moenne-Loccoz, Y. (2003): Phylogeny of HCN Synthase-encoding *hcnbc* Genes in Biocontrol Fluorescent Pseudomonads and its Relationship with Host Plant Species and HCN Synthesis Ability. *Molecular Biology of Plant Microbe Interaction*, 16: 525-535.

Ramesh, K.S. Ravi, P.N.M. Hemant, K.J. Vinod, K. Shree, P.P. Sasi, B.R. and Annapurna, K. (2006): Isolation and Identification of Natural Endophytes Rhizobia from Rice (*Oryza sativa* L.) Through rDNA PCR-RFLP and Sequence Analysis. *Current Microbiology*, 52: 345-349.

Rani, Y. Sauche, Y.S. and Goel, R. (2009): Comparative Assessment of *in situ* Bioremediation Potential of Cadmium Resistant *Pseudomonas putida* 62BN and *Pseudomonas moneitali* 97 AN Strains on Soyabean. *International Biodeterioration and Biodegradation*, 63: 62-66.

Reinhold-Hurek, B. and Hurek, T. (1997): *Azoarcus* spp. and Their Interactions with Grassroots. *Plant and Soil*, 194: 57-64.

Riggs, P.J. Chelius, M.K. Iniguez, A.L. Kaeppler, S.M. and Triplett, E.W. (2001): Enhanced Maize Productivity by Inoculation with Diazotrophic Bacteria. *Australian Journal of Plant Physiology*, 28: 829-836.

Saravanakumar, D.C. Vijaya, N. and Samiyappan, R. (2007): Solubilization of Zn Compound by the Diazotrophic, Plant Growth Promoting *Glucoacetobacter diazotrophicus*. *Chemosphere*, 66: 1794-1798.

Saravanan, V.S. Kalaiarasan, P. Madhaiyan, M. and Thangarju, M. (2007): Solubilization of Insoluble Zinc Compounds by Gluconacetobacter Diazotrophicus and the Detrimental Action of Zinc Ion (Zn^{2+}) and Zinc Chelates on Root Knot Nematode *Meloidogyne incognita*. *Letters in Applied Microbiology*, 44: 235-241.

Saveetha, K. Karthiba, L. Raveendran, M. Saravanakumar, D. Suresh, S. Raguchander, M. Balasubramanian, P. and Samiyappan, R. (2009): Understanding the Molecular Basis of Plant Growth Promotional Effect of *Pseudomonas fluorescens* on Rice Through Protein Profiling. *Protein Science*, 7: 47.

Senthilkumar, M. Govindasamy, V. and Annapurna, K. (2007): Role of Antibiosis in Suppression of Charcoal Rot Disease by Soybean Endophyte *Paenibacillus* sp. HKA-15. *Current Microbiology*, 55: 25-29.

Sevilla, M. Gunapala, N. Burris, R.H. and Kennedy, C. (2001): Comparison of Benefit to Sugarcane Plant Growth and 15N2 Incorporation Following Inoculation of Sterile Plants with *Acetobacter diazotrophicus* Wild-type and *nif* Mutant Strains. *Molecular Plant–Microbe Interactaction*, 14: 358-366.

Shaharoona, B. Arshad, M. and Zahir, Z.A. (2006): Effect of Plant Growth Promoting Rhizobacteria Containing ACC-deaminase on Maize (*Zea mays* L.) Growth Under Axenic Conditions and on Nodulation in Mung Bean (*Vigna radiata* L.). *Letters in Applied Microbiology*, 42: 155-59.

Siddiqui, I.A. and Shaukat, S.S. (2003): Role of Iron in Rhizobacteria-mediated Suppression of Root-infecting Fungi and Root-knot Nematode in Tomato. *Nematologia Mediterranea*, 31: 11-14.

Srivastava, J. Chandra, H. and Singh, N. (2007): Allelopathic Response of *Vetiveria zizaniodes* (L.) Nash on Member of the Family Enterobacteriaceae and *Pseudomonas* spp. *Environmental Microbiology*, 27: 253-260.

Suryakala, D. Maheshwaridevi, P.V. and Lakshmi, K.V. (2004): Chemical Characterization and *in vitro* Antibiosis of Siderophores of Rhizosphere Fluorescent Pseudomonads. *Indian Journal of Microbiology*, 44: 105-108.

Thakuria, D. Talukdar, N.C. Goswami, C. Hazarika, S. Boro, R.C. and Khan, M.R. (2004): Characterization and Screening of Bacteria from the Rhizosphere of Rice Grown in Acidic Soils of Assam. *Current Science,* 86: 978-985.

Trân Van, V. Berge, O. Kê, S.N. Balandreau, J. and Heulin, T. (2000): Repeated Beneficial Effects of Rice Inoculation with a Strain of *Burkholderia vietnamiensis* on Early and Late Yield Components in Low Fertility Sulphate Acid Soils of Vietnam. *Plant and Soil,* 218: 273-284.

Tripathi, M. Munot, H.P. Shouch, Y. Meyer, J.M.and Goel, R. (2005): Isolation and Functional Characterization of Siderophore-producing Lead and Cadmium Resistant *Pseudomonas putida* KNP9. *Current Microbiology,* 5:233-237.

Ueda, T. Suga, Y. Yahiro, N. and Matsuguchi, T. (1995): Genetic Diversity of N_2-fixing Bacteria Associated with Rice Roots by Molecular Evolutionary Analysis of *nifD* Library. *Canadian Journal of Microbiology,* 41: 235-240.

Upendra Kumar, Vikas, S. Vithal, L. Pranita, B. and Annapurna, K. (2010): Fluorescent Pseudomonads in Rapeseed Mustard. *ICAR News,* 16 (1):12.

Upendra Kumar, Vithal, L. Ramadoss, D. Parnita, B. and Annapurna, K. (2012): Microbial Consortium for Increased Nutrient Uptake from Basmati Rice Rhizosphere. *ICAR News,* 18(1): 14.

Vasudevan, P. Kavitha, S. Priyadarisini, V.B. Babujee, L. and Gnanamanickam, S.S, (2002): Biological Control of Rice Diseases. In: S.S. Gnanamanickam (ed.) Biological Control of Crop Diseases. *Marcel Dekker Inc. New York,* pp. 11-32.

Verma, S.C. Ladha, J.K. and Tripathi, A.K. (2001): Evaluation of Plant Growth Promoting and Colonization Ability of Endophytic Diazotrophs from Deep Water Rice. *Journal of Biotechnology,* 91: 127-141.

Vessey, J.K. (2003): Plant Growth Promoting Rhizobacteria as Biofertilizers. *Plant and Soil,* 255: 571-586.

Vivas, A. Biro, B. Luiz-Rozano, J.M. Baria, J.M. and Azcon, R. (2006): Two Bacterial Strains Isolated from Zn Polluted Soil Enhance Plant Growth and Mycorrhizal Efficiency Under Zn Toxicity. *Chemosphere,* 62: 1523-1533.

Wani, P.A. Khan, M.S. and Zaidi, A. (2007a): Co-inoculation of Nitrogen Fixing and P-solubilizer Bacteria to Promote Growth, Yield and Nutrient Uptake in Chickpea. *Acta Agronomica Hungarica,* 55: 315-323.

Wani, P.A. Khan, M.S. and Zaidi, A. (2007b): Effect of Metal Tolerant Plant Growth Promoting *Bradyrhizobium sp.* (vigna) on Growth, Symbiosis, Seed Yield and Metal Uptake by Green Gram Plant. *Chemosphere,* 70: 36-45.

Wani, P.A. Khan, M.S. and Zaidi, A. (2007c): Synergetic Effect of the Inoculation with Nitrogen Fixing and Phosphate Solubilizing Rhizobacteria on Performance of Field Grown Chickpea. *Journal of Plant Nutrition and Soil Science,* 170: 283-287.

Wani, P.A. Khan, M.S. and Zaidi, A. (2008): Chromium Reducing and Plant Growth Promoting *Mesorhizobium* Improves Chickpea Growth in Chromium Amended Soil. *Biotechnology Letters,* 30: 159-163.

Yanni, Y.G. Rizk, R.Y. Corich, V. Squartini, M.A. Ninke, K. Philip-Hollingsworth, S. Orgambide, G. De Bruijn, F. Stoltzfus, J. Buckley, D. Schmidt, T.M. Mateos, P.F. Ladha, J.K. and Dazzo, F.B. (1997): Natural Endophytic Association Between *Rhizobium leguminosarum bv. Trifolii* and Rice Roots and Assessment of its Potential to Promote Rice Growth. *Plant and Soil,* 194:99-114.

Yanni, Y.G. Rizk, R.Y. El-Fattah, F.K.A. Squartini, A. Corich, V. Giacomini, A. de Bruijn, F. Rademaker, J. Maya-Flores, J. Ostrom, P. Vega-Hernandez, M. Hollingsworth, R.I. Martinez-Molina, E. Mateos, P. Velazquez, E. Wopereis, J. Triplett, E. Umali-Garcia, M. Anarna, J.A. Rolfe, B.G. Ladha, J.K. Hill, J. Mujoo, R. Ng, P.K. and Dazzo, F.B. (2001): The Beneficial Plant Growth-promoting Association of *Rhizobium leguminosarum bv. trifolii* with Rice Roots. *Australian Journal of Plant Physiology*, 28: 845-870.

You, C. and Zhau, F. (1989): Non-nodular Endo-rhizosphere Nitrogen Fixation in Wetland Rice. *Canadian Journal of Microbiology*, 35: 403-408.

Methods for the Detection and Quantification of Vegetable Macergens

Bukola. Rhoda. Aremu and **Olubukola. Oluranti. Babalola**

Department of Biological Sciences, Faculty of Agriculture, Science and Technology, North-West University Mafikeng Campus, Private Bag X2046 Mmabatho 2735, South Africa.

ABSTRACT

The major constraint facing vegetable production is the problem of controlling macergens (pectolytic bacteria) that macerate the plant tissues both on the field and in storage. They cause high economic losses both in transit and storage hence, rapid identification of these bacteria need to be done in order to prevent them from causing total damage to the plant. But their identification and isolation were based on conventional methods which are majorly biochemical and phenotypic features that are slow and time consuming. This review highlights some of the molecular methods that are more recently applied in rapid and quick identification of these marcergens.

Keywords: Macergens, methods, detection, conventional, molecular.

INTRODUCTION

Despite advances in vegetable production and diseases management, many challenges face growers of vegetables, out of which the major one is the damage caused by macergens (Pérombelon, 2002). Macergens damage the tissues of vegetable thereby reducing the quality, yields and shelf-life and consumer satisfaction of these plants. They cause greater economic losses to vegetables in the field, transit, storage and during marketing of these vegetables. Due to the level of worldwide market of nowadays, which has extremely high expectation for farmers to supply crops of higher qualities and disease-free which have longer shelf life. In order to meet this great demand different ways of combating the macergens needs to be employed unfortunately all efforts to control these bacteria prove to be ineffective hence the only means of meeting the world market demand is to prevent macergens from attacking these vegetables and this could be done by checking the vegetables coming in and out of the country for any traces of these macergens at quarantine sector of ministry of Agriculture.

The traditional methods to identify these macergens are extremely slow, more complex and obsolete. Although resistance genes active against macergens have been found in multiple host species, but their sequences and mechanisms remain unknown (Lebecka *et al.*, 2005). Since the host for macergens have not been fully understood it is necessary to be quite sure of which of them is responsible for total tissues destruction in a particular host plant in other to ensure effect control measure of these macergens. However, the available method commonly used cannot meet this present demand for rapid and accurate identification. Hence, means of quick identification of these bacteria is very essential. Rapid and accurate identification of vegetable macergens is essential for modern agriculture, as it permits informed decision making with respect to potentially costly but necessary control methods that include quarantine and the destruction of infected plant material in the field (Gottwald *et al.*, 2001). Bacterial taxonomic were based on the various classification methods and as diagnostic methods evolved, they have been used in reclassification of different subspecies, species and even genera.

The modern methods for identifying macergens on the other hands turnaround time and eliminates the necessity of confirmation with the biochemical tests and always give instant and real time enumeration and quantification of these bacteria thus robust, accurate and efficient. These methods basically use molecular biology approach involving PCR protocols, DNA microarray assay and immunoassay for macergens identification processes. These will helps to in quantitative detection of macergens for rapid monitoring of the vegetables at the quarantine sector of Department of Agriculture.

So far the detection of these vegetable macergens are currently based on symptoms, host range, biochemical, serological and physiological properties, which are laborious and time consuming. Hence, this review article highlights the various methods of prompt and accurate diagnosis of these vegetable macergens for effective production systems. As a result of this, vegetable crops with commercially acceptable levels of yield and quality will be practicable for the farmers. Also, this will help in the understanding of the taxonomy of macergens to identify them accurately, understand their biology and ultimately to the best of controlling them.

Vegetables

Vegetables are one of the three major food crops along with fruits and grains. They are extremely important in human diet. They are highly perishable in nature hence have short shelf life. The internal tissues are very rich in nutrient comprising: 88% water, 8.6% carbohydrate, 1.9% protein, 0.3% fat, 0.84% minerals, fat and water soluble vitamin is less than one percent and their P^H tends towards neutral an ideal condition for the growth and survival of many microorganisms. Thus vegetables are good substrate for a wide range of microorganism including yeast, moulds and bacteria. Their structure is mainly made up of the polysaccharides cellulose, hemi cellulose, and pectin. The main storage polymer is starch. Microorganisms utilize host plant cell by degrading the polymer responsible for water release and other intercellular constituents for plant nourishment and growth with extracellular lytic enzymes (Miedes and Lorences, 2004). During fruit development, microorganisms can invade plant tissues either via the calyx or along the stem, or via various specialized water and gas exchange structures of leafy matter. Vegetables have natural barrier in terms of its outer protective epidermis covered with natural waxy cuticle which contain mainly the cutin polymer hence successful colonization depend upon the capability of spoilage microbe overcoming these multiple natural protective barriers (Lequeu *et al.*, 2003). Some spoilage microbes still have the ability to initiate and establish on healthy and undamaged plant tissue (Tournas, 2005).

Out of these microorganism, bacteria are accounted for the major loss in the harvested vegetables because they have more consequence in the spoilage of vegetables due to their rapid growth that out-compete the fungi for the substrate readily available in the vegetables and the intrinsic properties which enhance their growth. In order to meet the constant market demand for vegetables commodities supply of high-quality and disease free produce, it then becomes a great challenge for the farmers in the world to detect these bacteria before the deed is done to the plant (Bartz, 2006).

Types of Microorganisms on Vegetables

Both the gram negative and positive bacteria can be found on the vegetable surface and tissues. The gram negative rods commonly isolated from raw vegetables are fluorescent *Pseudomonads* spp., *Klebsiella* spp., *Serratia* spp., *Flavobacterium* spp., *Xanthomonads* spp., *Chromobacterium* spp. and *Alcaligenes* while the gram positive rods are predominant isolated from broccoli, cabbage, mungbean sprouts and carrots. *Coryneform* bacteria and catalase negative *Cocci* can be isolated from broccoli, raw peas and raw sweet corn. In India, the mesophilic microflora of potatoes mainly comprised gram positive bacteria, Bacillus spp., *Micrococcus* spp. as fluorescent *Pseudomonads*, *Cytophaga* spp., *F.* spp., *X.* spp. and *E.* spp. The most frequent and abundant species of lactic acid bacteria found on vegetables is *Leuconostic meseteroides* (Andrews and Harris, 2000).

Vegetable Macergens

Vegetable macergens are bacteria that can cause vegetable plant cell separation leading to total tissue collapse (Gwyn, 2007). They are pectolytic bacteria that can destroy the cell wall barrier of the vegetable tissues. There are two major types of macergens namely: primary and opportunistic macergens.

Primary Macergens

Erwinia species are the primary macergens because they possess the ability to invade both healthy (undamage) and unhealthy or wounded plant. Hence have extensive host range as well as wider distribution. These primary macergens are *E. chrysanthemi* and *E. carotovora* subsp. *carotovora,* which exhibit a broad host range, and *E. carotovora* subsp. *atroseptica,* which infects primarily potatoes. These macergens can also be called *Pectobacterium chrysanthemi, P. carotovorum* subsp. *carotovorum,* and *P. atrosepticum,* respectively; however, but these are not generally accepted by the taxonomist.

Opportunistic Macergens

These macergens can only invade plant tissues when the condition is favourable for their growth and the plant is unhealthy that is having an opening which can serves as their route of entering to the plant tissues. A range of opportunistic macergens, include: *B.* spp., *X.* spp., *P.* spp. and *C.* spp.

Mechanism of Infection

Soft-rotting bacteria are known for the speed at which they promote soft rot to the extent that stored produce may liquefy in only a few hours.

Identification Methods

Understanding the ecology and epidemiological potential of pectolytic bacteria requires methods to selectively detect isolate and quantify them in their different habitats (Hélias *et al.*, 2012). There are two major methods of detecting macergens; namely traditional or conventional method and molecular or modern method (Table 1).

Conventional Approach in Identification of Macergens

The conventional approach depends solely on the biochemical and phenotypical attributes of the macergens. This involves the use of physiological, biochemical and serological methods. Currently, the major macergen erwinias are identified by their growth and cavity formation on pectate-containing selective media, such as crystal violet pectate (CVP) which is one of the most useful techniques to track these bacteria in the environment (Hyman *et al.*, 2001), at differential temperatures, i.e., *E. carotovora* subsp. *atroseptica* grows at 27°C, *E. carotovora* subsp. *carotovora* grows at 27 and 33.5°C, and *E. chrysanthemi* grows at 27, 33.5, and 37°C.

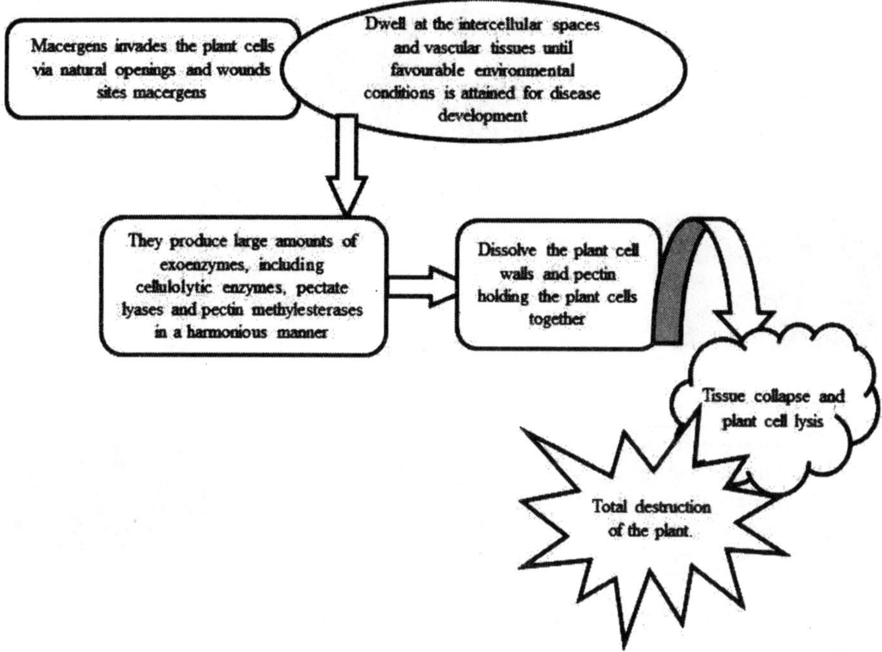

Fig. 9.1: Mechanism of the Disease

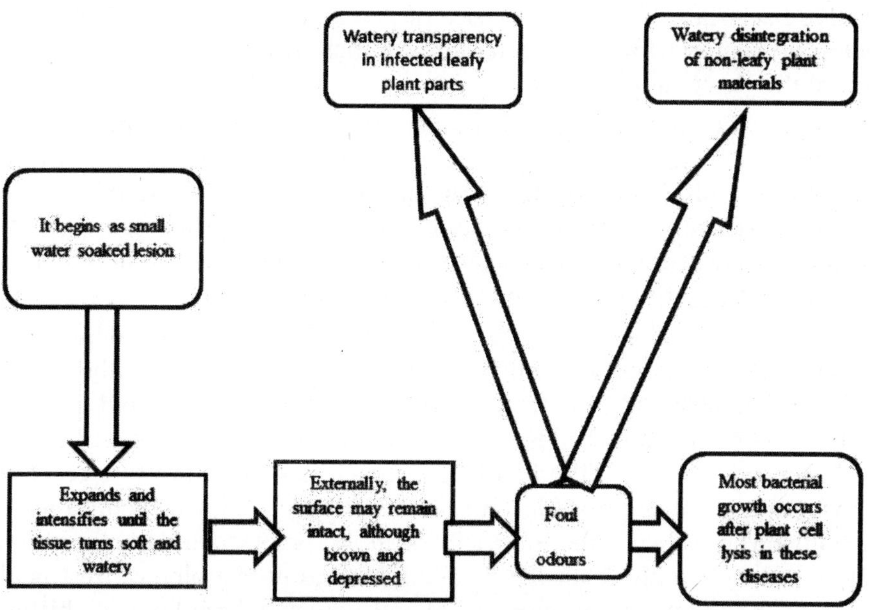

Fig. 9.2: Symptoms of Disease Caused by Macergens

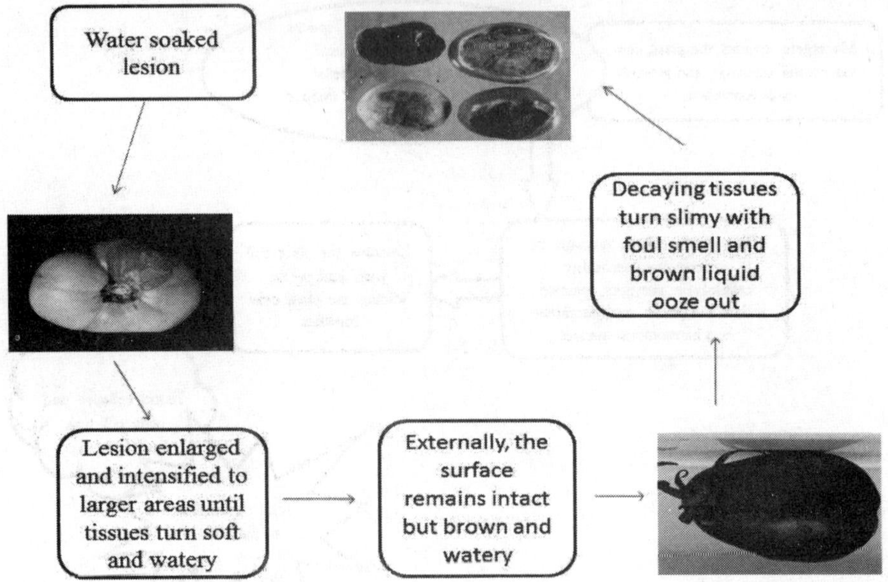

Fig. 9.3: A Cycle Showing Symtoms of Macergens in Tomato

However some of these isolates may grow outside their expected range of temperature, making the differential temperature inaccurate thus this identification method often remain unfit (Pérombelon, 2002). Their selectivity is based on the inclusion of crystal violet, which inhibits the growth of Gram-positive bacteria and in the presence of pectin as the major carbon source. Pectolytic bacteria form characteristic cavities in the medium, because of their ability to metabolize pectin.

The biochemical method used for standard identification and taxonomy macergens can only be applicable to purified cultures and allow the differentiation of all subspecies but can take up to 14 days for the identification to be done hence it is a time consuming method. Also, this method is very sensitive in the sense that if it is carried out by non-specialist laboratories it always gives indefinite identification (Verdonck *et al.*, 1987).

There are a lot of other conventional approaches used for identification of soft rot erwinias but they all have limitations in one area or the other as with biochemistry and growth on CVP. These methods can be tedious and a lot of time is wasted in samples processing. The uses of serology for macergens are limited due to the high serological heterogeneity and cross-reactivity found among subspecies (Singh *et al.*, 2000). Serological techniques are basically on efficiency of the specificity of antibodies used and not the bacteria isolation thus usually regarded as being inaccurate. Serological test is also based on the specificity of monoclonal and polyclonal antibodies which can be affected by the high number of serogroups among subspecies

(Fraaije *et al.*, 1997). Monoclonal antibodies have lower affinity for the antigens but are more specific than polyclonal antisera (Gorris *et al.*, 1994) . This technique is incapable of detecting very low bacterial populations but can only identify epidemiologically significant bacterial populations. *Erwinia* species with the exception of *E. carotovora* have been differentiated and identified using fatty acid profiling method (Persson and Sletten, 1995).

However, these conventional methods are basically on biochemical and phenotypic attributes of these bacteria but rapid and accurate detection of these macergens cannot be ascertained. This technique is not always conclusive with many drawbacks and require expert to carry out this techniques and can be acquired in lengthy years. As a result of this, isolate can be misinterpreted when effective results are not gotten. Hence, there is need for alternative methods to fill this gaps, that can be handle by any staff whether skilled or unskilled personnel.

Molecular Approach in Identification of Macergens

Many problems encountered by conventional methods of detecting microorganisms have been resolved through the emergence of molecular methods that are able to detect smaller quantity of these bacteria. As a result of this breakthrough, serology, enzymology, and metabolic analyses that normally used for plant pathogenic bacteria identification are gradually been surpassed by this molecular techniques (Babalola, 2004). The standardized molecular techniques that have been used for bacteria identification is based on nucleic acid based techniques which can be the use of probes or polymerase chain reaction (PCR). Clarification and acceleration of the in vitro amplification process of nucleic acid come true through PCR and other recently developed amplification techniques. These amplified products, referred to as amplicons may be characterized by different techniques namely: nucleic acid probe hybridization, restriction endonuclease digestion followed by fragment analysis or direct sequence analysis. These rapid techniques of nucleic acid amplification and characterization have significantly expanded the distinctive tools of the microbiologists.

Probing Method

Probes are the single stranded DNA or RNA molecules usually labelled with radioactive isotope, an enzyme or a fluorescent dye that binds to the complementary DNA sequences on the macergens of target which can be detected. It has been used for the detection of *Erwinia* spp., *Pseudomonas* spp. and *Xanthomonas* spp. The specific hybridization probes for *Erwinia* were produced through subtractive hybridization of the *Erwinia* genomic. But the invention of PCR-based methods that are simpler and cheaper made these probes for *Erwinia* strains detection and identification not to be widely used.

Macroarray techniques for identification and detection of potato-infecting bacteria which include soft rot *Erwinia* were recently described by (Fessehaie *et al.*, 2003). This array is made up of 40 different 16 to 24-mer oligonucleotides which are homologue of the 3′ end of the 16S rRNA gene and the 16S-23S spacer region. Macroarrays like these are relatively cheaper to produce.

DNA Hybridization

Although DNA-DNA hybridization is an accurate techniques but cannot be used for routine identification and characterisation of large quantity of macergens especially especially when large numbers of strains are involved due to its time-consuming factors (Vandamme *et al.*, 1996). PCR-restriction fragment length polymorphism (PCR-RFLP) analysis of a pectate lyase gene has been used but has been unsuccessful in identifying all *E. carotovora* subspecies (Hélias *et al.*, 2012). Amplified fragment length polymorphism and repetitive sequences can be used for fingerprinting of the macergens but also require computer analysis for this identification which may not be available to many laboratories (Louws *et al.*, 1999).

Automated DNA Sequencing Technology

This is also fast and accurate for DNA product amplification. It determines the amplicon sequence then analyses the DNA-sequence based on phylogenetic analysis to identify the macergens specifically. Currently, this can be achieved in two ways namely: electrophoretic separation and solid-phase sequencing which are based on the principle of polyacrylamide slab gels or glass capillaries and matrix determination respectively hybridization. In future, DNA sequence may be used for macergens strain typing because of their readily available and their data are very useful in phylogenetic placement. The sequence of *Xanthomonas axonopodis, X. campestris* and *X. oryzae* genomes have significantly helped in identifying virulence determinants of plant pathogenic bacteria (Qian *et al.*, 2005). The genome sequences of one strain of each of *X. oryzae,* and *X. axonopodis* as well as two strains of *X. campestris* have been completed and are available in the public domain (Lee *et al.*, 2005). The genomes of several other *Xanthomonads* including *X. campestris* are also being sequenced (Büttner *et al.*, 2003). These genome sequences have been analysed to identify genes that are peculiar to particular species or strains of *Xanthomonads*.

The phylogenetic relationships among *E.* spp. were studied using 16S rRNA gene sequencing (Gardan *et al.*, 2003). This techniques has been used to cross checked the taxonomy of the *E. carotovora* subspecies and does permit these identification of species and subspecies presently sequencing is not applicable for routine identification. In addition, this method reaches its limits of sensitivity below the species level. The rRNA genes are separated by the multicopy 16S-23S intergenic transcribed spacer (Sakamoto *et al.*), which possess greater sequence and length variation is also suitable for differentiating below the species level and can be used in a simple PCR-RFLP-based test (Guasp *et al.*, 2000).

Polymerase Chain Reaction (PCR)

High specificity is been maintained dramatically as the nucleic acid amplification increase sensitivity. The best developed and commonly used nucleic acid amplification technique is PCR. The principle of operation of PCR is based on the ability of polymerase DNA to copy a strand of DNA by extension of complementary strands started with a pair of closely spaced chemically synthesized oligonucleotide primers. A PCR technique is basically on three major steps: DNA denaturation (separation of target DNA double strand), primer annealing at lower temperature (primer cling to their complementary target sequences) and extension reaction step (DNA polymerase extends the sequence between the primers). The quantities of PCR product are doubled theoretically at the end of each cycle (made up of three steps) and this done in a thermal cycler.

PCR-based method is used for rapid synthesis of millions of copies of specific DNA. The conserved ribosomal genes are now commonly used in microbial taxonomy and detection. There are two main categories of PCR-based assays for macergens; the first category can determine if a disease plant sample is infected with marcegens and the can be used to characterize their isolates. Several PCR-based detection techniques operate on the basis of the *hrp* gene sequences and have been utilised for macergens such as *P. syringae pv* tomato, *P. syringae pv papulans* and *P. avellanae* (Loreti and Gallelli, 2002). These assays started before the description of the newest *E. carotovora* subspecies, *E. carotovora* subsp. *brasiliensis*.

Hence, no successful detection and diagnosis of *E. carotovora* by these primer sets is known. Most of these assays afore mentioned are been utilised before the invention of the real-time PCR and arrays and it is likely that these technologies will overrule many of the assays described for macergens detection with time. However, the conventional PCR-based assays described, are able to type more strains than the real time PCR and array assays but these primers sets in future will be more useful macergens detection (Amy, 2007). As a result of failure of conventional PCR to allow quantitative detection of the target macergens but real-time PCR with species-specific primers can give a precise quantification method through the measurement of the amount of PCR product in each cycle as fluorescence (intensity of SYBR Green I) (Sakamoto *et al.*, 2001).

Table 9.1

MACERGENS	PLANTS	METHODS	REFERENCES
Erwinia sp.	Carrot, potato, cucumber, onion, tomato, lettuce, sunflower, artichoke, chicory, leeks, spinach, broccoli, pepper	CVP medium, Chemical methods, RFLP, DNA hybridization, Serology, DNA sequencing, Enzyme profiling	Cuppels and Kelman (1974) Gardan *et al.*, (2003) Darrasse *et al.*, (1994), Fessehaie *et al.*, (2003) Yap *et al.*, (2005)
Xanthomonas sp.	Cabbage, cauliflowers, brussels, pepper	Chemical method, Fatty Acid Methyl Ester (FAME) Analysis, DNA fingerprinting methods, Polymerase chain reaction methods DNA barcoding methods Serological methods immunofluorescence or ELISA	Weller *et al.*, (2000) Fessehaie *et al.*, (2003)
Pseudomonas sp.	Onion, potato	CVP medium, Conductimetry method, DNA sequencing, ELISA, PCR	Fraaije *et al.*, (1993)

CONCLUSION

Current identification methods for the macergens are both imprecise and time-consuming. The detection of these vegetable macergens are currently based on symptoms, host range, biochemical, serological and physiological properties, which are laborious and time consuming. However, there are currently no commercial agents available specifically for controlling macergens (Dong *et al.*, 2004). Hence, need for cheaper and rapid molecular techniques that can be handled by both skilled and unskilled personnel. This call for further studies on how to produce primers based on the 16S rDNA genes of these macergens and optimization of the polymerase chain reaction (PCR) conditions for rapid, specific and sensitive detection of these macergens.

REFERENCES

Amy, O.C., (2007): The Soft rot *Erwinia*. In: S.S. Gnanamanickam (Editor), Plant Associated Bacteria. Springer, Netherlands, pp. 423-485.

Andrews, J.H. and Harris, R.F., (2000): The Ecology and Biogeography of Microorganisms on Plant Surfaces. Annual Review of Phytopathology, 38: 145-180.

Babalola, O.O., (2004): Molecular Techniques: An Overview of Methods for the Detection of Bacteria. African Journal of Biotechnology, 2: 710-713.

Bartz, J.A., (2006): Internalization and Infiltration. In: G.M. Sapers, J.R. Gorney and A.E. Yousef (Editors), Microbiology of Fresh Fruits and Vegetables. Taylor and Francis Group, New York, pp. 75-94.

Büttner, D., Noël, L., Thieme, F. and Bonas, U., (2003): Genomic Approaches in< i> *Xanthomonas campestris*< /i> pv.< i> *vesicatoria*< /i> Allow Fishing for Virulence Genes. Journal of Biotechnology, 106: 203-214.

Cuppels, D. and Kelman, A., (1974): Evaluation of Selective Media for Isolation of Soft-rot Bacteria from Soil and Plant Tissue. Phytopathology 64: 468-475.

Darrasse, A., Priou, S., Kotoujansky, A. and Bertheau, Y., (1994): PCR and Restriction Fragment Length Polymorphism of a pel gene as a Tool to Identify *Erwinia carotovora* in Relation to Potato Diseases. Applied and Environmental Microbiology, 60: 1437-1443.

Dong, Y.-H., Zhang, X.-F., Xu, J.-L. and Zhang, L.-H., (2004): Insecticidal *Bacillus thuringiensis* Silences *Erwinia carotovora* Virulence by a New form of Microbial Antagonism, Signal Interference. Applied and Environmental Microbiology, 70: 954-960.

Fessehaie, A., De Boer, S. H. and Lévesque, C.A., (2003): An Oligonucleotide Array for the Identification and Differentiation of Bacteria Pathogenic on Potato. Phytopathology, 93: 262-269.

Fraaije, B., Appels, M., De Boer, S., Van Vuurde, J. and Van den Bulk, R., (1997): Detection of Soft rot *Erwinia* spp. on Seed Potatoes: Conductimetry in Comparison with Dilution Plating, PCR and Serological Assays. European Journal of Plant Pathology, 103: 183-193.

Fraaije, B., Franken, A., Zouwen, P., Bino, R. and Langerak, C., (1993): Serological and Conductimetric Assays for the Detection of *Pseudomonas syringae* pathovar pisi in pea seeds. Journal of Applied Microbiology, 75: 409-415.

Gardan, L., Gouy, C., Christen, R. and Samson, R., (2003): Elevation of Three Subspecies of *Pectobacterium carotovorum* to Species Level: *Pectobacterium atrosepticum* sp. nov., *Pectobacterium betavasculorum* sp. nov. and *Pectobacterium wasabiae* sp. nov. International Journal of Systematic and Evolutionary Microbiology, 53: 381-391.

Gorris, M.T., Alarcon, B., Lopez, M. M. and Cambra, M., (1994): Characterization of Monoclonal Antibodies Specific for E*rwinia carotovora* subsp. *atroseptica* and Comparison of Serological Methods for its Sensitive Detection on Potato Tubers. Applied and Environmental Microbiology, 60: 2076-2085.

Gottwald, T.R., Hughes, G., Graham, J.H., Sun, X. and Riley, T., (2001): The Citrus Canker Epidemic in Florida: The Scientific Basis of Regulatory Eradication Policy for an Invasive Species. Phytopathology, 91: 30-34.

Guasp, C., Moore, E., Lalucat, J. and Bennasar, A., (2000): Utility of Internally Transcribed 16S-23S rDNA spacer Regions for the Definition of *Pseudomonas stutzer*i Genomovars and Other *Pseudomonas* Species. International Journal of Systematic and Evolutionary Microbiology, 50: 1629-1639.

Gwyn, A.B., (2007): Pathogen that Cause Soft Rots. In: S.S. Gnanamanickam (Editor), Plant Associated Bacteria. Springer, Netherlands, pp. 34.

Hélias, V., Hamon, P., Huchet, E., Wolf, J. and Andrivon, D., (2012): Two New Effective Semiselective Crystal Violet Pectate Media for Isolation of *Pectobacterium* and *Dickeya*. Plant Pathology, 61: 339-345.

Hyman, L., Sullivan, L., Toth, I. and Perombelon, M., (2001): Modified Crystal Violet Pectate Medium (CVP) Based on a New Polypectate Source (Slendid) for the Detection and Isolation of Soft Rot Erwinias. Potato Research, 44: 265-270.

Lebecka, R., Zimnoch-Guzowska, E. and Kaczmarek, Z., (2005): Resistance to Soft Rot (*Erwinia carotovora* subsp. *atroseptica*) in Tetraploid Potato Families Obtained from 4x-2x Crosses. American Journal of Potato Research, 82: 203-210.

Lee, B.-M. et al., (2005): The Genome Sequence of *Xanthomonas oryzae* Pathovar Oryzae KACC10331, the Bacterial Blight Pathogen of Rice. Nucleic Acids Research, 33: 577-586.

Lequeu, J., Fauconnier, M. L., Chammaï, A., Bronner, R. and Blée, E., (2003): Formation of Plant Cuticle: Evidence for the Occurrence of the Peroxygenase Pathway. The Plant Journal, 36: 155-164.

Loreti, S. and Gallelli, A., (2002): Rapid and Specific Detection of Virulent *Pseudomonas avellanae* strains by PCR Amplification. European Journal of Plant Pathology, 108: 237-244.

Louws, F., Rademaker, J. and De Bruijn, F., (1999): The Three Ds of PCR-based Genomic Analysis of Phytobacteria: Diversity, Detection, and Disease Diagnosis. Annual Review of Phytopathology, 37: 81-125.

Miedes, E. and Lorences, E.P., (2004): Apple (*Malus domestica*) and Tomato (*Lycopersicum esculentum*) Fruits Cell-wall Hemicelluloses and xyloglucan Degradation during *Penicillium expansum* Infection. Journal of Agricultural and Food Chemistry, 52: 7957-7963.

Pérombelon, M., (2002): Potato Diseases Caused by Soft Rot Erwinias: An Overview of Pathogenesis. Plant Pathology, 51: 1-12.

Persson, P. and Sletten, A., (1995): Fatty Acid Analysis for the Identification of. Erwinia Carotovora: 151-156.

Qian, W. et al., (2005): Comparative and Functional Genomic Analyses of the Pathogenicity of Phytopathogen *Xanthomonas campestris* pv. *campestris*. Genome research, 15: 757-767.

Sakamoto, M., Takeuchi, Y., Umeda, M., Ishikawa, I. and Benno, Y., (2001): Rapid Detection and Quantification of Five Periodontopathic Bacteria by Real-time PCR. Microbiology and Immunology, 45: 39.

Singh, U., Trevors, C., De Boer, S. and Janse, J., (2000): Fimbrial-specific Monoclonal Antibody-based ELISA for European Potato Strains of *Erwinia chrysanthemi* and Comparison to PCR. Plant Disease, 84: 443-448.

Tournas, V., (2005): Spoilage of Vegetable Crops by Bacteria and Fungi and Related Health Hazards. Critical Reviews In Microbiology, 31: 33-44.

Vandamme, P. et al., (1996): Polyphasic Taxonomy, a Consensus Approach to Bacterial Systematics. Microbiological Reviews, 60: 407-438.

Verdonck, L. et al., (1987): Genus *Erwinia*: Numerical Analysis of Phenotypic Features. International Journal of Systematic Bacteriology, 37: 4-18.

Weller, S., Elphinstone, J., Smith, N., Boonham, N. and Stead, D., (2000): Detection of *Ralstonia solanacearum* Strains with a Quantitative, Multiplex, Real-Time, Fluorogenic PCR (TaqMan) Assay. Applied and Environmental Microbiology, 66: 2853-2858.

Yap, M.N., Yang, C.H., Barak, J.D., Jahn, C.E. and Charkowski, A.O., (2005): The *Erwinia chrysanthemi* Type III Secretion System is Required for Multicellular Behaviour Journal of Bacteriology 187: 39-648.

Index